LONG WAY BACK

FROM OBSCURITY TO PROMISE

JACK CUMMINS

Long Way Back: From Obscurity to Promise

ISBN 979-8-218-64775-9

Long Way Back Publications
Louisville, TN

Printed in the United States of America

DEDICATION

I dedicate this story to my lovely wife for all her sacrifice to achieve its outcome.

I also wanted to dedicate this story to Mr. Karl Beyersdorfer for his life leading examples. Karl's exceptional insight help pave the road for Long Way Back.

And of course, I wanted to thank Dr. John Riehm for being so inspirational in having me write this story.

And last, but not least, I wanted to thank Mr. Tony Collier for all his insight and wisdom on how to structure such a story.

I have known the above gentlemen for literally decades of my life and found all of them to of made quite an impact on my life. This goes without mentioning their acute ability to guide and settle life challenges during my journey

And as to my wife, well, that obviously goes without saying. A man couldn't ask for a better wife even if he were asked to.

CONTENTS

Introduction 1

Chapter 1: An Abrupt Halt 3

Chapter 2: Hard Road to Travel 27

Chapter 3: Observations of a Growing Child 47

Chapter 4: Mother and Son Share Life Stories......................53

Chapter 5: A Perspicacious Mother 89

Chapter 6: Searching for a Missing Life 97

Chapter 7: Differing Perspectives..117

While this story is based on true events, certain incidents, characters, organizations, timelines, dialogue, and names in the story have been altered for dramatic purposes.

With respect to such alterations, any similarity to the name, character or history of any person, living or dead, or any actual event is coincidental and unintentional.

INTRODUCTION

I was standing in a novelty shop one afternoon while vacationing. The shop displayed many unique items that one could desire. Suddenly, in front of me, I noticed a closed glass case. As I scanned the case with eager eyes on a peculiar book that caught my attention. The book had appeared to be at least a hundred years old. Asking the store manager if I could observe it, she told me the book had been written by a black slave woman just short of the Civil War. Of course, I realized right away the woman would have been one of the very few granted an education, largely due to the black oppression. As I commenced reading her book, I was mesmerized with the introduction and couldn't put it down for the first several pages. So, I asked the storekeeper, "How much do you want for her book?" She replied, "Well, since it is an antique, and about 125 years old, we are asking one hundred dollars for it." I raced to pull out my wallet, only to discover I had already used up my vacation allowance. I cringed at the thought in knowing I couldn't obtain that book any time soon. You see, with the book already being 125 years old, I could only imagine it serving the author as a, sort of, true statue representing the life she once beheld. Yes, a book that could have been exciting and wondrous for all of us. I shared these same thoughts one day with a gentleman I so often met in a coffee shop. He immediately felt compelled to ask me, "So why are you writing your book, Jack?" I said, "You really want to know?" He answered, "Of course I do." So, I said, "Well, her statue I don't need. And yet I know the experience she exemplified in her life can be a benefit for all of us. But more than that, like the slave woman, I didn't want to go to my grave without telling someone this story and what really happened.

•

CHAPTER 1

AN ABRUPT HALT

Only out of prison for a year, I stood at my bedroom window gazing over a parking lot where I had once lived. Appreciating my new home, I contemplated the many things my brother, Jerry, and I had already been through. At just twenty-six years old, Jerry and I were convinced that we had never understood the long-term ramifications of a criminal life. It certainly goes without mentioning the three organized crime families he and I were once associated with. One of which is an international crime family. Jerry and I were drug dealers during the 1970s. Two of these crime families were of Italian descent, and the third was the Cuban Mob just south of Miami. While serving my last year in prison, Jerry went to Chicago to close a deal with two Italian gangsters he knew there. The deal closed for half a million hits of blotter acid. Returning to Cincinnati, Jerry began distributing his acid to two men he and I had grown up with. Thinking of these two men brought to mind a former prison guard who handed me a pass to proceed to the Chaplin's office.

Arriving at the Chaplin's office one morning, I could see that the Chaplin's face wasn't exactly indicative of pleasure. He asked me to have a seat as my sister, Dorthy, and my father, Jake, walked into the room. They had a look on their face that definitely suggested that maybe someone had died. Not to my surprise, their focus that day was on my brother, Jerry. My sister asked me to remain calm while she tried to explain Jerry's sudden death. Without my sister's knowledge, I had already been informed of my brother's death just two days earlier. One of Jerry's prior associates had just arrived at the same penitentiary where I was doing time. Oddly enough, he was a member of a crime family with whom Jerry had often done business. I noticed the man in the prison yard a few days earlier, and he brought one of his messengers to inform me that he would like to speak with me. After conversing with his messenger for a few moments, a meeting had been set for later that afternoon.

Upon his arrival, I observed a sleek, medium-sized man encroaching on me with murderous eyes and a complete entourage that would have done well at intimidating anyone. His final approach clearly made way for what could have been perceived as an inquisitive conversation for the two of us. Positioning himself right in front of me, he opened up with brazing confidence and asked, "So, I take it you're Jack Cummins?" I replied, "And whom might be inquiring?" The gentleman said, "I'm Pete Paluci. I used to split some of the Chicago runs with your brother, Jerry." I reached out to shake Mr. Paluci's hand and said, "Oh yes! Mr. Paluci, Jerry told me a lot about you. However, I noticed you mentioned you used to split some of those runs with Jerry. Am I to take it you no longer do?" Paluci said, "As I was saying, your brother and I used to split some of those Chicago runs together when, one day, these two guys showed up wanting our whole load. I had a bad feeling about these two, but your brother said not to worry about them because you and he had grown up with them. And yet I still found it rather odd that your brother would want to front them our whole load." I asked, "And why's that?" Paluci said, "Because Jerry always split those runs with me." I said, "So what exactly does that mean?" Paluci said, "Well, it means that Jerry fronted them our whole load against my better judgment. After completing the transaction with these two, Jerry looked at me as if to insinuate that he had something far more lucrative for us." So, I asked Paluci, "Who were these two guys Jerry and I had supposedly grown up with?" With Paluci disclosing their identity, I knew it wouldn't be a Sunday walk through the park. In fact, when Paluci announced who they were, I was stupefied for what seemed to be an eternity. I found myself momentarily in a daze. I asked Paluci, "Now that we are sharing this moment together in our wonderful prison yard, what seems to be your sense of urgency in wanting to speak with me?"

Paluci said, "These two guys who Jerry turned our load over to ripped your brother off for the whole load." I said, "What!?" Paluci said, "That's right. Jerry told me he couldn't pay Antonio back in Chicago for the load. So, Jerry contacted Antonio to avoid any unnecessary bloodshed. Antonio reluctantly agreed to front your brother another half million hits of acid to cover the profit from the first load. Jerry agreed with Antonio to drop his profit down considerably on the second load to cover the loss on the first." I asked, "How much was the first load?" Paluci said, "A hundred and twenty-five grand." I said, "Nice price; Jerry should have done well, even losing on the first load." So, I asked Paluci how things went on the second load. Paluci said, "That's the thing, Jack. Things didn't go so well with the second load." I said, "What do you mean?" Paluci said, "The same two guys that ripped your brother off the first time decided to rip him off again for the whole second load." I yelled, "You've got to be kidding me!!!" Paluci said, "I wish I were, but I guess you know what comes next?" I said, "Yes, I do!!" So, I asked Paluci, "So, was Jerry able to salvage any part of the second load?" Paluci said, "No. You know how those things work, Jack. You can't sell what you don't have." I said, "No doubt, so it looks like these two guys really boxed Jerry in a corner with Antonio in Chicago." Paluci said, "By all means, Jack, it looked that way to me as well."

Paluci said, "You see, Jack, Jerry didn't want to believe he had been ripped off by two of his best buddies he had grown up with. Much less seeing them do it to him twice. When Jerry discovered he had been ripped off the second time. He knew Antonio would want his two hundred and fifty grand." As Paluci spoke, I paused, knowing Antonio probably already sent someone to whack Jerry for his money. After all, these were 1970s dollars, and the Mob was still at the height of its power. And they didn't have a problem making examples from people who interfered with their cash flow. With Jerry and I having dealt with men like these before, we knew they'd bury you in the middle of a cornfield if something should go wrong. With these thoughts dangling in my mind, Paluci suddenly snapped his fingers in front of my face, bringing me back into our conversation. So Paluci abruptly blurted,

"Hello!! Is anyone in there?" I said, "Yeah, I'm still with you, Paluci. By all means, proceed with what you were saying."

Paluci said, "What made things worse was after these two ripped your brother off, they suggested that maybe he should whack himself before one of Antonio's boys got the chance." I said, "Really!!" Paluci said, "Yeah, really!!" Then Paluci proceeded to tell me, "The thing is, Antonio had already contracted with somebody out of Detroit to make sure your brother wouldn't make it through the week. So, Antonio's button man is already on the way to Cincinnati. Your brother Jerry sat at a bar in Norwood doing three hits of acid, trying to figure out what he was going to do next." I said, "Well, I don't think anyone can figure out anything doing three hits of acid." Paluci said, "I totally agree." Paluci began to elaborate, and I got a little pissed off when I learned what these two jokers wanted Jerry to do in order to rectify the situation. I said, "OK, I give up. What did they want Jerry to do?" Paluci said, "They planned to convince Jerry to whack himself so as not to attract any undue attention to themselves." I said, "And so, how in the world were they ever going to do that?"

Paluci said, "They figured since Jerry already knew he was going to be whacked anyway, why not try convincing him to hit himself as opposed to one of Antonio's boys finishing him off? After all, they thought they would have a much better chance talking Jerry into whacking himself while he was still under the influence of that acid." I said, "What were they trying to accomplish in having Jerry whack himself?" Paluci said, "Well, they knew if Jerry had told Antonio that two of his buddies ripped him off, Antonio would have just hit the two of them for his two hundred and fifty grand. They also knew that Antonio knew nothing about their existence or dealings with Jerry, which would have definitely prolonged their life expectancy if their plan were to work.

Yet, on the other hand, they knew if they could get your brother to whack himself, things could work out far better for the cops and Antonio." I said, "How do you figure that?" Paluci said, "Well, let's face it, Jack, if the police were to see your brother's death as a suicide, as opposed to a hit, they'll just rest their hats on the suicide and make it home for dinner." I said, "Well, that's true, I can't argue with that." Paluci continued, "Furthermore, once Antonio discovered your brother died over trying to collect his money, he would just write it off knowing that Jerry's debt was paid in full with his own blood." Paluci asked, "So far, so good?" I said, "I must admit, it sounds pretty ingenious on their part." Paluci said, "Yeah, we thought so, too. It doesn't look like these two were so stupid, after all. Do they?" I said, "No, it doesn't look that way at all." Paluci responded, "Of course, when they went to execute their plan, it didn't take me long to figure out that I was their only loose end. I realized they would want me just as dead as Jerry if their plan were going to work full proof. After all, they knew they stood to make a cool million on the retail market with your brother's dope, or shall I say, Antonio's dope.

Nevertheless, with them not knowing who I really was at the time, I called our good friend in Jersey and asked him to fly to Cincinnati to empty both of their lives out. Have I ever told you about our good friend in Jersey, Jack?" I said, "No, Paluci, I don't believe you have." Paluci said, "Well, it goes without saying, they don't call him the grinder for nothing." I said, "Yeah, I don't think I'll need to meet him." Paluci said, "No, Jack, you're right. I don't believe you'll need to make his acquaintance. After all, your brother and I were good friends, and there's no reason why you and I can't be the same. At any rate, your brother and two buddies thought they could make off with all that acid and whack both me and Jerry at the same time. You know, like I didn't see those chumps coming!!! Who the hell do they think they're dealing with? That's why I ordered our friend from Jersey to pay them a visit right away."

In the meantime, during all that stupidity, some of Delvecio's boys and I picked up eighteen hundred keys of Coke out of Miami the same day the grinder arrived in Cincinnati. After we got our cocaine, the DEA busted us just thirty minutes later. Some of the Delvecio's boys were arrested with me. When the Hamilton County Sheriff transferred us all out, they ensured we were split up in different penitentiaries. I always knew you were here in Lebanon because Jerry told me a little while back that you were. Soon after our arrest, I had Delvecio cancel the grinder's flight to Cincinnati." I said, "Why would you do that? I thought you wanted Jerry's rip-off buddies dead?" Paluci said, "Hey, make no mistake, I still do. It's just that I found our arrest a little more than a coincidence." I said, "What do you mean by that?" Paluci said, "Well, we were arrested thirty minutes after picking up our coke. What I don't know is how much Jerry's ripped-off buddies knew about me or our daily operations. Or if they had anything to do with the DEA popping us. And since I don't know how much Jerry may have disclosed to them while they were still bosom buddies, I needed more time to learn whether or not they helped the DEA arrange for our current accommodations here with you." I said, "And if they did have something to do with your arrest?" Paluci said, "Well, that goes without saying, Jack. If they helped the DEA, I'm sure our associate out of Jersey won't mind making a second trip. Besides, it puts me in a much better position to make sure their experience with him is at least excruciating before he empties their lives out."

I said, "You have my vote on that." Paluci said, "Thank you, Jack, but I won't need your vote on anything. I'm accustomed to emptying out whomever I deem necessary whenever I want." Talking to Paluci that day was like being addressed by Satan himself. So, I said, "Well, Mr. Paluci, I appreciate the heads up about my brother Jerry, but I have to move on now, and maybe we can talk some other time." I started to walk away when suddenly Paluci blurted out, "Wait a minute, Jack, there's more!" Turning around, I said, "Oh yeah?" Paluci said, "That's right, there's more. Jack, I wasn't so taken back by your brother's buddies wanting him to whack himself." I said, "Really!! It sure caught my attention." Paluci said, "No, what actually caught my attention is how they wanted your brother to whack himself." I said, "Oh yeah, and why is that?" Paluci said, "One of them wanted Jerry to pop himself with a pistol that they had just sold him." I said, "You gotta be kidding me!!" Paluci said, "No, I'm not. You know how that stuff goes, Jack. You can talk anyone into doing anything while they are on acid. So, while Jerry was doing the acid, they finally convinced him to pop himself. I assumed while your brother was doing acid, he probably concluded it was better to whack himself as opposed to one of Antonio's boys doing it. What other conclusion could I have come to? I have no doubt they must have convinced Jerry how much worse things would be if one of Antonio's boys had to whack him themselves." I said, "Hey, are you trying to tell me something?" Paluci said, "I'm sorry for your loss, but that's exactly what I'm trying to say. Your brother, Jerry, isn't with us anymore. Believe me, Jack, I had no idea I'd be standing in front of you today telling you something like this." I said, "To say the least!! But I haven't heard anything about Jerry's death." Paluci said, "I'm not surprised, considering it's only been 24 hours ago. However, I have no doubt you'll be hearing from our prison staff soon." I said, "Yeah, let's hope so!" Paluci said, "As I said, Jack, I'm sorry for your loss." I said, "Thanks." Walking away from Paluci with news of Jerry's death was the most awkward feeling anyone could have ever felt. Just a few moments later, Paluci summoned me back again. When I arrived a few seconds later, I asked him, "Have we missed something?" Paluci replied, "Again, Jack, for what it's worth, you have my condolences."

"Thanks, Mr. Paluci, I appreciate that."

Paluci said, "Pete is fine, Jack." I said, "OK, Pete!" I knew when men like Pete Paluci requested someone to use their first name. It wasn't because they wanted to throw a birthday party for you. Knowing how these men operated was the equivalency of witnessing madness in progress.

Finally, Paluci bowed out of our conversation, leaving me with all he knew about Jerry's death. I couldn't contact anyone pertinent to our prison staff to corroborate Paluci's story simply because our guards had already changed shifts. Walking around the prison yard that evening, I thought about how compelling Paluci's story was. It also had to be one of the longest nights I spent in my cell. I sat there thinking about how Paluci described Jerry's final hours. It didn't take long for me to figure out why Jerry elected Paluci to know precisely what happened in his deal with our two buddies we had grown up with. With Paluci knowing all the details that led up to my brother's death, it became evident to me that Jerry was reaching up from his grave to make sure I knew all the facts. Of course, I'm sure Jerry never calculated Paluci, literally ending up in the same prison I was just to disclose his demise. Who would have held the crystal ball for that occasion? If anything, I'm sure Jerry envisioned Paluci telling me about his death from some fine hotel as opposed to this prison cell. I had no doubt Paluci must have felt the same way. As the night dragged on in my cell, I contemplated all Paluci had said to me and realized one way or the other, the man had no ax to grind with me. But where was the word of my brother's death? According to Paluci, Jerry's death had just occurred in the last 24 hours. However, where was it validated, and why were there so many secrets surrounding it?

Nonetheless, visiting the Chaplain's office that second morning of Paluci's arrival gave plenty of corroboration to his story. This was the same day my father and sister walked into the prison Chaplain's office to tell me about Jerry's death. Sitting in his office that morning, my sister, Dorthy, began telling me her version of Jerry's suicide. About that time, my mind slipped into a daydream, analyzing all the details Paluci shared with me just two days earlier in the prison yard. I realized that my father and sister had no clue about what had happened in Jerry's final hours. I elected not to disclose much of that information for years to come. I knew they could never understand it anyway. It's like trying to explain a deeper depth of Satan's way of life and expecting a wholesome person to grasp it when there are too many twists and turns. But for these two guys to have convinced Jerry to whack himself while he was still on acid hadn't set well with me at all. I had no doubt they'd figure I'd want revenge upon my release. They were right. However, I knew it would take time to efficiently and effectively arrange for their departure. I knew they would want the same for me upon my release. The feeling was mutual on both sides and only stood to reason. I wanted them dead just as much as they wanted me dead. I knew taking someone out needed to be precisely how the Mob would handle such situations since our crew was accustomed to the Mob's approach in those years. I knew having all the necessary people in place would take time. Make no mistake, folks, when the Mob decides to walk someone out, it's not like the average murder the police deal with daily. No, it's more like, will the police ever find you?

At any rate, I was assured the police and the Mob were happy with Jerry's so-called suicide since his demise seemingly worked out for both entities. I had no doubt Jerry's two ripped-off buddies were operating under the same grand illusion. I had no doubt they probably thought they had gotten away with indirectly murdering my brother. I also suspected that their new "Utopia" outlook would only last as long as it would take Paluci to whack both of them. After all, the Mob takes it personally when someone wants to interfere with their cash flow. But, be that as it may, and still sitting in the Chaplin's office, my sister, Dorthy, snapped her fingers in front of my face, hoping to bring me out of my daydream. She blurted out, "Hello!!! Are you in there?" I said, "Oh yeah, I'm sorry, Dorthy, go ahead with what you were saying." Dorthy said, "Jerry had come over one day to tell all the kids and me goodbye. I asked him where he was going. Jerry said, 'It's not so much where I'll be going as opposed to what will be happening to me.'" Dorthy asked, "What the hell is that supposed to mean, Jerry?" Jerry said, "They've got a hit on me coming out of Detroit to ensure I don't make it through the end of the week. I just wanted to stop and say goodbye before they do me." Dorthy said, "Why do they want to hurt you, Jerry?"

Jerry said, "I don't think you get the picture, Dorthy. They don't want just to hurt me; they want to take me out altogether, and that's exactly what they'll do before this week is out." My sister asked, "Why do they want to kill you, Jerry?" Jerry said, "Because I'm into them for a quarter of a million dollars, and I can't cover it." Dorthy said, "Jerry!! We've always told you to stay away from those gangsters, so why do you keep going back to them?" The only response Jerry had was, "It's over."

So, my sister, Dorthy, continued talking to me at the Chaplin's Office that day. She said, "We couldn't make a lot of sense out of what Jerry said that day, but when he arrived earlier that week, we had no knowledge of him being armed. Sometime before the course of our conversation, Jerry managed to shove a 9mm pistol down between the couch where he sat. Jerry then looked at Dad and asked, 'Why didn't you raise me like Jack?'" Dad said, 'Jerry!! I was changing in those years, and I didn't feel it was necessary to raise you like your brother Jack.' Dorthy said, "Jerry wasn't satisfied with Dad's answer of not being reared like you, so he pulled the pistol out from where he sat and shot himself through the head. His body fell forward, draping itself across the coffee table in the living room. It shocked the hell out of both Dad and I." I said, "I bet it did." Dorthy said, "After a few seconds of disbelief, we could clearly see Jerry was ferociously bleeding from both sides of his head. Dad called an ambulance right away, and when the police arrived, they removed a bullet from the woodwork next to where Jerry was sitting. A few minutes later, I left in an ambulance with Jerry while Dad followed behind in his car. After being at the hospital for several hours, the doctor claimed that if Jerry were to live, he would be no more than a vegetable at best. Dad reluctantly requested that all life support be removed. The whole day was absolutely unbearable in every way. After Jerry passed, Dad signed papers donating his eyes to medical science. Upon signing the papers, the doctor explained that the donation of Jerry's eyes could possibly open the door for two other people to be able to see. Dad and I were just glad that something positive came out of such a deplorable and gut-wrenching day."

I knew my sister and father only had bits and pieces of what really happened in Jerry's final hours. Again, I could only assume that the two men Jerry and I had grown up with knew I would want revenge. They were right; I did; I just kept it to myself. I'm sure it was written all over my face the following day when I entered our prison yard to speak with Paluci. I was equally convinced that Jerry's two ripped-off buddies wanted to whack me as soon as they could for more than obvious reasons. But I also knew they wouldn't be able to, knowing that Paluci protected me while I was incarcerated. Paluci had already put the word out that if anyone touched me, they'd experience spontaneous health failure. Paluci was a madman, and no one dared to fool with him. With Paluci being new to our prison, he already had an entourage of suckers who were more than eager to do any of his beck and calls. It's like getting brownie points with Satan himself. They would do anything to gain his favor, and the guards knew it.

Paluci's protection was A-OK with me because I didn't exactly want to lose my life while I was still in the joint. Besides, it's too easy to get hit in prison, much less being linked to the Mob. However, it only made sense to me that the two men Jerry and I had grown up with differently expected Paluci to hit them as soon as possible. They weren't too far off in their calculation. Of course, Paluci wanted them dead for interfering with his Chicago runs. Trust me, Italian gangsters have a way of being totally ruthless regarding their money. As for me, I wanted to send them a clear message of how much I didn't appreciate them having my brother whack himself while he was taking acid. I thought that was a low blow for anyone, much less knowing there was a trusting relationship growing up with these two. They boxed Jerry in a corner, making him choose how he wanted to die. Of course, their efforts in seeing my brother dead were to conceal their own part in the same crimes—that way, they still could make off with a cool million bucks. I have to admit, it was a nice try on their behalf. But with Paluci angered about his Chicago runs with Jerry and Antonio wanting his quarter of a million bucks back, I had a bad feeling these two idiots were about to run out of life.

It's like what Paluci once said to me, "Jerry thought it was better to whack himself as opposed to having one of Antonio's boys do it for him." I was quietly angry and wanted to see those two boxed in the same corner they boxed my brother in.

I wanted them to know what it was like to scramble like a rat for their lives, just as much as Jerry had scrambled for his life. I wanted them to know what it was like to fear the same things Jerry feared in his final hours. Yes, to never have known how or when their departure would come. I wanted them to bleed through their nose the same way Jerry bled through his. I wanted them dead!! And as far as I was concerned, both of them richly deserved it. At that time in my life, I had the fullest intention of making sure they wouldn't be with us anymore. You see, my brother, Jerry, and I didn't operate in a make-believe world back then. Plain and simple, the people Jerry and I dealt with in those years played for keeps, and so did we. You did what you had to do, and if you didn't have a stomach for it, you were obviously in the wrong business. So, in the coming days, I was somewhat reluctant to ask Paluci for help whacking Jerry's two ripped-off buddies. If Paluci wanted them dead for his own reasons, why rock the boat? I hoped Paluci would empty them out before I was forced to deal with the situation myself. He already knew I was pretty capable of getting the job done without his intervention. But I knew men like Paluci love to plan your future. They look for people like my brother and me to advance their criminal aspirations. So, I had not suspected it would be too long before Paluci wanted to speak with me. I was right. A few days later, I received a fake pass to an obscure area in our prison, where I found Paluci waiting for me.

For me to ask Paluci to help me whack these two was the equivalency of owing him a favor. I knew Paluci would try to bait me with the idea anyway. Wise guys like Paluci know that after they do you a favor, it's now your turn to do them one. And it's always on their terms. I didn't need that kind of action at that time in my life because I had plans to work things out. It just so happens that I had a solid connection to the Cleveland syndicate from being formerly associated with Al Sinclair from the old days. When I was released, I knew Sinclair would make the necessary call to take care of things. It's not that I didn't like working with Italian gangsters. That's not the case at all; it's just that I knew some crime families prided themselves on not making a lot of noise. So, I had learned well from men like Paluci to see when you are better off not accepting an offer. I figured, why go through the trouble if you don't have to? Our crew found mimicking Mob operations didn't necessarily entail adopting some of their same mistakes. I knew because they taught us. We'd much rather do business with the Mob than owe them a favor. They, in turn, respected us for being good students, for their sole purpose was to channel their drugs through our crew. We made them a lot of money in those years, and they made us a lot of money.

On the other hand, when one deals with the Mob, you can always anticipate circumstances arising that will require you to do something totally against your constitution. Trust me, these moments do arrive; when they do, you will do what has to be done, whether that appeals to you or not. Some of my closest friends down through the years would hear me talking about how the Mob would have handled a particular situation. They automatically assumed that I was in the Mob because of some of my dealings with the Mob. The truth of the matter is, and what most people don't realize, is, if one elects to ring the doorbell of the Mob in wanting to do business with them, "They will hear you out!!!" And if they like your offer, "they will do business with you!!" However, chances are, those who are already ringing their bell are usually those who are already criminally acclimated themselves. And even if you are not an experienced criminal, it certainly doesn't mean that you are in any less danger if something goes wrong.

If anything, what it means is whatever your agreement was with the Mob, it better be everything you said it was going to be because if it's not, being buried in the middle of a cornfield shouldn't come as a surprise to you. Trust me, I barely escaped with my life when I unknowingly invited a lieutenant from a known crime family to finance a multi-million-dollar drug deal in L.A. in 1977. But more on that later. In short, for any agreement with the Mob not to turn out how you said it would be, you would have been better off making out your Will before the deal took place. On the other hand, if you were like our crew and had occasionally done business with the Mob, it certainly didn't mean you had a carte blanche pass of not being in danger. If anything, it meant just the opposite. That is to say, your chances were even greater in not seeing the trap spring that would have claimed your life. The makings of what I'm talking about are like those of an acquaintance I once had with a well-known Irish gangster many years ago. He was the Purple Gang's former WHEELMAN and bag carrier during the 1920s and 30s. Though he passed at eighty-three, and considering I hadn't been involved with organized crime then, he acutely shared a phrase with me one afternoon as he and I ate. He said, "The life I chose, Jack, is a very fearful one, and there are a thousand things that can go wrong." Even after hearing those words from Al Sinclair's mouth in 1972, I couldn't wait to be just like him.

So, to ask Paluci to help me whack these two guys wasn't exactly going to work in my favor. Besides, making it home from prison to do my own dirty work in those years was just fine with me. As I anticipated, Paluci began baiting me in our prison yard one day to allow him to whack Jerry's two associates. I wasn't disillusioned at all with his tactics. For I knew if Paluci had hit those two himself, it would have been inconvenient for me and my purpose. And, of course, Paluci knew that well. So, when Paluci approached me, I asked him not to do anything while we were still incarcerated. He responded by saying, "Jack!! Now's the time for us to whack these guys so they can't link their disappearance to either one of us." Notice Paluci's terminology here, "for us to whack them." So, I said, "I can't argue with what you're saying, Pete, and it certainly makes better sense to whack both of them while we're incarcerated. But doing so certainly doesn't mean you won't attract any new attention while being locked up, especially if the cops find out more than they already know.

Furthermore, what happens when Jerry's former associates in Chicago decide to dig deeper?" Paluci replied, "What the hell does that mean, Jack!!?" I said, "Well, Pete, now that we are on a first-name basis, if Jerry's associates in Chicago learn that his ripped-off buddies were whacked over their money, wouldn't they want to take a second closer look at you? And with you representing a totally different crime family altogether. Wouldn't that attract undue attention from opposing bosses? And what happens when the cops find out that their deaths are related to Jerry's demise? Wouldn't that be a new interest to the police?" Pete answered, "Hey Jack!! Are you watching too many movies, or do you want to whack these guys yourself and leave me completely out now? Which one is it?" Taking a big chance to answer Paluci, I said, "Are you in a big hurry, Pete!!!?" Pete said, "Well, no!" I said, "Then why the big hustle to decide to whack these two right now?" Pete said, "Jack, I reluctantly admit that maybe there is some validity in what you're saying. However, I hope you're not saying all of this crap because you want to whack these two yourself?" Paluci's statement basically meant that he was still willing to whack them in exchange for my loyalty in the future.

I said, "Look, Pete, you want them for one thing, and I want them for another. It doesn't matter if I whack them or if you do. I consider your offer very insulting to my intelligence when you know damn well you are just standing there trying to bait me for my future loyalty. I mean, what the hell is all that when I'm having a hard time grieving my own brother's death? It's a cheap shot at best, and you know it." Pete said, "Hey, bud!! Am I not the one who's saving your ass while you're walking around here in our wonderful prison?" I said, "Yes, you are, Pete." Pete said, "And have I not shown proper respect for your welfare and protection?" I said, "Yes, you have, Pete." Pete said, "I'll just drop it right now, Jack. I'm not going to try to convince you to do anything while you're still grieving your brother's death." I said, "Gee Pete, you're all heart." Pete said, "Don't be a smart ass with me, Jack. I can always lift my grace from your life. But for the sake of your brother's dealings with me, I won't. Jerry always made me a lot of money with plenty of solids to boot." I said, "OK, Pete, that sounds fair enough." I knew in my mind Paluci wasn't sorry. He just decided to abandon his idea of baiting me for a while. However, I knew he'd still want to whack those two guys for messing up his Chicago runs with Jerry. That fact hadn't escaped my mind at all. From what Jerry indicated to me before his death, those runs alone would have cost Paluci a cool twenty-eight million a year.

Just enough loss for Paluci to arrange for their demise as soon as possible. As far as I was concerned, why not let him handle the problem? Let's face it; Paluci whacking these two guys could have helped me in several ways. One, he could whack both of them relatively quickly while he and I were still incarcerated. And two, I could avoid owing him loyalty for a lifetime. That would have given me the best of both worlds. It's a good thing I was coming to my senses before it was too late. I knew if I'd agreed to allow Paluci to hit these two, it would have always assured my acquaintance with the Mob. I wasn't so sold on the idea at that point in my life. So, I decided to wait things out. If Paluci wanted their lives emptied out, let him do it on his own terms. Besides, if he decided not to whack them in the future, it would have forced the door open for me to whack them myself.

When you ask these types of favors from ruthless gangsters, you can always rest assured you'll be into them for something. They usually end up asking you to do something totally against your constitution at a later date. Most of the time, it's usually what you want them to do for you. However, to my surprise, Pete learned later that Jerry's two ripped-off buddies had nothing to do with his arrest. So, he canceled the grinder's trip to Cincinnati to whack them. It's not that I was convinced Paluci abandoned whacking them altogether. I just figured he wanted to do it himself upon his release, or he was asked to cool his jets by his crew boss. Sometimes these things happen. Whatever it was, it became apparent by Pete's behavior that I should take care of the problem myself if I wanted them emptied out. With that, Paluci agreed to provide any protection I would need until my release. But whatever changed his mind, I haven't the slightest idea to this day. I do know that these two men's lives once hung in the balance from a ruthless madman standing in the middle of a prison yard eager to empty them out. I was surprised to even see things turn out the way they had.

For rarely do they, when the Mob is hell-bent on taking you out. I had wholly understood that concept on several occasions in my own life. Meanwhile, the prison's Chaplin's office determined that since I wasn't armed during my arrest, I would be allowed to attend my brother's funeral. So, I took a trip to Cincinnati the following day with an undercover cop who elected to have a few words with me on the way. Riding down I-75 South to Cincinnati, the cop opened up with what I considered to be intimidating comments. He said, "Well!! It looks like I will be going down here to pay a visit to your dead brother!! However, I wanted you to know I'll be keeping a close eye on you all the time. I'll be sitting directly behind you, Jack, during the whole funeral procession. I'm going to release your handcuffs when we arrive, but your leg irons will remain on. That way, your hands will be free to do all your hugs and boohoos when those moments become apparent. But make no mistake, Jack, I will be sitting real close to you, so keep that in mind.

And incidentally, Jack, if any of your gangster buddies try to break you free from me, you can expect a sudden weight loss." I said, "Oh yeah, and how's that?" The cop said, "Well, that's when I commence pumping enough bullets into your back to drive a stagecoach through." I said, "Gee, are you always this compassionate when transporting prisoners to family funerals?" The cop said, "Not exactly. I just wanted us to be on the same page before we arrive; ya follow me?" I said, "Yes, I believe I do." The cop said, "Good." So, I assured the officer that there wouldn't be any trouble during Jerry's funeral and that I would humbly return to prison to do the rest of my time. As the officer and I arrived at the funeral home that day, I noticed the establishment was somewhat packed for the occasion. I didn't think many people would attend Jerry's funeral. I was glad, for Jerry's sake, simply because if he had been alive to have attended his own funeral, he would have realized more people cared about him than he would have anticipated. Sitting in the third-row back was one of two men who ripped Jerry off. It was Stocum. I became immediately concerned that he'd try to whack me right there if he had the chance. I remembered Paluci's story about Stocum's involvement with Jerry, and having known the man myself, I elected to sit in the row directly behind him. There was no way I would sit down with my back to him. Besides, I could definitely tell just by his body language he fully expected me to take revenge upon my release. Be that as it may, I was assured in my mind I had made the right decision to sit behind him. With me sitting behind him and a cop sitting behind me, I was hoping that if something were to go wrong, maybe the cop would shoot Stocum before Stocum had a chance to kill me. Or at least I hoped it would turn out that way. As I sat there for a few moments, it suddenly dawned on me that Stocum probably wouldn't run the risk of whacking me there simply because there were too many new faces in the crowd, especially with all the undercover cops that would have been intrigued to attend Jerry's funeral in hopes to obtain any new information about Jerry's former associates. I had no doubt the police knew there would be persons of interest attending that day. I tried my best to scan their faces for any anticipation that would appear odd or suspicious.

My effort bore no fruit, seeing that all the cops and gangsters wore the same stone faces. It wasn't the greatest feeling, considering why I was there. I found Stocum's entire demeanor to be somewhat disturbing, to say the least. Simply because he spent more time trying to convince me that he had nothing to do with Jerry being ripped off as opposed to focusing more on Jerry's death. He wore this disposition like a flag waving its meaning. Not to mention his willingness to stay away from our family for the next nine years. I guess he forgot that innocent people don't feel compelled to stay away for nine years, especially if they haven't done anything to hide. All of Stocum's actions that day added validity to what Paluci had already disclosed earlier that week in our prison yard. After hearing what Stocum had to say that day, I was convinced that he and his accomplice wouldn't be with us anymore. And I suspected I wouldn't have changed my mind upon my release. But again, and unknowingly, God had a different plan for my life. In the meantime, Stocum continued to fall all over himself by trying to convince me he had nothing to do with ripping Jerry off much less instigating his death.

I suddenly and abruptly walked past him to approach my brother's casket. Arriving at Jerry's casket, I noticed two patched bullet holes on each side of his head. It appeared the funeral home had done the best work they could to camouflage Jerry's wounds. Before my brother lost his life, he had completed a short term in the Ohio State Penitentiary under the number 111949. Standing there and quietly weeping at his casket, I removed a small Bible from my back pocket. I silently read a few scriptures over his body. I had never done anything like this before and found it rather arduous under the circumstances. After regaining my composure at Jerry's casket, I wrote a short line in my small Bible that read Life for 111949. Placing my Bible under Jerry's hands, I walked away from his casket.

The ride back to prison proved to be long in thought, to say the least. It reminded me of my arrest just a few years earlier. As the officer and I were in transit back to the prison, I couldn't help but think how I once arranged for four keys of cocaine and thirty thousand Quaalude's to be sold at my partner's choice of place. With no knowledge we were being taped during the sale, that day would undoubtedly bring about a new conviction for me. Just eleven months earlier, I was arrested for aggravated trafficking of cocaine exceeding bulk amounts more than five times. With this latest arrest, it would have totally sunk my ship for no less than 8 to 25 years in an Ohio State Penitentiary. With being on probation from a prior conviction, there was no way I could have escaped from doing time on this new arrest. With our last drug deal in progress that day, my partner realized at one given point that the cops were taping our deal. With that being the case, we had no idea that the local police and federal narcotic agents had the whole city block locked down. Some were across the street under porches with rifles pointed up at us while others were in the tree tops pointing their weapons down at us. During the course of the deal, my partner realized we were being filmed and threw all the drugs over the back seat to announce that he didn't want anything else to do with the deal. Of course, the cops caught wind that we were on to them and immediately took us down. Our car was rushed from all sides, with numerous narcotic agents screaming and informing us not to move. We broke a cardinal rule by doing business in the general public, where the police could gain control of our activity right away. Of course, it was too late to switch gears at that point; they had us, and we knew it.

I happened not to be armed that day, but my partner was. Some cops take it personally when one is armed during an arrest. When they discovered my partner was armed, they elected to pistol whip him across the hood of one of their police cruisers. With my partner's teeth bleeding, he abruptly announced to one of the arresting officers that they were pretty brave to beat him up while he was hand-cuffed. The officer said, "Oh yeah!!?" My partner, The Bear, said, "Yeah!!!" Then, my partner would commence to spit in the officer's face only to provoke even more of a beating. Seeing my partner being beaten so bad that day helped encourage me not to be as resilient as he was. So, I elected to keep quiet during his misfortune. But I must admit, The Bear had a lot of heart in taking all that was dished out. With the cops beating him the way they had, I thought maybe the problem lay more with the police having to wait so long to catch The Bear. With new federal funds on the table from President Reagan's war on drugs gave federal narcotic agents a far greater reach in arresting both The Bear and I. After they beat The Bear good and proper, we all took a little trip downtown. Of course, all the agents involved in our arrest that day wanted The Bear and I to snitch on one another. What else would they have wanted? When one of the federal agents discovered my partner wasn't so willing to snitch on me, he immediately headed for my cell, hoping I would snitch on my partner. The agent spoke with me briefly, only to learn I wasn't up to the task. So, the agent concluded his interview with me by announcing,

"Loyal to the end 'ha! Cummins!!?" I said, "Yes, and considering that I'm still breathing, it may be a good idea to stay that way." The cop said, "Oh, don't tell me you're worried about one of your associates whacking you for talking to us?" I said, "No more than your concern of having one of your copper buddies snitch on you when your hand is caught in the cookie jar." The officer said, "Hey, hey, hey!!! Now don't we have a real smart ass here?!!" I said, "No, just checking into reality." The cop said, "Well, check this out, Mr. Reality!! Your ass is on the way to prison if you don't help us, and trust me, Jack, it will be a *long way back* before you ever see the light of day again! So how does that grab you, Mr. Reality!!?" I knew the officer was agitated by my comments.

Nevertheless, I also knew deep inside that he hadn't known how long of a way back things had already been in my life, nor was it his objective that day to find out. The life I had led up to at that point had utterly exhausted me in every way. But for the sake of answering the officer's question as to snitch on my partner, I simply said to him, "Knowing that my breathing is still in tack, I'd much rather elect to do my time as opposed to my body being found in an obscure area." The officer replied, "So be it, and make no mistake, Cummins, your journey will begin in just a few short weeks with a first-class ride to the big house. I hope you find your breathing in good working order there as well. But for some reason, you don't; I have no doubt your arrival will be breathtaking in every way. So, enjoy your visit to hell, and may the devil bite you in the ass." The officer walked away from me, laughing so ever enthusiastically at my inevitable fate. Some cops have a tendency to get jacked out of shape when one doesn't snitch for them. The truth of the matter is they really don't respect snitches. They actually think less of them for snitching. Of course, if you're a snitch, they don't tell you that. The only real snitches that are generally accepted by both our community and the police are usually those who haven't been involved in a crime. And even those have to be careful. It's not like now, where one can pretty much get away with snitching. Allow me to elaborate.

In short, even the cops don't want their partners snitching on them, especially if they're wrong. When it comes to snitching, the rules for the public differ from those of the police. That is to say, when the cops ask you to snitch on someone, they inform you that it is a good deed to help the general public stay safe, and likely so. However, snitching is still something that the police department would never consider doing with their own colleagues. Here's why. They can care less if you end up dead for assisting them with your snitching because, after all, you are the bad guy. But if the tables are turned and a cop is asked to snitch on one of his partners, chances are the cop being asked to snitch won't react any differently than you did when you were asked to snitch on your partner. In other words, it's okay if you die in the name of justice because, after all, you're still a criminal. But, if an officer is asked to give up his partner for the same justice, don't kid yourself; all bets are off. How's that for a two-edged sword? Now, it's not quite like that today because both cops and crooks are all too often willing to snitch on one another. And all too often, one can't tell them apart. But in my time, it wasn't so. So, it's still a double standard at best.

I don't mean to fixate so much on the snitching game. Still, the game has seemingly mystified some of our general public and those who are convinced they'll never get caught. Allow me to clear up any mystery with a classic example of what I'm talking about. There never really was any way of knowing how many federal dollars were spent to secure mine and The Bear's arrest, or if any amount at that. In mine and The Bear's arrest, there was at least one snitch in the wood pile to secure our apprehension. I had known our snitch for about five years at the time, and we had no idea he had problems with the police himself. He appeared to have been enjoying the good life with some medical doctor who suddenly became his new girlfriend. Yes, I know most of you wouldn't think so. Still, sometimes white-collar professionals get involved with people of questionable character. So, let's briefly examine how such associations may turn out occasionally.

Now, our snitch's girlfriend, the doctor, had a whole host of problems with the police herself. Instead of being willing to hold a bag of uncertainty, she decided her new boyfriend, "our snitch," would look much better at carrying that bag. After all, the doctor didn't want to risk losing her license. Yes, to roll over on her new boyfriend seemed to be an obvious solution at the time. With our snitch and his new girlfriend's hands caught in the cookie jar at the same time, no doubt one of them would bring about truth or consequences. Well, wouldn't you know, the doctor wasted no time telling the police everything they wanted to know, and the consequences immediately fell to our snitch. Now, the police were more than happy to have the doctor's ex-boyfriend run with his new bag of snitching tricks. And believe me, that bag would get really tricky before it was over. It's what some gangsters would refer to as a trick bag!! So, for the sake of this story, let's give our snitch a fictitious name. After all, we wouldn't want to see him under any undue stress at such a late time in life. So, I will just call him Pat the Rat. Now, Pat happened to know a significant number of gangsters from his own comings and goings. And yes, that included The Bear and myself. When the FBI wanted Pat to take off with his new bag of snitching tricks, Pat suddenly discovered a tremendous pitfall along the way. That is to say, when The Bear and I were in prison, we learned that Pat had already aided the FBI in arresting four more major drug dealers.

Why The Bear and I even helped make some of their acquaintances to better help us buffer our stay in prison. With all of us so closely fitted together, it definitely looked as if President Reagan's war on drugs was getting the most bang for their buck.

Meanwhile, I'm sure Pat the Rat probably felt he was a good citizen in helping the police and the FBI make all those new arrests. How else would he have felt? The problem with Pat's new perspective of working with the FBI he probably forgot that he was still considered a criminal in the eyes of the law. I have no doubt the police and the FBI assured Pat he was doing the right thing!! The only problem with Pat's efforts to cooperate with the FBI was that he hadn't considered that the FBI was operating on new federal dollars. This basically meant Pat would probably run out of people to snitch on long before the FBI would run out of money to catch criminals.

So, one day, things got a little bit out of control when the FBI decided to close in on two Italian gangsters dealing Quaalude's in the millions. Of course, our boy Pat happened to be there that day. Naturally, the two gangsters in question didn't want to give up their half million Quaalude's, so they shot it out with the FBI. One of them was killed in the exchange of fire while the other lay critically injured. Pat probably came away with a whole different perspective on what a snitch's life really comprised of. Not to mention how he was now running out of people to snitch on. And don't you know, with Pat running out of people to snitch on, the FBI didn't quite have the same enthusiasm for Pat's services anymore. Now, isn't that sad? And to top things off, Pat discovered that the FBI didn't have the same sense of urgency in protecting him as they once held. Now, isn't that a shame!! If anything, Pat could now see he had stirred up quite a bee's nest with a few gangsters that were looking for him, including myself. All this was still during a time when the federal witness protection program was still ironing out its kinks. Yes, for Pat, it was a bad day in the neighborhood!! Here, Pat thought all along that he was just doing his patriotic duty. Hello!!! If one elects to be a criminal who talks to the police, that can get you killed, and they won't miss you!!! Remember, you are still the crook!! And when you elect to snitch for the police, they pretty much forget you right away when they are finished with your services. Don't kid yourself, you would-be gangsters.

At any rate, eventually, two other hoods I hadn't known learned of Pat's whereabouts. They slowly pulled up one afternoon at the foot of the old Alms & Deputy building in downtown Cincinnati. Many people were in transit that day as they were leaving their offices for lunch. Pat was supposedly scheduled to exit the same building that day for lunch. With many people already in transit, no one seemed to notice two windows of a black sedan being rolled down just twenty-five feet away. Of course, there were two gangsters that Pat had no idea were waiting there for him to appear. Upon what was thought to be Pat's arrival, a whole mirage of bullets began flying as soon as Pat stepped out of the doorway. When the shooting started, the crowd responded right away by dropping to the ground and running in assorted directions. Fortunately, no one was hit or killed. Just several dozen bullet holes struck the entrance way where Pat once stood.

Interestingly enough, it was later learned that Pat wasn't even in the vicinity when the shooting began. The gunman was actually shooting at a man they thought to be Pat. An unfortunate misunderstanding in Pat's identity surely caught the general public off guard. The irony was that some of the case workers employed at the Alms & Deputy building knew of Pat's complicated lifestyle with his girlfriend. Those same case workers decided in the following days that the best way to leave for lunch was to wear signs on their backs that read, "We're not Pat."

And so, the signs remained worn until the heat was off. I had the same luck in not finding Pat like the two other gangsters I hadn't known. I, too, was prohibited from plugging Pat a few times before leaving for my prison sentence. I thought if I could empty him out before I went to prison, it surely would have made me feel a lot better that he was no longer with us. As desperate and evil as this type of mentality could appear, it would dissipate over the years by drawing closer to God. The closer I got to God, and the more converted I became, the more I realized Pat had done me a favor. Of course, not all ex-gangsters become Christians. I say this because I have no doubt that if some of Pat's former associates knew his whereabouts, they'd have no qualms in arranging his immediate departure.

That's the bad thing about becoming a snitch on any scale. It never goes away. And the police you assist, when they retire, they leave you looking over your shoulder for the rest of your life. And they never shed any crocodile tears in remembrance of your services. Not much of a deal, is it? Pat would have been far better off just doing his time when things went south with his doctor's girlfriend. Now, the time Pat is doing is forever, hoping someone doesn't eventually whack him. And, of course, the chances of being whacked for being a snitch are far greater than that of winning the lottery. Especially when circumstances present opportunity. It was not much of a life to live, considering the FBI had promised Pat so much for his services. The truth of the matter is some of them jokers Pat busted are probably still hoping they can find him. And I have no doubt some of them will wait for years to see if they can make his acquaintance again. That's how the snitching game really goes. Hopefully, Pat's story clears up any mystery about anyone contemplating being a snitch or a would-be criminal. You see, if a criminal chooses to snitch, the cops pretty much chalk it up to help society rid its scum. And, of course, the general populist couldn't agree more.

However, don't take me wrong. I firmly believe that we need a police force because all cops aren't bad. It's just our cities do employ some law officials that have developed into the same type of scum they are trying to get rid of. Whether you are a cop or, instead, if you are a civilian, we all tend to have our brand of scum, don't we? Some have a little, and some have a lot. Remember this, the cops nor gangsters like snitches. The thing to do if you're in a mess with the cops is to keep your mouth shut until you get your head up out of the noose. That way, you'll have ample opportunity to live a better life upon your release. But bear in mind, when one lives the right way of life, it's always okay to tell the police what they want to know. And it's even the right thing to do. But if you're busy trying to be the bad guy and you tell the police what they want to know, that can get you killed every time from either side.

CHAPTER 2

HARD ROAD TO TRAVEL

At any rate, when I returned to the big house from Jerry's funeral, I knew I'd be gone for at least three years of my sentence. Words can't adequately express how one feels at a time like that. But, be that as it may, I obviously had broken the law, and being punished for it shouldn't have surprised me. Plain and simple, I had it coming. True to my arresting officer's word, it only took a few weeks to transfer me to Mansfield State Penitentiary in Mansfield, Ohio. The place was well-built shortly after the Civil War and looked much like a medieval castle. The bars on the outer windows were just as thick as those that once held the apostle Paul in Rome. I arrived at Mansfield Reformatory when the old cell blocks were still in use. This is where *Shaw Shank Redemption* was eventually filmed, with Morgan Freeman being their lead actor.

I often wondered how Morgan was able to play his part so well. I learned at a later date that Mr. Freeman spent an ample amount of time with inmates in order to perform his character. By the grace of God, I only had to spend six weeks at Mansfield Reformatory because, at the time, that's where the State of Ohio had conducted its orientation procedures. This basically meant I'd have an adequate chance of being transferred somewhere else and, hopefully, to a better prison. At the end of the six-week orientation, most inmates transferred to other penal institutions around the state. Many times, inmates were assigned to institutions that were closest to their families. Once in a while, an inmate would have to serve the remainder of their time at Mansfield. Some of us gathered around in the prison yard after six weeks just to find out where other inmates would be transferred. Some prisoners had to remain at Mansfield to finish out their sentence. When news like that was learned from other inmates, a certain sadness fell across the faces of most. For Mansfield, State Reformatory was no cakewalk, to say the least. Hard, hard time and easy to be raped or murdered. If one opened his mouth back then, he had better be all that because someone was always willing to close his eyes permanently. And from time to time, the closing of someone's life would occur.

After all, Mansfield Reformatory was equipped with its own graveyard right there in the backyard of its own prison. How convenient for those who would not be leaving any time soon. I was fortunate to have been transferred to Lebanon Correctional Institution to finish out my time. It, too, eventually became a maximum State Penitentiary, just like Mansfield. But that transformation wouldn't take place until after my time. Going back to prison that day from Jerry's funeral brought to mind the many crazy things he and I were involved in before our arrest. Without glorifying it, I could honestly say Jerry was a real stand-up guy with a lot of heart. And I appreciated that about him. I knew I had lost my right arm when I lost Jerry. With my brother gone, so was a big part of me. His absence gnawed at me through the years of my life. Especially when I needed someone to take care of something that no one else was willing to do. Jerry was always there to make sure those things were sealed. During my and my brother's criminal career, we had accepted two different contracts to ensure two other individuals wouldn't be with us anymore. Those two hits were prohibited for unknown reasons and with extra extraordinary circumstances. One of those contracts was given to Jerry by the Cuban Mob, and the other was given to me only to be stopped short by police intervention. Even with the police intervening during the act, I was still able to avoid conviction because of the circumstances. I had always been unsure whether Jerry had ordered someone else's departure during his affiliation with the Cuban Mob. If he had, I never knew anything about it simply because he never elaborated on such things with me. But for the record and how he spoke about things, I wouldn't have been surprised to learn he had. But being back just a few weeks from Jerry's funeral, I sat in my cell one evening thinking about a kidnapping my brother once contracted with the Cuban Mob. I remember Jerry trying to dodge me because he knew I'd ask for half the money to ensure his man got delivered. Jerry's main concern at that time was not to share the contract money with me. The Cuban Mob was offering Jerry thirty grand to kidnap this guy for ripping them off for forty keys of their coke. With Jerry moving a lot of their cocaine in those years, they naturally gave him the contract.

If my memory serves me right, at that time, that much cocaine would have been the equivalency of more than several million dollars. Of course, with the Cuban Mob losing that much money, they had no qualms about giving Jerry thirty grand for their man. After all, they had their own specialty of taking care of people who wanted to rip them off. And yes, it was rather unique, to say the least. That is to say, people who ripped the Cuban Mob off were usually escorted several miles offshore in one of their yachts. After a significant distance out to sea, they'd cut their engines to allow their yacht to settle in the water. They would then Lower a 12×30 steel cage into the water that housed their killing machine. That is to say, their yacht carried two large plastic containers full of water that contained their own sharks. If one decided to cross them, they'd beat their victim to a pulp until he or she was delusional. After the Cubans got their fill of the beating, they would cut the bottoms of their victim's feet just before throwing them into a barred cage just beneath the sea. Of course, with that much blood lingering in the water, it wouldn't take too long before their victims were torn apart. Whatever was left over of their bodies would be gathered up with a net and thrown back into the sea. Really lovely people, aren't they? From what Jerry told me, they really enjoyed their killing machine and couldn't wait for the next fool to cross them. He also mentioned that he felt some of their tactics were far more ruthless than those of the Italians. As far as I was concerned, both the Italians and the Colombians were some of the most ruthless gangsters I had ever known. Or shall I say at least our media thought so, especially during the 1970s.

At any rate, one day, Jerry, also referred to as "The Cowboy," set out to bring the Cuban Mob back their man. With the kidnapped not knowing my brother, it appeared Jerry's kidnapping would work very well. Or at least "The Cowboy" thought so. Jerry maintained not soliciting my help, knowing I would want half the money. So, he decided to recruit someone unknown to our crew in the hope of keeping most of the money. He and his accomplice met up with their target one day outside a business that the kidnapped was using for a front. Jerry slowly pulls up in a van with a gunman in the back, ready to snatch this guy up. At the time, their target was up on a ladder, supposedly working on an old gingerbread overhang. With the man not knowing what was about to happen, Jerry invited him down to help him make a mechanical adjustment to his van. My brother explained to the man that it would take two people to complete the task in order to start the van engine.

Meanwhile, Jerry's accomplice was still hiding in the back of the van, waiting to spring the trap. At first, the man seemed somewhat reluctant to help my brother but then decided to do so on a whim. When the man got off his ladder, Jerry directed him to the side of his van, explaining that the tools they needed could be found there.

Suddenly, the side door of the van swung open from inside, with a man shoving a gun in the victim's face. "Get in, stupid," said the man. With the victim knowing his fate was at hand, he immediately tried to attract as much attention as possible. So, he raised his hands, hoping that someone in the vicinity would suspect a robbery in progress. Jerry shoved a gun in the man's ribs and said, "Put your hands down, dummy. It's your kidnapping, not a robbery." Pushing the man in the van, the victim definitely knew he was on his way to becoming shark bait. Within seconds, all three of them were headed for Miami. With the victim convinced of his fate, he decided to attack Jerry's accomplice in the back portion of the van. My brother looked eagerly into his rear view mirror, trying to keep up with their struggle. A full-blown fight was now in progress for their victim's life. Struggling back and forth, the two men slammed into one wall of the van and then the other. At one given point, Jerry's accomplice had his victim penned down on the floor with a gun to their victim's head. The next minute, Jerry would look through his rear view mirror only to discover Jerry's accomplice was pinned down with a gun to his head. It was absolutely bazaar in a way. With the circumstances producing absolute chaos, my brother was now in a state of agony, hoping his accomplice could help deliver their man. Suddenly, during the fight, the two rear doors swung open, to everyone's amazement.

Surly, their victim was terrified and leaped for the back doors, hoping to escape with his life. Jerry's accomplice managed to tackle their victim before reaching the back doors. With both men landing at the back edge of the van, the victim's body hung partly swinging outside the van. Jerry's partner held on to their victim's legs for dear life in fear of not collecting his part of the loot. With part of their victim's body dangling outside the van, it forced a scenario where the victim's head was being beaten against the two rear doors. Their kidnapped man again eagerly screamed for his life, hoping to attract any attention that would save his life. Suddenly, Jerry realized the police were closing in at a distance. In the heat of the moment, my brother ordered his accomplice to let the man go. His partner replied, "Are you crazy!!!" Jerry answered, "Either that, or we will both be arrested for kidnapping!!! How do you want to do it!!!? Let him go!!!" With their victim still screaming and the police closing in, Jerry's accomplice decided to drop the man out of the van while it was still moving about thirty to forty miles an hour.

Fortunately for the victim, he rolled away through a heavy snowdrift that seemingly cushioned the impact of his fall. With the police suddenly making a left turn, it became painfully clear to Jerry and his accomplice that the police never once knew of their doings. Jerry's agonizing thoughts of a small fortune went up in smoke. And yes, the Cuban Mob eventually got there; man, it's just they decided not to use any of Jerry's kidnapping services anymore. At that point, the Cuban Mob felt they were much better off allowing Jerry to move their cocaine as opposed to contracting their kidnappings with him. I used to tease Jerry about the incident by reminding him of the incredible circumstances that had him lose his thirty grand. I would say things like, "If you weren't so greedy, I could have ensured your man would have been delivered. But because you wanted it all, you forfeited the whole thirty grand. Of course, fifteen thousand of it would have surely been yours if you hadn't been so quick to discard my services. Oh well, we live and learn, don't we?"

My brother would just become furious at me and walk away. Thinking of such things in my cell that day, I realized Jerry and I had already lived a horrific lifestyle, only for him to end up dead over a lousy two hundred and fifty grand of the Mob's money. Jerry never disclosed to me how often the Cuban Mob used their killing machine at sea. But he did tell me they'd have him sit in on some of those occasions to witness others losing their life over drug deals gone south. Jerry said, "The effect of such observances helped me maintain a proper business relationship with the Cubans." After the Cuban Mob had done business with my brother for a while, they decided to nickname him, Gringo, the Cowboy, which later became known in the international drug community as "The Cowboy." Though Graciela Blanca's Cocaine Cowboys ruled most of the cocaine distribution of the 1970s,

31

the single name of "The Cowboy" was none other than Jerry Rufus Cummins of Cincinnati, Ohio, dealing Cuban Mob cocaine and their bootleg Quaalude's. He was also known as Rufus Cummins, a name that very few people even knew him by. His middle name, Rufus, would clearly turn ruthless if someone decided not to see things Jerry's way. Soon, other large drug dealers from Cincinnati, Chicago, Detroit, and Los Angeles just called him "The Cowboy." Many local drug dealers feared my brother because of his international connections and what he could arrange for their lives and their families should something go wrong. As I said, we played for keeps in those years, and one had to act on such things if need be. Making a fatal mistake wasn't hard to achieve in those times, and it always had inevitable consequences regardless of who you were. In short, one learned quickly that Satan's way of life had many twists and turns and always had dire consequences at the edge of every choice. It was indeed a way of life that would sicken most people. It was Satan's arena, and he was the ring leader.

As Jerry's older brother, I, too, have to admit here that I feared my brother's reputation and the influence he once held with two powerful drug lords out of Columbia as well as the Cuban Mob. I simply never would admit that to him out of my own pride. So, I cooperated with him because I knew that angering him was equivalent to running unnecessary risk. I didn't feel Jerry would whack me on a dime, but why rock the boat. After all, the Bible says that a brother offended is harder to win than a strong city, and their contentions will be like the bars of a castle, Proverbs 18:19, KJV. At any rate, Jerry's Cowboy nickname became household of the day in the international drug community, negotiating some of the largest cocaine deals ever. And the irony? Unlike Pablo Escobar, neither Federal Narcotic Agents nor the DEA could ever nail down my brother's operations. Though Jerry was clearly under the radar of the DEA, he, in fact, was one of the few international drug dealers of its time who was never indicted. And that, to Jerry, spelled success. So long live "The Cowboy"!! I know you may be wondering why I would say such a thing as if raising a flag in my brother's honor for being a drug dealer. Before you adopt a jaundiced outlook, allow me to elaborate. I by no means condone drug dealing. After all, that trade not only partly helped destroy my life, it almost got me killed on a few occasions. But having grown up like Jerry and watching him get beat within an inch of his life with an ironing cord, for Jerry, to beat the DEA at their cat-and-mouse game made him feel that he had some type of self-worth. Of course, he obviously enjoyed the action as well. There's no doubt this type of lifestyle definitely becomes addictive to whom it lands, especially on the level Jerry was dealing. After a while, you start feeling better about yourself, but only in all the wrong ways.

And I, for one, knew precisely how Jerry felt. I was trapped in the same illusion. And yet, the two of us grew up believing we could never really achieve the proper type of success. Being subject to an abusive background will many times produce negative outcomes with many families. Many studies have proven those things for decades. And the irony is that all too often, our parents seem to be at a loss when the truth begins to unfold. Jerry used to look up to me, thinking that I was the one that had it all together. Unknown to him, I was just as crippled inside as he was but didn't have the honesty to reveal the same weaknesses to him for fear of being thought of as less. Dealing drugs for both Jerry and I became the only self-worth we could turn to and understand. Having been crippled inside from our childhood, we both bought into a way of life that provided Satan's greatest illusions of grandeur. Sadly, my brother fed those illusions all the way to his grave, and they essentially landed me in prison. That same illusion had me barely escape with my life on two separate occasions. But all is not lost, and Satan doesn't win them all.

In short, when Jesus Christ comes back to set up His Kingdom on earth, even people like the "The Cowboy" will have their real first chance of living a full life. So Long Live "The Cowboy," and may he rest in peace until that day. Sitting in my cell that final day of my sentence reminded me of how my and Jerry's life panned out. Suddenly, at that moment, a guard entered my cell, telling me that my time was up and it was time to go home. What a breath of fresh air, to say the least. It was sure nice for a change not to wake up in the morning and hear our prison intercom screaming out loud commands. Just to be able to enjoy the simple things in life was very much appreciated. After being home for a while, I gazed through my new bedroom window one day, contemplating how Jerry and I had grown up.

Of course, not being able to remember the exact moment I arrived on our planet, I can tell you that Dwight Eisenhower was our President, and Dick Clark hosted the American Bandstand. Yes, the year was 1957, and God had blessed me with such a good memory that by 1959, at just two and a half years old, I can remember walking across the beautiful wooden floors of my parent's first home. As I walked through our first new home, I'd gaze up at the stained-glass windows, wondering where I was. Growing older, I was amazed that a child of two and a half could even have such thoughts, much less retain them. Like any other infant, I wanted to know who, what, where, when, and why. And, oh yes, let us not forget how. In just a short time, I'd walk around the neighborhood wondering how long the buildings had been there. You may ponder why young children just walked around unattended in those years. It's because our Charlie Manson hadn't arrived yet. It was still during a time when most people didn't even lock their doors. But we did have our challenges, and you'll be able to assess one of them in just a moment. I attended an elementary school about ten blocks from where we lived. And yes, we walked to school. It wasn't optional; it was automatic, and we enjoyed it. It was undoubtedly a time when a boy could ask a girl to carry her books home from school without worrying about whether or not it would be politically correct. Life was far simpler in those years, with most having their common sense still intact. Of course, common sense today is usually buried under a pile of philosophy that is generally engineered by idiots.

I noticed a pretty little girl in the first grade with beautiful blue eyes and blond hair. I would see her almost every day during recess. I always asked her if I could carry her books home. She always said yes with a warm smile, and I always obliged her. As I grew older, some thought it was unusual for me to be interested in girls at such a young age. Allow me to elaborate on those circumstances if I may. On my fourth birthday, my sister and I had just finished our baths when our mother asked us to have a seat in the living room. Her tone of voice certainly suggested that maybe something was wrong. My sister and I patiently waited in our grandfather's old rocking chair to hear what our mother had to say. Suddenly, our mother entered the living room, announcing that she would leave the family and never return.

Naturally, my sister and I were taken aback by her announcement. Our mother had requested that my sister Dorthy hand deliver a letter to our father upon his arrival from work that day. Essentially, the letter explained to our father why our mother was leaving the family. The next thing I saw was my sister Dorthy tip-toeing over a banister on our porch to watch our mother pull away in a taxi. Words couldn't express how my sister and I felt that day. We spent most of the day trying to figure out why our mother decided to abandon us. A time span of twenty-two years would go by before ever seeing my mother again. I was twenty-six at the time and really hadn't entertained any thought of ever seeing her again. Especially after being recently released from my incarceration period. Starting a new relationship with my mother not only didn't make any sense, but it seemed not to fit at all in the scope of things.

My release from prison would open the door to cultivating a new relationship with my mother. When my mom learned of my release, she asked her brother, Wally, to contact me. So, my Uncle Wally approached me in a parking lot one day and asked if I'd be interested in renewing a relationship with my mother? Realizing my mother abandoned me at such a young age, I wasn't so quick to jump aboard. After not seeing her for all those years, I wasn't convinced this new opportunity was the right thing to do. So, I asked my Uncle Wally to let me think about it for a while, and he said, 'Okay.' Noticing my Uncle Wally in the same parking lot some three weeks later, he asked me again if I would be willing to meet with my mother.

Responding to his request this time, I said, "Uncle Wally! If Mom wants to have a relationship with me, I'll only do that under one condition." Uncle Wally said, "And what might that be, Jack?" I replied, "If Mom is willing to remain persistent in the relationship, then I'll be willing to build one with her. But if she is not going to remain persistent, then I'd rather pass." Uncle Wally said, "That sounds fair enough, Jack, I'll get back with you soon." I said, "Okay, I'll see you later." I really hadn't known my Uncle Wally too well at the time. I remember being affiliated with him briefly when I was nineteen. Our relationship was good, and I found him a trustworthy person, at least on my behalf. He helped me in every way he could back then, so I was willing to trust his intuition when it came to revamping my relationship with my mother. So, another three weeks had passed since I saw my uncle in the parking lot. This time, he approached me and said, "You've got a deal, Jack. I talked to your mother, and she's willing to remain persistent in the relationship if you want to move forward."

For unknown reasons, and not completely to my understanding, were my thoughts on what I should do next. So, I found myself candidly waiting outside my mother's door for Mother's Day with a bouquet of flowers in hand. Standing there in a suit and tie, I knocked on her door, not knowing what to expect. Waiting a few moments for her to arrive, I felt the atmosphere in the corridor thicken with anticipation of what to say as she opened her door. For the first time in twenty-two years, my mother stood in her doorway, greeting me and telling me to step inside. She said, "Hello, son, please come in and have a seat. Oh! I love your flowers. Thank you so much for bringing them. They're beautiful. Here, let me put them in a vase of water." We sat down for what would develop into a short visit. We elected to take things slow, with both of us not knowing one another. It was awkward at first, to say the least. And yet, neither one of us anticipated a relationship that would encroach sixteen years before she died.

As I left our visit that day, it reminded me of the little curly, blond-headed girl I so often walked home with from school. After mom abandoned us, I frequently talked with that little girl in front of our schoolyard. Sometime after Mom's departure, I hadn't realized how fulfilling my talks were with the little girl. Standing there speaking with her one day, I noticed the fall winds gently blowing through her hair like an ocean wave, wanting to repeat its glory and grandeur. Her name was Valerie, and we met almost every day for recess. As soon as I noticed her appearance in the schoolyard, I'd ask her if I could carry her books home that day. She always said yes, and the emotion from her answer always made me feel like a million dollars. I was later to understand that it was my mother's abandonment that had me wanting to walk Valerie home so much. I simply didn't feel rejected by Valerie as I had with my mother's abandonment.

Walking home with Valerie one day, we both encroached a place on the road where she and I would have to detach in order to arrive at our separate homes. As she and I prepared to go our own way, I gently laid her books on the ground so I could kiss her goodbye. Rising up from placing her books on the ground, I asked her for a kiss. Her beautiful, soft voice always invited a reply of "Yes!!" Gradually approaching her face for the kiss, I could clearly see how innocent and trusting her eyes were of me. It was as if her whole physical persona was screaming out that she was a special girl in need of being treated like a princess. Drawing ever so closely to touch her lips, I pondered what she thought of my request to kiss her. With the two of us embracing our arms together, I admired her beautiful curly blond hair and those gorgeous marble blue eyes. As I drew near to kiss her, I suddenly felt the sun's warmth on my back. The next thing I noticed was the light of the sun's gentle rays blanketing her entire face, only to exhibit the extraordinary beauty of her innocence. Moving gently forward to kiss her lips, I wondered if our kiss could last a lifetime.

That was sixty-two years ago. After losing contact with Valerie by second grade, I thought of her many times down through the years, wondering if she had a good life. But as for my new relationship with my mother, I knew it would be some time before she would fully disclose why she abandoned me at such a young age. Driving home that evening from my mother's first visit, a whole mirage of thoughts eclipsed my mind on what it was like to have grown up without her. But with my sister, Dorthy, and my brother, Jerry, suffering from the same abandonment, it's probably better to start with what life was like to live in the late fifties and early 1960s.

Spiraling through the years of my life, my mind seemingly wanted to focus on the tender age of five. With some of the kids returning home from school one day, many of them elected to take detours through the local woods. The children had lots of fun in those years following these old dirt trails. It appeared those ancient paths had been worn for at least several generations. As we traveled these paths, some kids were eager to throw rocks at each other while passing through. Caught in the crossfire one day, a seven-year-old boy decided to beat me with his stick. Because he was a few years older, I immediately feared him. I tried to avoid any physical conflict at all costs. In doing so, my first reaction was to try to outrun him. There was no such luck, and he soon caught up to strike me even more. At just five years old, I was terrified at the thought of having to engage in violent behavior to resolve any problem. Temporarily managing to escape the boy, I fled through a particular part of the wooded area and headed for our neighborhood corner store. I thought maybe if I were to step inside the store long enough, my bully would some-how just go away. Unfortunately, the boy eventually made it to the store himself. Only this time, he was conveniently accompanied by two of his buddies. Exiting the store that day, I found my bully awaiting me in the hope of continuing his abuse of me. If the conflict were to continue, I had no doubt his two new friends would have possibly jumped me as well. I must admit things began to look bleak. Finally realizing something had to be done, I dropped my candy bar and grabbed Mr. Jerk by his ears. I don't know why I decided to grab his ears, but I did. I hung on to them for dear life and pulled his ears in a downward motion ever so forcibly. As my fingernails began to dig into the back of his ears, his immediate reaction was to scream with an announcement to let him go. However, I didn't trust the situation for a quick solution, so I continued to pull downward on his ears even harder. Blood began to protrude from the back of his ears as he screamed again to let him go. With the boy unable to free himself, he quickly and ferociously grabbed my forearms and swung me in a clockwise motion. Eventually, the centrifugal force of his effort threw my body away from his.

A few seconds later, I landed on my face with new scratches covering my forearms, accompanied by a bloody nose. Fighting my way back to my feet, the boy announced how crazy I was for the way I treated him. Thankfully, the fight ended, and he elected not to bother me anymore. I certainly didn't expect such challenges at the age of five, but nonetheless, they were there. It seemed like the corner store was the hot spot where things usually took place in those days. Watching people drive by in their vehicles with signs posted on their back windows, "Just Married," was always uniquely pleasant. Beeping horns and dragging empty food cans made plenty of noise as newly married couples would pass by. Passing pedestrians were always willing to offer jesters of good luck with warm, sunny smiles. As children, Dorthy, Jerry, and I were fortunate enough to have witnessed some of America's last innocent times. It was definitely a time of peace that one could feel for the inter of their being. Receiving our first dog, Tramp, proved challenging in keeping him from being hit by passing cars. Grandpa sat on the back porch watching us run with our carefree lives. He would correct us gently and always for our own good if we needed it. I remember once thinking he was really going to spank me good for accidentally injuring my brother, Jerry. Jerry was three years younger than me. He and I had gotten a bow and arrow set for Christmas one year. These types of arrows had rubber cup tips; one could lick and stick to a wall. Jerry and I thought removing the rubber tips and sharpening them in a pencil sharpener would be much cooler. That way, they could stick to almost anything.

Needless to say, Jerry and I spent the rest of our day shooting our new pointed arrows all over the place. With the day lingering on, Jerry and I somehow became separated. Not knowing where he may have been reminded me that the bow and arrow set was now in my possession. Unannounced, Jerry had drifted off to the side of the house, where I couldn't see him at all. Not thinking of his whereabouts, I fired an arrow into the air, assured Jerry was no longer in the vicinity. Suddenly and without warning, my brother decided to magically reappear from his absence. Suddenly, his body aligned perfectly with the flight pattern of the arrow that I had just fired. With the arrow rapidly falling from the sky, Jerry's current position invoked the strongest feelings of what it would be like to experience a spontaneous heart attack. Our grandfather was eating his beets and crackers on the back porch as he grimly watched my and Jerry's situation unfold. The final seconds of the arrow flight suddenly struck Jerry on his forehead. Fortunately, there wasn't enough impact to penetrate his skull. However, the arrow had lodged itself beneath a piece of Jerry's forehead skin, with the arrow not having the capacity to sustain itself in place. It simply dropped and dangled to the left and right of Jerry's body. Each swing of the arrow worked its way loose from Jerry's forehead and had essentially dropped to the ground. With my grandfather sitting on the back porch and witnessing the whole ordeal, he just stood up and abruptly announced, "The show is over!!!" Not knowing if my grandfather knew the circumstances to be an accident, it would require him to walk by me in order to attend to my brother's wound. As he did, I could feel his parsing eyes looking right through my very soul. With his walk being closely quartered to my body, I wondered if any of his comments would bring about a new revelation or my resurrection. Knowing my grandfather could quickly exchange my life for Jerry's, I kept quiet as he passed by. Much to my surprise, he just asked me to sit quietly on the back porch while he attended to Jerry's wound.

It never dawned on me at that point I'd eventually see Jerry lying in a casket one day with bullet holes on each side of his head. Jerry was our grandfather's pride and joy. Our grandfather was fifty years older than our father, so we found him to be much sterner than our father. He was a former mountain man who homesteaded four hundred acres for the Canadian government. Though he was gentle with us as children, fighting off bears and wolves as a younger man would befall his lot. With that being his background, no one really cared to fool with that old man. I remember once my grandfather had gotten into an argument with our dad about coming home drunk on Christmas Eve. By the time the disagreement was over, our grandfather had broken our father's nose with a hammer and thrown him down the steps of his own home. Our grandfather always had a way of getting your mind right if you weren't with the program. Of course, extreme methods were never used unless one demonstrated that there was no other way to learn. Grandpa wanted the best for us and wouldn't tolerate Dad coming home drunk, regardless of the occasion. I remember our father bringing one of his drinking buddies home one night. His name was Oscar.

At the time, I was sleeping in an over-sized walk-in closet closest to my grand-father's bedroom. With Oscar being drunk and not able to see me sleeping in the closet, he landed right down on top of me without him knowing I was asleep in that particular place. I was suddenly awakened from the pressure of his body. An alarming gurgling groan suddenly blurted from me as my grandfather quickly got up to see what the problem was. When my grandfather turned the light on in his bedroom, he could clearly see Oscar's body draping mine in a smothering way. Oscar was so drunk he hadn't noticed he was lying on top of me. Oscar was about twenty-eight then, and my grandfather was about seventy-five. Grandpa went over and picked Oscar's body up off of mine and threw him across the room. As Oscar reached the other side of the room, Grandpa walked over and stood him up, ulti-mately slapping him to the other side of the room.

In one way, I felt sorry for Oscar because my grandfather was about 6'2" and had those big, thick hands that were slapping Oscar into oblivion. I sat on the edge of my bed that evening and watched Oscar travel from one side of the room to the other in a mirage of slaps. It appeared to me that my grandfather had literally slapped Oscar totally sober. When Grandpa finished slapping Oscar, he'd ask him, "Is your mind right now?!!!" Oscar answered, "Yes sir" so many times that I thought maybe he was ready to be inducted into the United States Marine Corps. Though Oscar thought of himself as one of my father's best drinking buddies, he elected never to return. I do declare I think he got his mind right. As our grandfather aged, he'd sit around the house watching us kids get into mischief. My sister, Dorthy, and I felt we had a worthwhile pursuit of seeing who could get the other brother or sister in the most trouble. We even looked at some of our attempts as sort of a sport. The problem with Dorthy's attempts to get me in trouble was they never worked. I had always gotten away with my attempts. Still, Dorthy always suffered brutally for her attempts to get me in trouble. One day, Dorthy was on the same side of the house where Jerry unfortunately was met by my flying arrow. She decided to bite herself on the arm and tell Grandma that I had bitten her. The only problem with her story was the woman living next door observed Dorthy biting herself. Of course, the women found my sister's behavior to be somewhat perplexing.

Meanwhile, Dorthy had already told Grandma that I had bitten her on the arm. Suddenly, our grandmother received a call from the woman next door telling her that she had watched Dorthy bite herself and was wondering if everything was OK. Grandma thanked the woman for her observation and politely hung up the phone. Grandma further examined Dorthy's arm and found that the teeth marks on my sister's arm matched that of her own.

Considering Grandma was from a different era, she found Dorthy's plot to get me in trouble was asinine altogether. So, my grandmother asked my sister, "Dorthy!! Why did you tell Grandma that Jack bit you on your arm when, in fact, you knew all along it was you?" Well, needless to say, it wasn't long before Dorthy's face wasn't exactly indicative of pleasure. Dorthy's second plot was even more clever than her first. My brother, sister, and I happened to have our own shower stall located in the basement. Of course, we'd take our showers there most often. Dorthy would note as to when I would be taking my shower. As she did, she would sort of hover around the shower stall, waiting for me to rinse the shampoo out of my hair. She knew as I rinsed the shampoo from my head, I would be at least temporarily blind until the shampoo cleared from my eyes. Of course, when this occasion occurred, it left the door wide open for her master plan. And that, of course, was to unleash her moment of glory. With my inability to see during my final rinse, Dorthy would slip her hand through the shower curtain, turning off all the cold water. Her deed would only allow hot water to protrude from our shower spigot. Within three seconds, I'd emerge like a rocket from our shower stall to avoid further burning from the hot water. The only problem with her plan was that when she reached the shower stall to change the water temperature, Grandma came down the basement stairs to catch her in the act.

What a nightmare it was for my sister. She was constantly being royally busted to the max in her plans for me. The look on my sister's face when our grandmother appeared was like a Rembrandt painting displayed in a public museum for its best angle. I must admit that I found my sister's plots rather creative for a seven-year-old girl.

Finally, the day came when Dorthy and I would no longer think about getting one another in trouble. The reason is that our following incident would be the closing act of our madness. The stage was set with all of us playing in the backyard that day.

With our father, being a hard worker and a good provider, he decided to buy me a bicycle one afternoon. He took me to the old Sears Roebuck store on Glenway Avenue in Price Hill to select the bike. I always enjoyed doing things like this with Dad because it made things special for both of us. Returning from the store, I rode my bike all around our backyard. Dorthy and her girlfriends decided they wanted to play horseshoes in the backyard where I was riding my new bike. The following incident wasn't planned at all but reeked with stupidity waiting to happen. But it definitely ended our sport of trying to get one another in trouble. Well, my sister's girlfriends arrived that afternoon, and all proceeded to the backyard to play with their horseshoes. Our horseshoe pit was located in the deepest part of our yard, which was the largest section of our yard. It provided plenty of room for both riding bikes and playing horseshoes. As the girls played horseshoes, I rode my bike around the edge of our horseshoe pits. Finally, it became Dorthy's turn to throw her horseshoe. Just as she released the horseshoe, Grandma stood there to watch Dorthy's throw's glorious flight pattern.

Suddenly, Dorthy's horseshoe fell from the sky, delivering a sharp blow to my head that far exceeded the whistling arrow that once struck Jerry. Great was my fall to the ground, where I lay entangled in my twisted bike. And great were the gigantic steps of our grandmother moving ever so quickly toward Dorthy. Her brisk steps appeared to have no lake of agility in wanting to totally eradicate my sister's madness. With Grandma witnessing Dorthy's last two attempts to outwit me at our getting one another in trouble game, Grandma was now convinced Dorthy was seriously trying to hurt me. Well, needless to say, it wasn't long before Dorthy's face wasn't indicative of pleasure. Meanwhile, when Jerry realized I had ridden my bicycle too close to the horseshoe pit, he insisted on telling me that I should be crowned "King Stupid of The Day." Much like our grandfather, our grandmother wasn't anyone to fool with either.

When our grandmother was a young teenage girl, she worked long hours as a cook at a logging camp in the northern hemisphere of the state of Maine. She knew what it was like to put up with rougher type men and their foul mouths. So, when Grandma saw Dorthy's horseshoe hit me that day, she knew it would have been better for Dorthy to have made her escape. Well, it goes without saying our sport of getting one another in trouble ended abruptly. It was a blessing to have our grandparents step in after our mother abandoned us. They both provided a happy atmosphere and good memories in our formative years. We remember our grandfather sitting on the front porch, always eager to give us his time, love, and attention. He was just as accustomed to giving us his very last nickel or dime so we could visit the corner store for a push-up ice cream. When playing in the streets, we always remembered grandma's rule to come in when the street lights came on. As the evening came, our grandmother would sing Twinkle Twinkle Little Star to us in our backyard. We'd awaken to the best golden brown cinnamon toast imaginable the following day. You could definitely say we were happy kids with our grandparents living with us. There's no doubt suffering abandonment and divorce by the age of five can punch holes in one's foundation, but having a hard-working father and loving grandparents sure helped make up the difference. With our grandparents at home, we began to experience some stability from our parent's divorce. Many neighborhood kids gathered to play at the corner store in those years. So, taking a trip to the store one day seemed to fit. Upon entering the store, I sought to purchase some penny candy, which was common in those times. A woman by the name of Irene ran that store for many years. We thought the world of her and always looked forward to stopping and seeing her again. In her comings and goings that day, she noticed my shoes were being worn backward. So, with a polite smile, she sat me on top of an old wooden candy counter that had been left over from the 1920s. The counter had a round bubble glass look that held some of the best-assorted candy a five-year-old could ever feast his eyes on. Irene sat me on top of that counter to help me put my shoes on straight.

As I walked away from Irene that day, she requested that I use the front door of her store. I approached the front door and saw myself looking through a plate glass window just before exiting. It appeared a man had pulled up in a 1949 Chrysler. I could see the car was about thirteen years older than most other vehicles parked in front of the store that day. Looking through the store window, the old car reminded me of a bygone era. Noting the car's history gave one the feeling of just wanting to hang on to every fiber of life for what it was worth. Intently observing the old car's condition brought to mind what once was and what was yet to be. For some reason, continuing to fixate on that old car had brought some of the most profound thoughts a child could ever have. The gazing of the car was as if I stood in the midst of time and space, cherishing the very life God had given me. Sobered by such thoughts, I was brought to a glimpse of eternity for a fleeting moment. The experience had exuberant existence of my being and everything I knew up until that moment.

Realizing my mind couldn't grasp the depth of any other profound thought I might have. I exited the store only to be interrupted by an arriving coal truck. Two men stepped from the truck, extending a conveyor belt to the basement window of the store building. Of course, the conveyor belt carried coal to the building for heating purposes. The year was 1962, and it proved to be some of the last times to see coal being used to heat public buildings. I stood there, asking the workmen multiple questions while they were transferring the coal. I didn't realize it at the time; however, I still had a sensational urge to learn everything I possibly could about life. As the two men struggled with their work, they reached a point in their patience where they were no longer willing to answer any more of my questions. So, they abruptly assured me that they wouldn't be the ones to further enlighten my curiosity.

As I walked away, I noticed a man standing across the street. He stood at the edge of the trail where kids so often played. He appeared to be a nice man and invited me over to join him. I hadn't felt alarmed by his demeanor or invitation, so I joined him at his request. He took me to the back woods, where I soon discovered I was in over my head. He appeared to be in his early twenties and coached me in having oral sex with him. He caught me twice more on those trails and repeated that same process until releasing me. After this, I never looked at our back trails as a safe haven anymore.

Furthermore, I had no idea what the long-term ramifications of abandonment, molestation, physical abuse, and verbal abuse would be in the long run. But I can say this: I would never have thought life would have so many twists and turns in the coming years. The state of feeling sane and being at peace wouldn't come for many years. One of the purposes of writing *Long Way Back* is so that some people may know there's real redemption and hope for people who have lived an abusive life. There is an ample amount of people out there who have been socially challenged because of past abuse issues. If you're one of these, then small portions of this book are specially designed for you. Many people have experienced long-term consequences from multiple abuse issues. If you're one of these, then identifying with some of these stories can possibly arm you for further personal growth. Realizing many of you haven't suffered from any type of abuse at all, I applaud you. If you are this type of person, great, I wanted you to know this book is not about making people such as yourself feel uncomfortable. So, you can relax and brace yourself for the strikingly unanticipated.

Last but not least, if you're the type of person who enjoys action, my story has a hard time escaping it. So just sit back and enjoy the movie. Dr. John Riehm is a friend of mine out of Louisville, Kentucky. Unfortunately, he passed from Covid-19 complications in 2020. It was sad because he had genuinely helped many people for nearly four decades. And, of course, many will miss his personage as well. Fortunately, I was able to speak with Dr. Riehm three days before his demise. As I spoke with him one afternoon, I mentioned to him that I had seen about four different movies that had depicted many parts of my life.

I told Dr. Riehm that when those things really happened to me, I never felt adequately compensated for all my performances. I have no doubt some of you can probably say the same thing. So, Dr. Riehm casually asked me why I hadn't written my autobiography to share some of those stories. I remarked, "I don't know." When I finally started writing *Long Way Back*, I realized that Dr. Riehm's final influence convinced me to write this story.

As you can see, it was my very intention to have shown ages one to five in a diverse setting. Notably, there are good things in life as well as bad. I'm sure glad

God provided an adequate amount of good things to help alleviate the bad. It would be the good things in life that would give a much stronger foundation later in life. When one is taken advantage of at such a young age, it clearly points to questionable character. Most people know that questionable character has the capacity to strike anytime, anywhere, and for any reason. It's not biased when it hits and usually performs evil when it does. And, it enviably strikes when one is least expecting it. In the upcoming chapters, the road is paved with a mixture of human frailties and strengths. This book is designed to see human nature at its worst and best, but certainly with a desirable outcome that too few ever achieve.

CHAPTER 3

Observations of a Growing Child

Achieving a wholesome outcome from a shattered background would prove very challenging without the help of God. In short, for most of us to attempt to do this, you'll find yourself up against something a lot bigger than you. Allow me to elaborate not only on the good but also on how the bad can overwhelm someone, and you suddenly find yourself lacking the ability to conquer deficiencies that are far greater than yourself. To this degree, I needed help and didn't realize it at the time, nor did I know how to tap into the answer. But more on that later. Our grandmother and father would often take us to an amusement park located in the small town of Ross, Kentucky. The park establishment stood out for its day. The closest amusement park of its kind would be on Cincinnati's east side. Ross Park, of Ross, Kentucky, and Coneys Island of Cincinnati, would be considered amusement park King of Hill for decades. Later, the spotlight would shift from these two icons. Breaking ground for Kings Island just north of Cincinnati would soon pave the road for future success in the amusement industry. However, Ross Park of Ross, Kentucky, was unique in its day. Its reign would last from about 1920 to 1970. The park staff prided themselves on the ability to serve as many individual families as they possibly could. Being recognized as a special family, each family was cared for the duration of the day. I haven't seen the makings of Ross Park or its services since its era. Our family would often visit the park in its hay day. There was singing, dancing, swimming and so on. The park provided a setting where my sister, Dorthy, and I learned how to jitterbug.

Interestingly, my sister and I learned much later that our parents were jitterbug champions during the 40s and the 1950s. They had won awards from many dance competitions they had entered. Numerous times, our parents would take to a dance floor in many establishments only to have their spectators in awe of their ability to jitterbug. There was no doubt Ross Park played a significant role in providing a wholesome atmosphere for many families during its reign.

Forty years would pass before revisiting the park. Stumbling across the park's ruins one day reminded me of past centuries gone by. I once managed to get my sister Dorthy to visit Ross Park to witness its final decay. Walking through the park one day with my sister Dorthy reminded us of the good times we enjoyed so much as children. She took a picture of me play-acting a jitterbug on the very floor we had learned to jitterbug some forty years earlier. As we continued our walk, we both encroached a patch of concrete where we stood for a moment or two. Dorthy looked at me and asked, "Where are we?"

I commenced pulling back some bushes that exposed faded blue paint on a concrete wall. It was the remains of a swimming pool where Dorthy and I had swam many years earlier. With my sister's sudden recognition of where we were, she wept, knowing that God had richly blessed us with this wholesome time in our lives. Some years earlier, our whole family had occupied that same park. One day, it was time to leave, and this is when I noticed both our father and his mother had a drinking problem. Leaving the park that night, our grandmother decided to have a verbal confrontation with a police officer who happened to be guiding outbound traffic from the park. Our grandmother was intoxicated and quickly became very belligerent with the officer. With the officer busy directing traffic, Grandma became impatient with his performance. She felt that the officer could do far better by allowing our vehicle to leave the park first. So, she proceeded to tell the officer that he was nothing but a "public servant" and that he needed to act accordingly. Of course, this was still a time when most people just didn't have the gull to approach authoritative figures with such a disrespectful attitude. Grandma continued to taunt the officer and made several stabbing remarks about his insufficiency. With the officer quickly eroding from our grandmother's comments, he acutely informed her that he would be more than happy to jerk her out of the car to help her gain a totally new perspective. Our father instantaneously implored our grandmother to stop agonizing over the officer's performance. With our grandmother quickly considering our father's request, she decided that the officer's totally new perspective wouldn't be necessary. So, regarding the officer's disposition, our grandmother elected to keep her mouth shut.

Seeing that the officer was clearly agitated by our grandmother's comments, I was somewhat surprised when the officer allowed our vehicle to pass anyway. To me, Grandma's belligerent demeanor toward the officer just wasn't warranted. But upon exiting the park that day, most everyone concern was if our father would consider driving while intoxicated. He would take sharp corners at high rates of speed that would scare the fire out of us. This was during a time when the automobile industry was slow to install seat belts. Our grandmother would ask our father to slow down in response to our father driving recklessly. Not acknowledging her request, Grandma would encourage all of us to lie down on the back floor to help minimize harm should our father wreck. As children, this type of behavior certainly frightened us, and it was clear that such actions were unacceptable and weren't the norm. Like anyone else, our father had good qualities as well as bad. We'd often play in the backyard just to catch Dad arriving home from work. He would usually get out of his truck and walk down the side of our house, headed for the back door. As he'd walk down the side of our home, we'd climb all over him, yelling, "Hi, Daddy!! Hi Daddy!!" When our father left for work the following morning, we'd persuade him to play a little baseball with us. We took much pride in watching our father hit the ball farther than anyone else. He was indeed our Superman, and we all loved him. As a child, and for unknown reasons to this day, God allowed me to see human strengths and frailties at a younger age. I think most kids do. It's just that most of us aren't equipped to know how to handle the bad when it rears its ugly intent.

In the coming years, we saw our father at his best and worst. I think most kids want to spend as much time with their father as possible. I certainly did. I have to admit here, I wasn't expecting such a rolling coaster ride with my dad. So, I write the following not to throw darts at him but to set the stage for how life would proceed for both my father and me. I remember once begging him at five years old to go to work with him. Of course, any father would find such a request rather tricky to fulfill during the early 60s. Dad was self-employed and owned a rather lucrative cleaning and painting business. He worked at his own company for fifty years and then retired. My younger brother Jason assumed operations of my father's company when Dad decided to retire. Jason would have been my father's first son from his second marriage to Jeannie Elam. Fortunately, our half-brother and sisters experienced a relatively good childhood, according to what they had reported to us some years later. Jason essentially joined the United States Navy years before assuming my father's business operations. With our father operating his own business for fifty years, seventeen of those years would be devoted to a part-time position with Uniroyal Incorporated. Dad began his part-time employment with Uniroyal Incorporated in 1955. But Uniroyal wasn't always known as Uniroyal Incorporated. When Dad was initially hired, the giant corporation was still referred to as the US Rubber Company. Which, of course, stood for United States Rubber Company. This company would impact my life as a child and even as a young adult. I still sometimes reminisce on the unique grandeur it held so high for so many of its days. In my father's retiring years, I'd call him occasionally and ask him if he had ever missed working at Uniroyal. He'd reply, "All the time." At any rate, here I was, five years old and wanting to go to work with my father. He had been refusing me for a little while when, one day, I suddenly decided to go to work with my dad.

So, one morning, I made it to my father's truck before he did. I managed to hide inside his truck without him noticing I was there. He proceeded most of the way to work before discovering I was hidden in the back of his truck. Once my presence was discovered, Dad became a little disgruntled but soon got over it. As Dad worked that day, I was playing in a large conference room in the main sector of Uniroyal's office. In the conference room, a red toy fire engine truck lay on a large oval table that was used to help promote Uniroyal's tire selection. And wouldn't you know, the truck was just the right size for me to ride in. Boy, how I wanted that fire truck!!! Much to my surprise, Dad brought it home with him one day. This wasn't one of those cheap plastic toys so commonly seen in today's market. This was the real deal!! One could clearly see the truck was made of real metal and ripely displayed in its deep red enamel finish. I'd run to our backyard almost every morning to make sure I had a chance to ride it. As I would mount the truck to play, it was refreshing to see those real rubber tires with full-body chrome reflecting my very image. It had all the bells and whistles any kid would die for. The truck was battery-propelled, and I ran it until it died.

As with most kids, the love of any new toy fades with time. Wondering around our backyard one day, I realized I had never told Dad or our grandmother about the man who lured me into the woods to have sex with him. People didn't talk about such things in those years. Nevertheless, between abandonment, divorce, and the little trip to the woods, these things would have quite an impact on my life in the upcoming years. As I continued my visits with my mother shortly after my incarceration, I'd share with her these many things that had come to pass in the early 1960s. Sometimes, she'd cry. Other times, she'd just say, "I wish I was there to have helped you in some way, Son." I would just reply, "Mom, even if you were there, there would have been some things you just couldn't have fixed."

CHAPTER 4

MOTHER AND SON SHARE LIFE STORIES

When you are seven years old, and all these things are happening to you, you don't just stop the world and get off. Obviously, life isn't designed that way. But, be that as it may, signs of me being abused started to stick out like a sore thumb. As I entered second grade, our teacher instructed us to learn cursive writing. For unknown reasons, she would punish me by putting my desk in a corner facing a wall when I fell behind in my assignment. As she did, this always made me feel less than and some sort of outcast. Surprisingly enough, our teacher continued to practice this approach well into the third grade. She isolated me to a corner, forbidding me from communicating with other students. It worked well. The only problem with this arrangement was I wasn't getting any of my work finished by staring at a wall. It saddened me, and I had hoped the nightmare would just go away.

Emotionally and physiologically, I was beginning to "completely withdraw from society and reality." That is to say, this became some of my behavior patterns shortly after being molested. I started getting into more trouble and seeing the principal on a regular basis. In short, I watched my world fall apart and didn't know how to stop it, much less fix it. But I do remember desperately wanting things to be normal. However, it just wasn't working out that way. Soon, our father would marry again. Our new stepmother came on the scene, portraying herself as "the mother of the millennium." That is to say, she willfully painted a picture that basically encompassed her being more of a Mary Poppins-type stepmother if she were to marry our father. Being kids, my sister Dorthy and I bought her story, hook, line, and sinker. It hadn't taken long after Jennie's marriage to our father to see right through her charade. Eventually, my sister Dorthy and I came to see Jennie as no more than an opportunist. Our maternal mother from our father's first marriage bore four children. Those children, in order, would have been Dorthy, Jack, Billy and Jerry. Our maternal mother's maiden name was Elsie Smith, but she was also known to answer to the nickname of "Tiny" when she and our father were still married.

The economy thrived in those years, and Dad was making a lot of money. He would need to because he and our new stepmother, Jennie, moved forward in procreating four more children. The four children born to our father's second marriage were Louise, Jason, Jordan, and Jill. Jordan and Jill were twins. These second four children were primarily reared in Indiana. Dorthy, Jerry, and I coincided with them briefly at the beginning of their lives. We hadn't really got to know them until the death of their mother, Jennie, some twenty years later. Surprisingly enough, Dorthy, Jerry, and I always thought it was just the three of us in our father's first marriage with our maternal mother, Elsie.

There were actually four of us, counting Billy. But Dorthy Jerry and I never knew anything about Billy's existence while growing up during our father's first and second marriage. As I continued cultivating my relationship with my maternal mother, one day, she disclosed that I had another brother. So, I asked her one afternoon, "How could this be?" She said, "Son, you have another brother named Billy." I said, "That's funny; Dad never mentioned anything to us about Billy when we were growing up." Mom said, "I'm not surprised." I asked, "Where's Billy now?" Mom said, "I don't know, Son." I said, "What do you mean you don't know?" Mom said, "Well, when your brother Billy was born, I nicknamed him Billy, but his full name at birth was William Benjamin Cummins. I had him adopted out at my bedside immediately after his birth. That's why you, your sister Dorthy, and your brother Jerry never knew anything about him, including your father." I said, "Wait a minute, Mom, why wouldn't Dad have known anything about Billy's adoption?" Mom said, "He just didn't. And I suspect your father wasn't quick to tell your sister Dorthy or your brother Jerry anything about it, was he?" I said, "That's true, but why all the secrecy about Billy?" Mom said, "Immediately after Billy's birth, I decided he would be the one child your father would never lay his eyes on." I said, "What do you mean by that?" Mom said, "Oh yeah, your father entered the hospital room that day, fully expecting to see your brother Billy there.

However, when your father entered my hospital room that day, I knew he had been drinking the night before. I had already filled out the adoption papers. I said my goodbyes to Billy before your father entered my room that day." My mother had wept for a moment or two after telling me that. Regaining her composure, she decided to complete what she started to say. A few seconds into her explanation, she said, "I really didn't want to adopt your brother Billy out, Jack. I carried Billy under my heart for the same nine months I carried the rest of you. I really didn't want to give up my baby, for what mother would? You see, Son, in those years, the authorities only needed one signature from a parent to adopt a child from your bedside. Of course, when your father arrived at the hospital later that afternoon, he was taken back from the circumstances. He immediately announced, 'Where's my son!!! Let me see my son!!!'" My mother continued and said, "I knew your father had been drinking the night before because his body reeked from the smell of alcohol. But your father continued shouting anyway, 'Where's my son!!! I'm told he is a good-looking boy!!'" So, my mother answered my father's inquiry about Billy. She said, "Yes, Jake, he is a good-looking boy, but you won't be able to see him today. Your father said, 'Well, why not babe?'" Mom said, "Because I had him adopted out this morning. Your father replied, 'What the hell are you talking about?'" Mom said, "It is plain and simple, Jake. He was adopted from my bedside this morning, and he won't be coming back for you to see. So, your father said, 'Well, how can you do something like that without telling me?'" Mom said, "Jake, when I was delivering your son last night, had it ever occurred to you, it would have been nice to see you here by my bedside as your wife delivering your son!!! Or were you too damn busy occupying that bar stool!!! Where was all your interest in your son then!!! Hey, Hell!!! As I remember it, I even had to find my own way to the hospital to have your son!!!" I said, "What did Dad say to all of that, Mom?" Mom said, "He just stood there dumbfounded and bewildered as if he didn't know what the hell I was talking about!! So, I proceeded forward in telling your father, "Jake!!! This is one child you'll never lay your eyes on. Nor will you ever be able to affect that boy's life in quite the same way you're getting ready to affect Dorthy, Jack, and Jerry's life. And that, my dear man, you can take to the bank!!"

I said, "Mom, why would you say something like that to Dad?" Mom said, "Son, Mom witnessed, first hand, all those destructive behaviors your father so willfully displayed during our seven-year marriage. And make no mistake, they were enough to last me a lifetime!! Jack, Mom has never been sorry for giving up your brother Billy for adoption. Someone had to make sure that boy would escape the hell I lived with your father for those seven years. So, I decided it would be your brother Billy who would escape. When I told your father in the hospital that he would never lay his eyes on Billy, I meant it then!!! And I damn well mean it now!!! And your father never did lay his eyes on that boy. He didn't deserve to have a son because he was an animal!!! And I had to do something to save my boy's life!!! I had to ensure Billy would never be subject to the same things. You, Dorthy, and Jerry were distended to suffer. And as to my decision to adopt your brother Billy out, I still feel it was the best decision for his life at that point as opposed to anything else. I stood by that decision then and still stand by it to this day!! If I had to do it all over again, make no mistake, Jack, Mom would have done the exact same thing again. You never have to kid yourself about that, Son!! Mom prayed to Almighty God that your brother would end up with a good family, hopefully, placed with a doctor or something like that. Do you think I really wanted to give my boy up? Don't you kid yourself? My heart still aches to this day, not knowing where my Billy is or how he's doing.

It hasn't been fun not knowing what happened to your brother. No mother in her right mind wants to give her child up. But not to have adopted Billy out was to subject him to the same life you, Dorthy, and Jerry would undoubtedly live. And Mom wasn't having any of that!! And I was going to make sure your brother Billy didn't have any either!! You see, Jack, the reason why your father didn't care enough to tell you, Dorthy, or Jerry that you had another brother was because it would have put him in a bad light. And trust me, Son, the great JC wasn't having any of that!! You see, there would have been far too much on your father's part to explain. And Mom has no doubt your father wouldn't have been up to the task of explaining anything! Mom doesn't care who you are; no one wants to put themselves in a questionable light, especially your father. His ego wouldn't have tolerated that for one second.

Think about it, Son. This is not rocket science what we are talking about here. Any man, that's to say, any kind of man, would have wanted to share their story of his lost son regardless of the circumstances. Why, that's just common sense. Simply put, your father was more interested in saving face than exposing his own evil. Make no mistake, he was just like his mother!!!" I said, "What do you mean, Mom, when you say Dad was just like his mother." "Well, Son, let us visit another time. I'm tired right now and want to go to bed." I said, "Sure, Mom." Mom said, "Maybe we'll get together tomorrow?" I said, "OK, Mom, that's fine." Mom said, "Come on, Son, I'll walk you to the door." We hugged and kissed and said good night.

Driving home that night, I couldn't help but think about my mother saying our father was more interested in hiding his evil as opposed to telling us we had another brother. The thought disturbed me because I naturally wanted to know what my mother meant by our father's evil. When I returned the next day to visit my mother, she asked if I could find my brother Billy. I said, "Mom, I wouldn't even know where to begin." Mom said, "If it will help you, Son, Billy was born in September of 1958 under the name of William Benjamin Cummins. That was his birth name before he was adopted from my bed side.

Do you think you can find him, Jack?" All I could do was listen to my mother's grief and hope she'd heal from the matter in time. So, I said, "Mom, I'm under the impression that when they closed the adoption records in the 1950s, they were truly closed. Trying to find Billy thirty years later in the 80s would be beyond anything I know how to do." Mom said, "Well, I guess I'll just let it go for now." I knew my mother didn't have the money for a private investigator, nor did I. So, I inconspicuously drew my mother's attention to the courtyard to begin our visit that day. It was a beautiful sunny day, and I thought to myself if Mom couldn't find Billy soon, she'd probably die before ever meeting him. I felt so bad for her, and yet I couldn't help her, nor would I ever meet Billy myself. Mom said, "Well, Son, did you enjoy your evening last night?" I said, "Yes, I did, Mom." Mom said, "It's hot, Jack. Let us go inside where it is a little bit cooler." I said, "OK." Walking down my mother's corridor, she unlocked her apartment door. She said, "Well, if you ever decide to look for your brother, just remember he was born in General Hospital here in Cincinnati. As you well know, that hospital is now referred to as University Hospital." I said, "OK, Mom, I'll keep that in mind." Mom said, "Come on, Son, tell me more about your four other brothers and sisters your father had with his second wife, Jennie." I said, "Well, in retrospect, Mom, I naturally focused more on Louise. She suffered bitterly from an inflamed case of asthma that she had grown up with. As a child, it was brutal to watch her suffer so much from that dreadful disease. Next in line would have been Jason. I barely knew him because I was taken out of our home and placed in Allen House when Jason was still an infant. But I learned that he had served in the United States Navy some years later. I had already been in Allen House sometime when the twins Jordan and Jill were born. So, getting to know them wouldn't occur for some years to come. Unfortunately, Jill lost her life at the hands of a UPS driver when the driver crossed over a double yellow line, hitting her car head-on. She ultimately died a few days later from her many injuries at the age of thirty-one. She was survived by her husband and two children. As far as Jill's twin brother Jordan, it appeared he managed to become a very successful landscaper who enjoyed sky diving as a hobby.

It was apparent our stepmother was pretty over whelmed with having to rear a total of eight children. Dorthy, Jerry, and I were left over from your and Dad's first marriage. Now, Louise, Jason, Jordan, and Jill were added to the mix in Dad's second marriage with Jennie." Mom said, "I thought you said there were eight children. I'm only counting seven, according to what I'm hearing." I said, "You're right. I forgot to mention that Jennie brought a three-year-old daughter with her into the marriage with Dad. The circumstances made things somewhat difficult for everyone." Mom said, "What was the eighth child's name?" I said, "Her name was Lucy." Mom said, "Oh, now I understand how the eighth child came in." I said, "You know, Mom, that family scenario created serious problems right away." Mom said, "What do you mean, Son?" I said, "Well, Jennie favored her daughter Lucy from her first marriage. She kind of wore that on her sleeve like a flag, if you know what I mean. Of course, Jennie didn't think Dorthy, Jerry, and I could see through that kind of thing, but we did. It's a hard road to hoe when it comes to making a family out of two former families. I think Jennie may not have expected the task to be difficult. And for that matter, neither had Dad." Mom said, "Well, it's like I said before; Jennie was overwhelmed with having to take care of all of you." I said, "Sadly, in order to make up the difference, Jennie drafted Dorthy as her new Cinderella. And make no mistake, she worked Dorthy's fingers to the bone, stealing much of her childhood." Mom said, "That Bitch!! If I knew where she was, I'd slap her face good!! I said, "Mom, if we are going to have these types of conversations, you can't just fly off the handle about it because there's nothing in the world you can do about it now. And I would appreciate it if you could watch your language when we talk about these things." Mom said, "I'm sorry, Son, please continue." I said, "Jennie would take her frustrations out on Jerry by beating him relentlessly with an ironing cord. She'd beat Jerry so bad that Dorthy and I had to walk down the street to escape the horrifying screams Jerry so ripely displayed. Trust me, it was far more than being corrected, plain and simple; it was physical abuse, and it appeared she didn't mind dishing it out.

At times, Dorthy and I would return from those walks only to find red welts all over Jerry's body, with blood protruding from some of those welts. I hated Jennie for beating Jerry like that, and I used to entertain thoughts of assaulting her when I grew up. It became clear by her abuse and her general attitude that she favored her first daughter Lucy from her first marriage and lacked the same interest for Dorthy, Jerry, and myself. Jennie continuing to favor her first daughter fostered an atmosphere of ambivalence with just the right mixture of absurd." Mom said, "Boy! I don't know if I can stand to hear anymore, Son." I said, "Well, stay tuned because it doesn't get any better. That atmosphere totally alienated Dorthy, Jerry, and myself and left us feeling like we were really all alone. On occasion, Jennie would try to convince our father that the real problem was with Dorthy, Jerry, and myself. We were quite capable of picking up on her antics when it came to those types of conversations with Dad." Mom said, "Boy, if I had been there, Son, none of those things would have ever happened." I said, "I know that, Mom, but you weren't there, were you?" My mother would just cry and say, "I'm so sorry, Son, I'm so sorry I wasn't there to help you, Dorthy and Jerry."

At the beginning of my and my mother's visits, I had such a hard time forgiving her for abandoning us. And yet, I knew she'd eventually disclose more on the subject in the upcoming years. I sensed her explanation of leaving us at such a young age would be rather complex to explain and not the easiest thing to cover in a few visits. I think most of us seek absolute understanding from a returned parent all in our first visit. I want my readers to understand something here, "It doesn't work like that." It takes TIME, UNDERSTANDING, FORGIVENESS, and PATIENCE, then you'll be able to piece things together. But without TRUE FORGIVENESS, which may TAKE TIME, you'll never reach your objective, much less have a MEANINGFUL RELATIONSHIP. Rarely is it wise to conclude an abandoning parent's motives without hearing all the facts over a period of time. Realizing this, I wanted to give my mother and me an adequate chance to develop a quality relationship without being biased one way or another. Both my mother and I found our task of getting to know one another very arduous at times.

There were times when Mom and I just wanted to pull our hair out. Nevertheless, we both elected to stay the course. Remember, folks, when you're building a late relationship with a returning parent, understand that both of you will have things you won't like about each other. Both of you will have foibles and idiosyncrasies from an earlier life that neither one of you will readily understand or like. So, get over it and get on with it. Even if you need to take short intervals of time-out to proceed with your relationship, do it, but then return to your efforts so as not to dismiss the whole process. Most of you will find that the above approach will pay off in the long run if we are willing to follow the above principles. *Just remember to stay the course if you want the benefit.*

On the other hand, I know some of you have a parent, or parents, who are still willing to continue to hold you at bay and seemingly never want to deal with you. Let them go until they are ready. And if they decide never to ready themselves, then obviously you have done your part. So, I would sit there telling my mother stories of Dad's second marriage and many things that had come to pass. Dorthy Jerry and I knew what it was like to grow up in an upper-middle-class neighborhood, have all the physical things in life, and still be miserable. No doubt, our father felt overwhelmed and had a drinking problem in addition. Continuing my visits with my mother, I told her one day that our stepmother Jennie was, in fact, the fourth cousin of the famous movie star, Jack Elam. She said, "Really, Son?" I said, "Yeah, Mom." Mom said, "I remember seeing Jack in a lot of western movies. He played with people like John Wayne and all those other western characters." I said, "That's right, Jack Elam played in many cowboy movies." Mom said, "Son." I said, "Yeah, Mom, what is it?" Mom said, "Have you ever told your father about your little trip to the woods when that man made you have oral sex with him?" I said, "Well, Mom, that's certainly a change of subject, but the answer to your question is no, I never did. I really didn't feel Dad would have the capacity to absorb all that, much less know how to deal with it. Besides, I wasn't out there looking for anyone to tell anyway. Nor did Dad realize many of our family's new problems stemmed from such behaviors. Furthermore, Dad simply hadn't come to grips with many of his own demons.

Unfortunately, he was pretty preoccupied with trying to drown out many of his own issues with the use of alcohol. I can understand his approach because I tried drowning out many of the same problems by using illicit drugs. I have known many people to choose drinking and drugging over getting help through counseling. They would rather die on that stuff than deal with the problem. In all fairness to these folks, many of them simply didn't know what the problem was. The irony is that most of them are convinced there is no problem; just ask them. And suppose they do acknowledge there's a problem. In that case, many are convinced there is no need to check in to it because, after all, they really have the situation under control.

What a crock!! You know what I say to that, Mom?" She said, "What, Son?" I said, "They better get a head start working on such matters now because when Jesus Christ sets up His Kingdom, it will truly require them to change. This so-called drowning in a bottle or sticking a joint in one's mouth to escape will no longer be tolerated. At any rate, Dad did the best thing he knew how to do in those years, and that was to take us to work with him as much as possible. This proved to be the only thing worthwhile that came out of my and Dad's relationship.

Though a good work ethic is critical in life, "it certainly doesn't address the life of the whole person." Mom said, "You know, Son, you are absolutely right in saying that because Mom can attest that your father was the hardest worker I have ever known. And if he took you and Dorthy to work with him, that's probably one of the best things he could have done for either of you. I have to give your father all the credit in the world for being a hard worker. Boy! That man could work any other man right under the table. And Mom really means it, Son. Your father really knew how to work!! And his father was the same way! You know, Son, let Mom tell you a story about your father's work ethic when we were still married." I said, "OK, by all means proceed." Mom said, "Well, your father came home after a hard day's work early in the spring one year.

I knew there was something wrong, so I asked him, 'What's wrong, babe?' He said, 'They just want to use me up, they just want to use me up!!!' I said, 'Honey, who wants to use you up? What in the world are you talking about?' Your father said, 'Well, when I'm at work, it never seems like I can get anywhere because I always feel like I'm being used up.' I said, 'Well, babe, why don't we start our own business?' Your father replied, 'Yeah, I already know how to do the work!' I said, 'That's right, babe, we can do it together for ourselves. I can do the clerical work and make our phone calls, and you can go and make sure the job is being done right. With my office skills and you performing the work, you'll never have to feel used up again.' Boy!! Your father took off like a bat out of hell, making good money right away. I was so proud of him! And he wasn't singing that tune anymore about how someone was using him up. He was so busy changing the quality of our lives that there wasn't enough time to pay attention to anything else.

The Korean war had just come to an end, and our country was at peace again. The economy started to thrive for most people with lots of promise. After a short while in business, your grandmother Victoria became jealous of our new lifestyle. She decided she wanted to pay us a visit. Before your grandmother arrived that day, your father had just finished one of his projects and received a completion check. So, your father went out and surprised me right away by buying lots of items that I had been wanting for a while. When he came home from shopping that day, he took the time to hang some beautiful curtains that I had always wanted. Well, needless to say, your grandmother made it over that evening with all her venom intact. She systemically and methodically took those beautiful curtains down after your father had worked so hard putting them up. And your father let her do it too!!! Your father began to explain his mother's actions away by saying, 'Ah!! Don't worry about it, babe; we'll just buy some more!!' But that wasn't the point, Jack, I felt terribly violated!! It was like our home was being constantly invaded by my mother-in-law, who had no respect for me at all!! None!! Zero!!! Bare in mind, Son, that her actions in doing these types of things were nothing less than appalling to me, not to mention how intimidating they were.

She didn't care how she treated me and couldn't care less how I felt about anything. Because after all, don't you know, I took her little boy away from her!!!

And she was damn well going to make me pay for it. Son, Mom didn't understand your grandmother's attitude or her actions when it came to your father. Why that old broad made me sick!!! She made me put up with her verbal abuse all through our marriage on a regular basis, whether I liked it or not. With your grandmother on the scene in those years, I couldn't have found a better jackass, even if it were granted by the United States Congress. I couldn't imagine what your grandmother had hanging over your father's head that would allow her to treat me like a fool!! What made things worse was that your father would get all drunken up with her and then try to make me out to be the bad guy. I could clearly see your father loved me, but when it came to his mother, it was like I didn't exist at all. Any time that old broad came around, I was always treated like a second-class citizen. It didn't take me long to figure out why my mother-in-law had so much influence over my husband. I thought I was fighting an uphill battle, especially when they drank together. Son, Mom was a young woman back then, and I had never contended with such things before. Oh, I'm sorry, Son. Mom didn't mean to interrupt you. It is just that all those things came back to me when you were talking about your father putting you and Dorthy to work. Please proceed with what you were saying." I said, "Well, with Dorthy and I out of school for the summer, Dad would take us to work with him. Dorthy would clean ash trays and wipe off the desk while I emptied garbage cans and dust-mopped the floors. I think it was Dad's way of breaking up the monopoly of a deplorable situation from his second marriage. He couldn't have picked a better way to do it. But at the same time, he was lost on how to fix his own family, much less himself. Living with our new step mother was like not knowing what to expect from one minute to the next. It wasn't like the early '60s when we'd ask Grandpa for a nickel to go buy a push-up ice cream at the corner store. Nor were we awakened to a happy dog wagging his tail. The fresh golden brown cinnamon toast also became a thing of the past. And Twinkle Twinkle Little Star, well, it, too, had gone right out the window. Those days were long gone, and so was the peace there of.

Our new life now consisted of whatever type of mood our step mother Jennie was in. And if that consisted of her being totally asinine, so be it. In short, Jerry, Dorthy, and myself were living in an absurd form of oppression and suppression. Especially Jerry. And there was nothing we could do about it." Mom said, "Son." I said, "Yes, Mom, what is it?" Mom said, "Had you, Dorthy, and Jerry really felt oppressed?" I said, "Yes, we did, Mom. We had nowhere near the same liberty and peace we had with Grandma and Grandpa when they lived with us.

My schoolwork continued to decline, and so did our morale. As both Dorthy and I attended school in those years, we both were forced to engage in violent behavior that was basically being fueled by the civil rights movement. Dorthy once got into a vicious fight at school, and the principal requested that Dad's appearance be made in order to get the situation under control. These types of incidents added stress to an already highly charged atmosphere at home. I continued to isolate myself from everyone. But I always enjoyed it when Dad awakened me at 4:30 in the morning to go to work with him. As I would rise to my feet to get dressed, Dad would ask me, 'Did you sleep fast?' I always answered him by asking, 'How in the world can I do that?' Going to work with him in the mid-1960s was my safe haven for a while. We'd stop at a restaurant to eat before work and sit there and talk about everything. I loved it when Dad shared his life with me this way. These regular stops provided the gentle and compassionate side of my father. So, I always looked forward to our stops before work, hoping they'd last a lifetime." Mom said, "Son, that's how your father was when we first got married. He was gentle and observant at the beginning of our marriage, and then, over time, he really began to suck that bottle." I said, "Mom, that's exactly the way it was in my first love with Sheryl. At the beginning of our relationship, everything was great, but soon, it went to hell in a hand-basket. And a lot of it had to do with me getting high, abusing Sheryl, and running around with those gangsters." Mom said. "Mom can only imagine, Son. When your father went to work for Ruble Bakery in the 1950s, he got in with a bunch of crazy hillbil-lies." I asked, "What do you mean?" Mom said, "Well, he started working for Ruble Bakery when I was big in the family way with your sister Dorthy.

Not long after your dad started working at Ruble Bakery, he and those hillbillies started drinking moonshine together. Your father really went crazy when he started drinking that stuff. Why, I remember one time your father went out drinking with those idiots, and he decided to bring a few of them home. You could tell all three of them were crazy drunk and out of their mind. Well, anyways, one of them decided he wanted to get down on his hands and knees and bark like a dog!!!" I said, "Really?" Mom said, "Hell yeah!!! Why that Joker thought he was a dog!!! When he started barking, I knew he had totally lost his mind!!! Your father was sitting there on the couch when I told him that he'd better get off his duff and get rid of those idiots. You know, Son, when your father drank moonshine, I really began to believe that stuff really started to pickle his brain." I said, "What do you mean by that, Mom?" Mom said, "Well, do you remember a couple years back when you and I were just renewing our relationship with one another?" I said, "Yes, I remember that." Mom said, "Well, one day, you mentioned to me what date your brother Jerry was born and how your sister Dorthy's name was spelled when she grew up." I said, "Yeah, so?" Mom said, "Well, Son, every mother knows what date her son was born on and how her daughter's name was spelled." I replied, "So, what's your point?" Mom said, "Why were you telling me Dorthy's name was spelled totally different from how it was spelled when your father and I were still married? And then you told me Jerry's birthday was July 30th. I realized neither one was true." I said, "Really?" Mom said, "Yes, really!!" I said, "Then what are the correct answers?" Mom said, "Well, when I was still married to your father, your sister's name was still being spelled Dorothy. And now you're telling me it's spelled Dorthy. And your brother Jerry wasn't born on July the 30th; he was born July 29, 1960." I said, "OK, and what does all this have to do with Dad drinking moonshine?" Mom said, "Well, that's just my point, Son. It's like Mom said.

After your father and I divorced, I wondered what could have caused him to forget how his daughter's name was spelled or what date Jerry was born on?" I said, "Oh yeah, I see what you mean now." Mom said, "Your father just wasn't that stupid, Jack. And for your father to have forgotten how to spell his own daughter's name or what date Jerry was born on really struck me as odd. That's why I thought maybe the moonshine your father had been drinking was really starting to pickle his brain," I said, "I really don't know, Mom. I can't rightfully say one way or another." Mom said, "Someone would have had to change the spelling of your sister's name and the date of Jerry's birthday after your father and I were divorced." I said, "Well, Mom, I really don't know." Mom said. Well, Son, I'd like to get back to what happened when your grandmother and father drank together. It seemed they both enjoyed making me out to be the bad guy when they drank together." I said, "OK, Mom, so tell me what you have to say." Mom said, "Well, sometimes I would get a break from all that nonsense and madness your father would pull when your grandfather would show up. It was as if your grandfather knew when I had enough with your grandmother and your father. No doubt about it, he knew exactly how your grandmother and your father were when they drank together. I remember once hoping your grandfather would come over because I knew there would be peace for a while." I said, "What do you mean?" Mom said, "Well, I always referred to your grandfather as daddy, so when he came over, he made darn sure your grandmother Victoria and your father wouldn't pull their shenanigans!!! And your father didn't like it one bit when your grandfather would stop over because your grandfather would have your daddy hopping' to the tune!!!" I said, "What do you mean, Mom, by hopping to the tune?" Mom said, "Well, one time your grandfather came over early in the spring when I was prominent in the family way with your brother Jerry. By that time, the handwriting was pretty much on the wall, whether or not my and your father's marriage would even survive. We had reached a point in our marriage where most of your father's friends and mine knew our marriage wouldn't last until the end of the year.

Your father and I were just going through the motions to have our friends believe that our marriage was just fine. Well, at any rate, I think your grandfather came over one day to smooth things over between your father and me, hoping our marriage would move forward. I was trying to get my windows washed for the spring season. But I was having a time of it because I was still big in the family way with your brother Jerry. When your grandfather saw I was having a difficult time washing the windows, he immediately enrolled your father's services as if he were in the Marine Corps. Yes Sir!!! You can believe your father didn't have any time to suck that bottle that day!!! Yes, sir, your father was hopping' all around there like GI Joe!!! Your grandfather had your dad washing all those windows and anything else he could find for him to do. Yes, sir!!! You better believe it!! And your grandmother Victoria didn't open her mouth one time!!! That old broad knew to keep her mouth shut when your grandfather was around. Yes Sir!!! You can believe that with all your heart. Victoria knew when she was in over her head with your granddaddy. So, she made darn sure she kept her mouth shut during the entire visit!! No, sir, they didn't fool with that old man! Son, don't take Mom wrong! Your grandfather was a kind man, but make no mistake about it, your grandmother and father knew not to fool with that old man. And Mom really means it too, Son." I said, "Hey, I believe ya." Mom said, "Well, it's a good thing you do because your grandfather was definitely from a different era altogether." I said, "What do you mean by that, Mom?" Mom said, "Well, Jack, your grandpa was fifty years older than your father. So, there was still plenty of room for another generation, if you know what I mean. He was a mountain man that lived up in the hills of Canada. He knew another mountain man up there who helped him build his log cabin. And in return, your grandfather helped the other mountain man build his log cabin. They became friends for life and never lost contact with one another. It was said that both men kept their friendship intact until one of them died some sixty years later.

Both men lived high in the mountains and, on occasion, were forced to fight Blackfoot Indians at the boarder of our country. Your grandfather knew what it was like to fight off bears and wolves. That's why Mom said your father and grandmother knew not to fool with that old man because of him being of a totally different mentality altogether. Why your grandfather still live during a time when your nays were nays, and your yays were yays. Hey, hell, Son, there was no gray in those years. If your yays weren't yays, and your nays weren't nays, you were likely to find yourself standing at the end of a gun barrel, hoping that your grays hadn't been discovered. So, yes sir, when your grandfather came over to visit that week, it was, yes sir, no sir, three bags full!! Now, you can believe that with all your heart!! And to be quite frank, I had hoped Daddy, your grandfather, would come over more often because of all the hell we were going through in those years. Mother, sorry, Son, I keep interrupting your story. Please proceed with what you were saying." I said, "It's OK, Mom, don't worry about it, I'm used to the abuse." Mom said, "Oh baloney, get on with your story, boy, before I really thump ya!!" I said, "OK, Mom.

Well, Dad would search for ways to soften the blows for Dorthy, Jerry, and myself, only to find he was dealing with something much bigger than himself. With heavier drinking, Dad really started to change. Once, I showed interest in playing football for a local team named Jake Sweeney Tomahawks. This wasn't a school team; it was a public team. And we all would meet for practice over in McAvoy Park in College Hill. I was surprised Dad was interested in seeing me make the team. So, he took me to a sporting store where he bought all that I would need to play the game. Those were times I felt close to Dad. I really believed Dad tried hard at times to be the best father he could possibly be under his own circumstances." Mom said, "Of that, I have no doubt, Son. From what I remember about your father, he had good qualities as well. I know we sit here and run him through the mill at times, but I also know you love your father. And there's not one of us that hasn't been wrong at times in our lives." I said, "You've got that right, Mom.

At any rate, after practicing football for several weeks, I was suddenly cut from our team. Somehow, I wasn't able to understand the plays that were being called in the huddle. Dad and our stepmother Jennie only attended one practice, so they really weren't able to note any problems that I may have been having. I'm not sitting here, Mom, and telling you that they never attended any of my practices. I'm just saying I found it rather odd that they only attended one practice. So, at any rate, I came home one day after being cut from our football team and found Dad lying on the couch watching television. I tried breaking the news to him in a nice way, saying that I had been cut from our team. I explained to him that I wasn't able to understand the plays that were being called in the huddle. I explained to him with the quarterback constantly changing the numbers in the huddle, it had me confused. And, of course, the results of that confusion had me executing the wrong moves as the play was in motion. I thought Dad would have understood what I was trying to tell him. But he grew impatient with my explanation and said, 'Just go. *I knew you couldn't make it anyway*!!' After being dismissed from him, I found a place in our house where I could hide and cry. His message was much the same as my teachers when they would elect to put my desk in a corner to face the wall. I was at a total loss in my mind on what to do, much less on how to feel about such things. Dad's drinking progressed, and things only got worse for everyone." Mom said, "What do you mean by that, Son." I said, "Well, there were a couple of separate occasions where our stepmother Jennie feared Dad would return home drunk and become violent. In order to avoid any conflict, she would rent a couple of hotel rooms so that all of us could spend the night until Dad sobered up. Most of us didn't have enough sense to know we were in danger. Jennie seemed to understand it. Don't get me wrong, as kids, we, too, felt something was really wrong with Dad's drinking. We just didn't know what to make of it." Mom said, "I'd like to elaborate a little bit on your father's drinking, Son, when your father and I were still married. But for right now, go ahead with what you were saying."

"As I was saying, Dad really started to change because of his drinking. Working together with him in the mid-60s was far better than trying to work with him in the late 60s. His behavior went from being my dad and my friend to a man I didn't even know at all. It was as if his anger was starting to turn against everyone. I was nine at the time, and his drinking continued to get worse. He and our stepmother, Jennie, would continually fuss and fight about his drinking. Dad began to have vicious bouts of violent behavior that truly frightened me. At times, he would stop to take me on his drinking campaigns. Not knowing how dramatic the campaign would proceed, there was never enough time to sell front-row seats." Mom started laughing and said, "Yeah!! You ain't telling me nothing!!! I definitely know how your daddy's drinking campaigns went. Hell, I had a front-row seat long before all you kids were even born!! And I didn't have to purchase any tickets to watch your father tear the place up. I remember once your father got drunk at a local bar in our neighborhood. As he walked home that night, he decided to tear up six or eight parked cars along the side of the road. He'd smash their windows out to gain entrance to the vehicle and then tear them apart inside the car. It was like watching a vicious animal go crazy. If the car were a convertible, he'd take a knife and cut through the canvas roof to gain entrance. Once inside the car, he'd rip the rest of the canvas off the metal frame. Then, he'd commence twisting the metal frame out of place so as to prohibit the top from operating correctly.

Man!! It was a mess, Son!!! And the courts would make him pay for all that non-sense, too. It kept us in the poor house for about a year and a half until he could pay all that back. Yeah, Mom saw those drunken rages first hand. It was horrific, to say the least." I said, "Wait a minute, Mom, allow me to finish what I was saying." Mom said, "I'm sorry, Son, go on with what you were saying." I said, "Once, Dad and I were on one of his drinking campaigns while a plainclothes detective decided to pull his car over. Dad had already had a few drinks, and it was raining pretty hard outside that day.

The officer and Dad were engaged in a heated argument on whether or not I would be taken into custody for safe keeping. Dad and I were sitting in a 1954 Chevrolet station wagon parked on the side of the road. It was raining so hard that day, and Dad decided to lower his window by about four inches in order to speak with the officer. As Dad and the officer talked, Dad found the officer's verbal demands somewhat agitating. The officer kept announcing to Dad that he was going to take me away for my own protection. Dad announced to the officer that he wasn't going to take anyone. With the policemen clearly bigger than Dad, I was convinced that the officer would seriously injure Dad in some kind of way. The atmosphere between the officer and Dad grew more and more highly charged on both sides until I began to cry. Suddenly, Dad emerged from our car at lightning speed to beat the officer with in an inch of his life. After the policeman lost consciousness, Dad took his necktie off to tie his hands behind his back. I was sobbing so hard I inadvertently opened the car door on my side. This gave me hope to escape the trauma I so desperately felt from the violence. With my car door opened, I momentarily contemplated my situation while observing about four inches of rainwater running through the gutter. I suddenly heard Dad's voice shout out, 'Shut the car door, Jack!!!' Shutting our car door, I looked on to see what would become of the police officer. Dad carried the detective's body across the street like a piece of rolled-up carpet that was flopping from both ends. As Dad approached the officer's vehicle, he quickly opened the back door. He threw the policeman's body in the back seat of his own cruiser. The officer's fate became sealed when Dad hog-tied the officer and left him unconscious in the back seat of his own car. While the detective lay unconscious in his own cruiser, Dad walked across the street and got drunk at a local bar. Being totally traumatized from the episode, I had no way of ever knowing when the next occurrence would take place. Or if I should automatically assign myself to another traumatic outcome. I witnessed these types of things at the age of six and will see much more in the coming years.

Dad's vicious and violent acts become regular procedure." Mom said, "Oh, I know, Son, you don't have to tell me at all!! Once, your father got in a fight with two policemen at a bowling alley. By the time the fight was over, one officer hung from his duty belt attached to an old iron hook on the wall. Your father then heralds the other officer down a bowling alley, explaining to him that he would be the best object to knock the pins down. It was like watching a gorilla manhandle two human beings in a circus. Truly a scene out of the movies," I said, "Wow, you must have gone through all that too?" Mom said, "Yes, I did, Son!! Mom knew exactly what all that madness was about. And like how!" I said, "As Dad suffered from his alcoholism, the violence continued. I started looking for ways not to attend his drinking campaigns anymore for fear that the violence would eventually turn against me. I was right. The violence eventually did turn to me.

One night, Dad and I stopped at a bar. I was seven at the time, and things seemed okay at first. Dad was supplying me with plenty of nickels and dimes to play the bowling ball machine while he drank at the bar counter. After several drinks, he suddenly asked me to sit next to him. Joining him, he began explaining to me not to ever take my eyes off of anyone walking through the door. He'd slap my face and say, 'Do you understand me, boy, when I tell you not to take your eyes off of anyone walking through the door?' I'd just reply, "Yes sir, yes sir." Mom said, "Ah, BS!! You had no damned business being in a bar at seven, much less having your face slapped!" I said, "Chill, Mom, just let me tell you what happened." Mom said, "I'm sorry, Son, go on." I said, "About that time, Dad noticed a huge man sitting in an obscure corner of the tavern. The giant man had six or eight other men accompanying him at his table. Dad could hear the big man convincing his company that he was the King. This giant went on to assure his company that he was the King and there was none other like him. So, the King's company responded by assuring him that he was truly great in every way. With Dad hearing and observing the King's approach to his company, he wasn't so convinced that the King was all he thought he was. So, Dad decided to introduce himself to the King. I stayed seated at the bar counter as Dad walked over to meet the man at his table.

Deep inside, I knew this wasn't going to turn out like another day at Disneyland. And for once, I honestly feared Dad being seriously hurt by this mountain of a man. After all, even with Dad weighing in about 250lbs at that time, he still looked like a pup compared to this guy." Mom said, "He must have been huge, Son?" I said, "Huge is definitely not the word, Mom. The man was ridiculously huge. As Dad approached the King's table, he asked if he could be seated next to him. I had the deepest feeling the King was about to experience what it was like to see a bomb go off. I just wasn't convinced that Dad's physical explosion of effort would be enough to overtake this man. A few men sitting with the King looked at Dad as if to say, 'Are you sure you want to sit next to this man?' Sitting down at the King's table, Dad asked the giant what was going on. The King replied, 'I was just telling these fellows that I'm the King and that there's none other like me.' The other men accompanying the King looked at Dad with eagerness, awaiting his reply. Dad asked the giant how long he had been King? The huge man stated that he had always been King and that there would be no other to challenge his excellency.

The King suddenly slammed his hand on the table to reinforce his message and announced, 'Isn't that right, boys, I'm the King!!!?' Heck, when the King's hand hit the table, I felt its vibration all the way across the room from where I sat. The other men sitting at the King's table were still in agreement with the King's outlook and sucked up double to his personage. The King continued to glorify himself while the other men at the table wondered if Dad had something else to add to the equation. Dad suddenly informed the King that he was no longer King and then told the King's men that they had nothing to be afraid of. In defense of the King, his men assured Dad that they weren't scared of the King and that Dad didn't need to defend them. Dad abruptly interrupted their claim and said to the King, 'By the time all of this is over, you may want to rethink your position altogether.' After Dad made his announcement, the King seemed to be somewhat perplexed by Dad's approach. With the bar currently under renovation, Dad and the King sat close to a wall that had just been installed. It may have been that the studs in the wall were positioned too far apart for what was about to happen, Mom, for I don't know. Nor have I seen the makings of it since. So, the giant looked at Dad and said, 'My dear boy, I believe you have something you'd like to get off your chest?' Dad answered the King and said, 'Yes, I do!! For I'm not here for pleasure purposes but to dethrone you and bring you to absolutely nothing in the sight of all your yes men.' The whole bar looked at Dad as if he had lost his mind. Suddenly, the giant slid his chair back in anticipation of battle. Dad immediately emerged from his seat, grabbing the King by his neck. Tightening his grip, Dad thrust forward, pushing the giant toward the wall that had just been installed. With only ten to twelve steps before both men would hit the wall, you could undoubtedly see the rest of the patrons were in total disbelief that Dad had even gotten that far with their King.

When Dad and the King hit the wall, they crashed through to the other side, leaving a vast hole where their bodies just passed through. It shocked the socks of everyone. All the bar customers were in disbelief at what they had just seen. Pieces of drywall and stud splinters were shattered everywhere. Hollywood couldn't have picked a better scene for a movie. It appeared the new room the two men crashed through was built for additional stock. With the light on in the room, the remaining conflict would be seen crystal clear, to say the least. As both men lay on the floor from colliding through the wall, Dad managed to make it to his feet first.

With Dad making it to his feet first, he kicked the King everywhere he saw an opening. It was terrible, Mom!!! Myself and the whole bar watched the King take the beating of his life. My stomach turned to knots as I watched this man get his guts kicked out. The violence itself forced silence and sadness on all other patrons. It was as if every kick the man received brought a new knot in my stomach. As Dad kicked the man repeatedly, he screamed at the top of his lungs, saying, 'You were nothing when I got here, and you still are nothing!!!' As I looked around the bar, the faces of its occupants were sorrowed with fear, hoping someone would stop the fight. There was no such luck for their King. When Dad had his fill of the fight, he walked away to take a sip of his beer. He then sat his beer down to inform the rest of the tavern that he was now the new King and there was none other like him. No one seemed to want to argue the point as they observed their former King's broken body lying on the floor. But for me, I had had enough. I never wanted to see any man be beaten like that again. Nor was I impressed with Dad becoming the new King. I didn't want to feel knots in my stomach anymore, nor contemplate what may or may not happen in Dad's next escapade. Or how traumatizing the circumstances could become. I simply didn't want to be traumatized anymore."

"My God, Son, I don't know how you could have stood up to all of that. I could only imagine how crazy all that stuff was." I said, "Yes, it was, Mom, and I didn't care to experience it anymore." Mom said, "You know, Son, it's funny that you should mention your father beating up a man claiming to be a king." I said, "What do you mean?" Mom said, "Well, when your father and I were young, oh, I'd say about twenty, we walked into a place one night where we used to dance a lot. We no longer got into the door when your father decided to announce in a loud voice, 'I'm the King!! I'm the King!!! Well, he no more than got those words out of his mouth when he was met with a punch that sent him across the bar room. It embarrassed the hell out of your father, and we both left right away.

I felt bad for your father, and I elected not to speak about the incident for fear of hurting his pride." I said, "Had the two of you known the man from a previous time?" Mom said, "Well, we knew the man had run around with another crowd that was about ten years senior to us. Other than that, we hadn't known the man personally or anything like that. The man in question was about thirty and had obviously been around. I was just glad he didn't hurt your father any more than what he had. Needless to say, your father didn't talk about being the King anymore." I said, "Mom." Then she responded, "Yes, Son, what is it?" I said, "I just didn't want to go out with Dad anymore when he drank like that." Mom said, "I know that, Son. It came to that same point long before your father and I were divorced. His own friends stopped coming around him. Your father would get drunk and become so obnoxious with his friends that they'd finally reach a point where they just didn't want anything to do with him anymore. And all of them were his friends, Son!! When your father and I started dating, I didn't know all of his friends. I really didn't!! They were mostly his friends before my time. And to be quite frank, your father was a very charismatic man who could attract and influence other people dynamically. For him to be basically an uneducated man by the world's standard, he did very well at attracting top-caliber individuals who really wanted to hear what your father had to say. But when his friends saw his persistent belligerence fueled by his drinking, they just got the hell away from him.

So, no sooner than he'd attract the right people, it usually became something short-lived. Some of those folks could have really helped skyrocket your father's business if he hadn't drunk so much. It was sad because both of us watched new opportunities go by the wayside as your father's drinking progressed down through the years. He and I would talk about lost opportunities at times, only for him to fluff it off by saying things like, 'Hey babe, I don't need any of those people; I'm already better than any of them will ever be. Besides, I've done forgot more than most of them will ever know.' Mom continued, "Well, the drinking systemically destroyed your father and gradually ran most of his friends off. He got in the habit of sabotaging relationships with people who were the closest to him. And at one given point, that would include me as well."

I knew my mother was right in her observation about Dad sabotaging relation-ships. I once had the opportunity to do business with a couple that my parents had known long before I was even born. Doing business with these two came many years after my parents divorced and long after my mother's death. This particular couple and my parents grew up together in the Avondale area in Cincinnati in the mid-1940s and 50s. Answering their service call one day, I introduced myself as

Jack Cummins. The gentleman answering the door inquired if my father's name was Jake Cummins? I said, "Yes, it is. How do you know that?" Before the gentleman could tell me how he knew my father's name, his wife interrupted and asked, "Had people referred to your mother as Tiny?" I answered, "Yes, how do you know that?" She replied, "My husband and I ran in the same crowd with your parents in the 1940s and 50s." The woman continued and said, "Boy! Your father was some character, to say the least, and everyone liked him." So, as I conducted business with these two, the time slowly drew near for me to finish their project. As I mentioned, my mother had already passed some ten years prior to meeting these two. And with both of them knowing my parents, I wanted to speak with at least one of them to corroborate some of my mother's stories. I knew it was rather unusual to discuss personal business with a client. Still, I suspected there could be some validity in the stories Mom shared with me when she was alive.

So, I sought the gentleman's wife out one day in the hope that she would elaborate more on their relationship with my parents. I asked her if she felt Dad had run people away with his drinking problem? She quietly and sadly replied, "Yes, Jack, he did. We all felt very sorry for your father because we all liked him and wanted the best for him as well. After all, your father was a very likable man and probably still is to this day. Unfortunately, we had to sit there and watch him systemically destroy himself with his drinking. After a while, your father's abusive behavior forced a decision on whether or not my husband and I wanted to continue our friendship. My husband and I felt bad for having to sever our acquaintance with your mother and father. Still, it obviously became necessary at one given point." I said, "Well, I kind of expected what you were going to say." The woman sighed and said, "If I'm hearing you right, Jack, I think you're probably wondering if your mother was correct in her assessment of your father's drinking problem?" I said, "Yes, ma'am, you're hearing me right." The woman silently and regrettably remarked, "Your mother was right in the things she has told you, Jack. But more than that, my husband and I still cherish the memories of your parents and miss the fondness we once held in such high esteem for both of them." I said, "Thank you, I really wasn't surprised by all that you've disclosed, and I hope I haven't overstepped my bounds from a professional stand point." She said, "Not at all, Jack." So, I gracefully bowed out of our conversation and finished the final makings of her work. Having studied the ramifications of abuse issues before, I knew sabotaging relationships was a common trait in people who had been abused themselves. Especially if they had been sexually abused. When my mother claimed that my father had sabotaged relationships, it rang a bell with me. For I had watched my father purposely sabotage relationships, one right behind the other, and was perfectly willing to do so. But interesting enough, I, too, had the same propensities and didn't understand why. Today, I realize some of those tendencies come from what a person has been exposed to, while other tendencies derive from the spirit of a man.

At any rate, getting back to my father's violent acts, I said, "Mom, it was as I anticipated. Dad's violent behavior finally turned against me." Mom said, "What do you mean, Son?" I said, "Well, once Grandma was visiting us, and she knew Dad would soon be arriving home intoxicated. I was in the backyard playing when Grandma suddenly opened the second-floor window to announce Dad would soon be arriving drunk. So, I asked her, 'Is there a reason why you're telling me this?' Grandma said, 'Yes, there is. It's because if he finds you here, he'll kill ya.' I didn't understand Grandma's reasoning of why Dad would want to kill me, but believing what she said, I quickly fled our home premises. Walking away to honor my grandmother's sudden warning, it dawned on me that my grandmother just told me that my father would be willing to kill me. At just eight years old, her comment didn't make any sense to me at all. Why would my father feel that he needed to kill me when he got home? And the answer is, it's not that Dad wanted to literally murder me physically, but more that he wanted to continue abusing me verbally, physiologically, and physically. Of course, with Dad being intoxicated, Grandma became more concerned about Dad's inhibitions to perform more violence. I remember witnessing on the news from time to time where an individual would lose their life from such notions springing up. After Dad had been home intoxicated for a while, he decided to leave the house to continue his drinking campaign.

Meanwhile, my sister Dorthy and my stepmother Jennie learned our grandmother had asked me to leave earlier that day to avoid any sudden conflict with my father. So, they drove around the neighborhood looking for me. I usually hid in the back woods of McAvoy Park, located in College Hill. Unfortunately, the day had finally come when Dad was ready to execute violence against me. The thought of it saddened me because I knew it was his progressive drinking that was causing his change of heart. It hadn't dawned on me yet that my father, being constantly molested by his mother as a younger boy, could have diffidently given way to his rage. He was no longer the man I knew who stopped with me at a restaurant to engage in pleasant conversation before going to work." My mother asked, "What do you mean, Son?"

I said, "Well, case in point, I was walking home from school one day when I accidentally dropped an empty coke bottle it the street. With the bottle breaking in the gutter close to traffic, I thought it would attract the wrong kind of attention when I got home. My inclination was right. When I arrived home that day, it appeared that someone had already informed my father about the broken bottle. Entering the kitchen, I discovered that Dad was already in a drunken rage. He spoke to me about the broken bottle in question and wanted to reprimand me for breaking it. So, he began screaming at me in a forcibly loud voice. He suddenly grabbed a broom handle out of the kitchen corner and viciously broke it over my head. Dazed from the broom handle striking me, I soon found myself hoping the situation would just dissipate. There was no such luck. The progression of my father's assault only grew worse. Jennie, Victoria, and my aunt Penny quickly got out of their kitchen seats to request Dad to abandon his assault against me. Dad was so drunk and out of his mind he just continued screaming at me. My stepmother, Jennie, and Grandma continued to ask Dad to calm down, but to no avail. With Dad largely ignoring the girls' request to calm down, he noticed one of them baking something in the oven for dinner. He spontaneously decided I should be thrown into the oven as my punishment for breaking the coke bottle in the street. So, Dad offered intense verbal and physical gestures to throw me into the oven. Frightened and already traumatized from the broom handle being broken over my head, I momentarily contemplated what it would be like to be thrown into a hot, burning oven. Of course, the thought was terrifying, to say the least. Dad's advancing physical gestures, coupled with his threats to throw me into the oven, had me really sobbing at that point. At eight years old, I just didn't know what to do. I could clearly see he was drunk and out of his mind. Suddenly and without warning, I was being hurled by my father across the kitchen and aimed for a hot oven. Mom said, "You mean your father was going to throw you in a hot oven, Jack?" I said, "Yes, he was Mom, and he wasn't kidding.

At any rate, with Dad now in motion to throw me in the oven, Jennie and Grandma screamed as they left their seats the second time to intervene in Dad's madness. 'STOP IT JAKE!!! STOP IT!!! The girls cried, hoping to sever Dad's grip on my head. As Dad and I continued his advance toward the oven, my head was tucked under his arm like a football. Suddenly, Jennie and Aunt Penny were struggling against Dad in the hope of stopping his advance. As both girts tried to subdue Dad, I could see their skidding feet across our kitchen floor in the hope of redirecting my father's steps.

'STOP IT JAKE!!, STOP IT!!! The girls would feverishly cry, trying to prohibit any further advancement. With the four of us scuffling at the front door of the oven, a vibrant, stale mate seemed to seize the moment. Not being able to see much of anything during the struggle, I could now feel the protruding heat from the oven encroaching on my face. The next thing I noticed was the oven door being swung open so that my body could be thrown into it. With Dad's final thrusting me to the oven, he managed to get part of my head frightenedly close to an oven rack that was cooking our meal.

Thank God he was drunk enough to where the girls were able to suppress any further advancement. For if they hadn't, I could see their fate similar to that of the detective that was hog-tied and thrown in the back seat of his own cruiser." Mom said, "Son, Mom has never heard of such stories before, and I'm so sorry those things happened to you." I said, "Mom, when I grew older, I tried to tell Dad how those things effected me." Mom said, "What was your father's reply?" I said, "He said not to worry about it because he was getting me ready for the world. That's what his explanation was. And, oh yes, I forgot, he asked me not to allow it to bother me. And Dorthy always wondered why my and Dad's relationship was so acrimonious in those years. She never understood, nor ever saw, Dad's basic approach to me. In short, Dad wanted me to except his abusive behavior as love and not to think of it as anything else. What a crock of baloney!! The man was a narcissist and couldn't see it. He simply couldn't see the forest for the trees when it came to dealing with other people. Such an approach would essentially cost him tremendous grief in much of his life. And he still didn't get it. In short, Dad lacked the Godly character and the willingness to help other people on a regular basis. Nor was he instrumental for his own good. Most people aren't.

Furthermore, he didn't want to accept any responsibility for his own actions. He downplayed anything that would suggest he should. Nor was he concerned about how his actions may have affected other people. And yet, the man wants me to believe that he loves me. Can you see a problem with that, Mom?" Mom said, "Yes, I can, Son." I said, "Mom, love is GIVING, CARING, and SHARING for the welfare of the other person. The actions Dad displayed were HATE, DESPAIR, HOPELESSNESS, and ABUSE. Hog wash!!! By the grace of God, I was able to see right through that malarkey. Let's not kid ourselves here.

Dad's behavioral traits were spiritually sick at best." Mom said, "Son, it took me years to see right through all that same BS." I said, "Watch your language, Mom." Mom said, "Okay, I'm sorry." I said, "Well, be sorry enough to discontinue it." Mom said, "You better get on with your story, Son, because it is clear to me that the church you are attending is starting to work on your head." I said, "Ok!! When I would talk to Dorthy about Dad's issues, she wasn't willing to comment on them because of the rose-colored glasses she so often loved to wear. She's of the opinion that real problems just somehow fade away on their own.

I would end up shouting at her. Baloney!!! Wake up!!! We realize our family is the way it is because of what we have been exposed to as children, adolescents, and young adults. And that's not to mention the former three generations. It's because of that type of behavior that Dorthy is contemplating who she's getting ready to marry. Let us not kid ourselves here." Mom said, "You've got that right." I said, "I know I do, Mom. Does Dorthy think I just sat in prison and did nothing while I was there? I decided to let that time pay me!! So, I read three hundred and five books when I was there, sixteen of which were devoted to the study of human behavior and why people do the things they do. I had already lived a horrific lifestyle to begin with. So, I adopted a sense of urgency!!! To find out what was wrong and how to correct that. By the time I was released, it was clear that most people don't take the time to develop that same sense of urgency to help themselves. I had to study and grow on a consistent base to live a better life. This idea of just coasting through life without any REAL personal or spiritual growth is like substituting water for one's gas tank.

This sense of urgency that I'm talking about, Mom, usually doesn't happen with people who are preoccupied with paying their bills on a regular basis. My study also included Bible study and reading as many church publications as I could possibly find. I read so many church articles from Ambassador College out in Pasadena, California, that they sent me a letter one day commending me on having such intense interest in wanting to know how to live life. So yes, I do know what's going on in part, and I really feel Dorthy is getting ready to marry this guy who dishes out verbal abuse like the Niagara Falls flows its water. Dorthy's boyfriend sits there all drunked up, as you would say, and then addresses her in total vulgar ways. Why, if that sucker ever talked to me like he does to Dorthy, I'd set him on the porch like a milk jug." Mom said, "It looks like you've done some growing up, Son."

I said, "You better believe I have, and I give all the credit to God. Without Him, none of my successes in any area of my life would have been possible. You can believe that with all your heart. Plain and simple, the end. Why my sister would consider marrying someone who verbally abuses her is beyond me." Mom said, "Well, Son, let Mom tell you something. We are all products of what we have been exposed to. And your sister hasn't escaped being a product of what she's been exposed to, either. However, she won't always have the time nor luxury of making incorrect decisions when it comes to a potential mate." I said, "What do you mean?" Mom said, "Well, if she is to marry this fellow, she won't be able to continue with him under the same circumstances as your father and I had." I said, "What does that mean?" Mom said, "Son, no woman is designed to put up with abuse forever; something has to give. Either she will essentially leave this man, or she will join him." I said, "Don't talk to me in riddles, Mom, just get to the point." Mom said, "Well, the point is this, if your sister marries this fellow, she'll subconsciously come to see that her marriage with this man is not what she anticipated for her life. She will even reason in her own mind that somehow his abuse is real love. It's common with people like your sister and their behavior traits. Such was the same case with me and your father.

But she'll eventually discover that she needs to do something about her marriage, or she will join her new husband status quo." I said, "What do you mean by his status quo?" Mom said, "Well, either she will leave him, or she will join him in his drinking and except whatever abuse he'll continue to dish out. That's the status quo Mom is referring to. So, she'll ether join him in his status quo, or she will leave him, plain and simple. If she chooses to put up with his verbal abuse and what other "jack in the box" may spring up in their marriage, it will certainly disappoint her in the long run. For your sister to stay in an abusive marriage will definitely assign her to his drinking habits in order to survive the marriage. Drinking with him will only serve as an outward expression to survive the relationship. Sadly, drinking with her new husband will drown out any hope of a better life and seemingly medicate any inward emotional pain stemming from her circumstances. And because I really don't believe her boyfriend will go to work on his drinking problem, she may just well join him in the long run." I said, "Don't you think he'll eventually stop drinking, Mom?" Mom said, "No, I don't, Son." I said, "Why not?" Mom said, "Because he's cut out of the same cloth as your father is; that's why your sister was attracted to him in the first place." I said, "What do you mean?" Mom said, "Well, like your father, your sister's boyfriend really believes there's no real problem with his drinking. Therefore, no reason to change. Son, your father had the same outlook as your sister's boyfriend when it came to his drinking, and he never changed. So, what makes you think your sister's boyfriend is just going to stop drinking on a dime? If the truth be known, Dorthy's boyfriend doesn't have the ability to stop drinking without help. And since he doesn't want help, he'll continue to drink. Furthermore, I personally don't believe the man has enough intestinal fortitude to pull up his boot straps and put his life together without the use of alcohol. Therefore, for your sister's marriage to end up as something meaningful has far less than an average chance. And why? Because your sister can't see she's a product of what she has been exposed to!! Nor will she consider another viable alternative to her circumstances. That, my dear boy, is the way it really is.

Like me, your sister grew up believing "subconsciously" that various forms of abuse and deviant behavior were acceptable. When your sister was growing up, she accepted all these different behaviors as normal without question. Therefore, she will have a much greater chance of marrying someone with the same similarities as your father. By the way, Son, most studies confirm what Mom is talking about." I said, "You should have been a psychologist, Mom." Mom said, "Well, Son, I've been seeing one long enough to have unlearned a few things." I said, "I respect the work you've accomplished so far." Mom responded, "Thank you. It wasn't exactly a walk through the park by any means." Mom continued, ("Here's the thing, if I had to learn these things the hard way where would your sister appear to be making the same mistakes?) And now that it has come time for your sister to choose a mate, she'll be at her greatest disadvantage because of her youth. You see, in part, it's your sister's youth that will blind her to make an improper decision in choosing a mate." I said, "How do you figure that?" Mom said, "Because your sister hasn't done enough healing from her childhood environment to make better choices. Nor could she 'subconsciously' see things in her adult life that would have been much better to counsel about first before making a major decision. You have to remember something; (your son and mom) have already been where your sister is getting ready to go. And like you have so often quoted me in the past, when it came to your business affairs, 'speed of the leader, speed of the pack.' And since I'm already of the opinion her boyfriend won't lead by example, I'm afraid your sister is getting ready to fall for the pack. I say these things, Son, because I have already made the living your sister needs to do in order to make better choices in life. However, just so you know, I chose not to stay in the so-called "status quo" with your father because I knew he would never change. And because of that, I chose to leave him. Hell! I had to learn all those things with my first husband, John. Damn, if I needed to learn those things over again. Unlike your sister, I not only had to put up with your father's verbal abuse, I also had to put up with his physical abuse as well. And that is something your sister doesn't like to look square in the face. With the physical abuse progressing in my and your father's marriage, it essentially forced a decision on rather or not I would stay in the marriage. Your sister Dorthy wants to hold me guilty for wanting to save my life from all that BS."

As mom was talking I responded, "Watch your language, Mom." Mom said, "Hey, hell, you watch your language. I'll damn well say what I please!! I've learned no matter what I say to your sister, it's just not good enough for her, is it? I don't know who the Sam hell she thinks she is because she didn't live my life back then. She didn't have to put up with quite the same things I had to put up with, especially when it came to your father. It seems to me that your sister and father can't find enough wrong to say about me. If all they have on me is being a bad house keeper, then I'd have to say they both have a lot of nothing, or I'm a real Bonnie and Clyde, which is it? Your sister has judged me, and that's all there is to it!! The end. Well, I'll tell you something, Son, it won't be until I close my eyes that your sister's eyes will open. So, she can sit over there on her high horse all she wants because when her youth starts to fade, and her so-called upcoming marriage starts to decline, she'll have a whole different perspective on that day. And her decision to marry her new boyfriend, only the wind tunnels of time will tell that story. For as sure as God made little green apples, her choice to marry this man will surely come out in the wash of life. I just hope her decision is the right one because if it's not, she'll know on that day what it's like to have made the wrong choice. And that story, my dear boy, is still yet to be told."

I said, "It sounds like you're a little ticked off at Dorthy?" Mom said, "Your damn straight I am. Son, I mean every word I've said for her sake. It's like I told you before; I've already been where she's getting ready to go, and then there are some. So, I don't feel like I need to apologize for anything I've said. And yes, I am a little ticked at her. When is she going to quit sitting over there, crucifying me? When will she finally start to forgive me? Or is she convinced that her own sin will be glossed over by our Maker? That girl needs to figure things out before it's too late for the both of us. Make no mistake, Son, we all have our appointed time with God, and your sister will have hers just as well. I wonder how things will pan out for her on that day? Will she feel high and mighty then?"

"Just calm down, Mom. She'll probably call you some time." Mom said, "Well, she better hurry before they put me in the bone yard. Son, all kidding aside, will you talk to your sister for me? You know, she is still my daughter, and I still love her. I carried her under my heart just like I did with the rest of you. Talk to her for me, please!! Just talk to her for me." I said, "OK, Mom, I'll see what I can do, but I can't promise you anything." Mom said, "I know that, Son." I said, "Good night, Mom." Mom said, "Good night, Jack. Are you coming tomorrow?" I said, "Yeah, I'll come over. Who else can torture as well as me?" Both my mother and I laughed as I left. Arriving the following day at my mother's home, I reminded her how Dad refused to take any responsibility for the way he treated me as a child. "It's plain and simple, Mom. People who love you don't abuse you. As I said before, love is *giving, caring, and sharing for the welfare of other people.* Abuse is hate and despair that readily often disguises itself as love." Mom said, "That's very true, Son." I said, "The irony is that Dad loves to portray himself to other people as all-wise and that they need to follow his example in order to have a full and abundant life. What a crock of BS that turned out to be."

Mom said, "Don't let it bother you, Son. We all have our brand of vanity, and evidently, your father's brand is having other people think he's a real cracker jack when it comes to being a wise man. Trust me, he is not the first one to have that approach. As you can see, it's just another smoke screen to protect himself and have other people think he's something that he is not. But he doesn't fool me at all. I saw that joker coming a long time ago, and plenty like him. Your father had that same cracker-jack opinion of himself when he and I first met. Yes, sir, he never grew up; he just grew old with the same old BS. See, y'all have to remember something. I knew your father when he was still a young man, so he can't pull anything over on me. I knew the great JC like none of you have ever known him. Yes, sir, he doesn't get away with any of that cock-en bull with me. And it was the same way with his darling of a mother. Why that broad made me sick!! You can believe that with all your heart. Your sister Dorthy thinks she really knows your grandmother. Why she doesn't see the half of it. And she better be damn glad she doesn't because it would just make her want to puke all over the place."

I said, "Mom, I believe deep down inside Dad's a broken man who really doesn't know how to pick up the pieces in his own life." Mom said, "And that, Son, you have said well. But make no mistake, as our visits progress, I very much intend to shed some light on why your father seems to be such a broken man. No doubt about it, we'll get around to it sooner or later." I said, "Well, I hope so because you've been telling me that for some time." The day was just about over when I grew tired of telling mom stories of things that happened when I was a boy. Mom said, "Well, Son, it definitely looks as if the madness continued even without me being around in those years." I said, "Yes, it had, Mom, yes, it had." Mom said, "I'm so sorry all those things happened to you." I said, "Well, Mom, that was then, and this is now. What can you say?" Mom said, "All you can do now, Jack, is move forward." I said, "You are so right, and that's exactly what I intend to do." Mom said, "I have no doubt that you will, Son." So, we kissed and said goodnight.

I was glad to be single in those years, for it gave me a lot of time to catch up with my mother and build the best relationship possible under the circumstances. My mother and I attended many outings in those years to occupy our time. We'd visit many local parks and attended recreational boat rides that seemed to come around during the fall. When we weren't doing those things, we'd visit the local art and history museums. I wasn't too distracted from my work at that time, so we were blessed to be able to do whatever we wanted. My mother told me one day that she didn't deserve the way I treated her. So, I asked her what she meant by that? She said, "Even the first two children I had with John Howler didn't treat me as well as you do, Son." I said, "Well, Mom, they didn't have to. They grew up with you. It was too easy for them to take you for granted." Mom said, "I hear what you're saying, Son, but that's not exactly what Mom means." I said, "Then what do you mean?" Mom said, "I just simply meant you treat me well for a man that I abandoned as a boy. And I'm very grateful for that, Son. Even your older sister and brother don't know me as well as you do." I said, "Well, it doesn't matter, Mom. We are going on with our lives now, and that should be good enough for both of us." Mom said, "Yeah, you're right, Son, and that's just what I will do."

I suddenly realized in my mind that I wasn't some little boy who grew up with his mother. It was more of a mother and her son growing older as grown adults. I'm glad God made so many allowances in those years for my mother and me to have gotten to know one another. Driving home that evening, I thought a lot about why my dad was so violent when he was a young man. I didn't realize my mother would help fill in so many gaps as the years passed. Trying to reason in my mind what triggered my father's violent tendencies brought me to mind what God once said, "violence would seek to over throw the violent man." Though our grandfather was very kind to us as children, it could be said maybe our father's violent tendencies stemmed from our grandfather being a former mountain man. I frankly didn't know.

I say this because of the rugged life style so many Americans were forced to live during the final settling of our country's frontier. Our grandfather was fifty years older than our father. He was, in fact, a mountain man who homesteaded 400 acres for the Canadian Government. He knew what it was like to kill bears, fight off wolves, and occasionally kill Blackfoot Indians that threatened his life. He lived in a cabin high in the hills of the Canadian Alps. He was married to a beautiful Blackfoot Indian woman. Shortly after they married, she got sick and died as a young woman. She hadn't born any children during my grandfather and her marriage.

A few years after Grandpa's first wife died, he met our grandmother in the state of Maine on his way back to the United States from Canada. They both married and soon settled in a small town known as Foster, Kentucky. Being a no-nonsense type of man, you always knew where our grandfather stood. It had been understood that our grandfather had killed two men in the City of Cincinnati, supposedly in self-defense. The first one occurred in 1926 when a man was riding the same street car my grandfather was on. While the man tried to impose his will, our grandfather drew a gun and shot the man off the street car. As the man lay dead in the street, spectators agreed to go to court and testify on our grandfather's behalf. The court soon ruled that self-defense would be the end of the matter. Some twenty years later, at the end of the second world war, an unknown man entered a public laundromat where our grandmother was "supposedly" washing her clothes. The man suddenly pulled a knife on our grandmother, wanting to rape her. At the exact moment, our grandfather entered the laundromat, seizing the situation. With our grandfather acknowledging our grandmother's screams, he immediately took battle with her assailant. The fight for the two men's lives became paramount. A few moments later, our grandfather emerged from the struggle, killing the man with his own knife. The police excepted our grandmother's report about her attacker trying to rape her. The incident soon led to our grandfather's second acquittal.

A few years passed when it became rumored that our grandmother's story of her attacker trying to rape her wasn't exactly accurate. With our grandmother giving a new twist on her story, our grandfather really never knew what to believe. Consequently, our grandfather felt very remorseful over killing the man, especially after hearing our grandmother's new story. Many years went by before our grandfather started to attend a corner Baptist church. One Sunday afternoon, another unknown parishioner was seated in the same chapel and overheard my grandfather's prayer as he stood at the altar. By the time the unknown parishioner reported what he had heard, it had become apparent that our grandfather was asking God to forgive him for what he believed was an unjustifiable death. With no one ever really knowing the attacker's original acquaintance with our grandmother, it indeed invited much speculation for its day.

In one way, I thought maybe our father had gotten some of his violent tendencies from our grandfather's experiences. But as I really took a square look at my grandfather's life, I could clearly see that wasn't the case at all. Our grandfather simply did what came naturally for a man who lived during the close of the American frontier life. So, as I really thought about it, there really was no evidence of our grandfather's lifestyle supporting our father's tendencies to be violent. Besides, I could clearly see that all the women in our family deeply admired him. I've known some people to overcome violent tendencies through counseling, and it wasn't as bad as they thought it would be. Of course, professional counseling is different for most people. I think when it comes to professional counseling, most people already naturally feel they don't need it. Some don't want to counsel for fear of being embarrassed or maybe thinking someone may think they're crazy. Yet most feel they are just fine. Just ask them. This point brings me to remember an evangelist I once knew. He once said, "Have you ever met anyone who didn't think they were a good person? Well, personally, I have met no such person. Why, everyone I ever met was definitely convinced that they were a good person. Just ask them, and they will verify it. But I'm here to tell you that human nature loves to think of itself as good but does not automatically produce good." The natural feeling many of us have when it comes to counseling seems to have stemmed from human nature itself. That is to say, human nature dictates there's nothing wrong with the self; therefore, there's no real reason to seek counseling of any type. In short, human nature usually thinks it's right. We see a perfect example of this when God asked Adam and Eve why they ate from the tree of knowledge of good and evil? Adam and Eve not only didn't want to be wrong in answering God, but they certainly didn't want to be right either. Of course not. In other words, often, mankind doesn't want to do the right thing. This approach has been at the core of human problems from its beginning.

This stubborn approach not only continues to assign some people to a very arduous life, but it also destroys any hope of healing. I found benefits with both psychological counseling and counsel with a minister of choice, which helped me get on with my life. So, I never wanted to throw the baby out with the bath water when it came to counseling.

CHAPTER 5

A PERSPICACIOUS MOTHER

"Your father was one of those good-looking guys that caught my eye. He was always the sharpest dresser in the crowd and wore the best duck tail hairdo one could imagine. Some of the other guys in our crowd were jealous of him but dared not fool with him because of his reputation. So, they bridled their jealousy for the sake of peace. Your grandfather knew your father and I were very much in love, and he wanted to see us marry. But your grandmother didn't want any part of her little boy being taken away from her! So, with your father being just shy of eighteen, it would require one of his parents' signature for us to marry. And since your grandmother wasn't up to the task at all, your grandfather gladly stepped in. He signed our marital papers against your grandmother's will. After we married, we set up our little happy home and got on with our lives. Your father and I weren't married long before your grandmother got a job offer in Columbus, Ohio. With her driving back and forth to Columbus almost every day, it became somewhat debatable if she could keep up with having to take care of your grandfather. So, they both decided to move to Columbus, which would only last for about a year. During the course of that year, your father and I had plenty of time to bond. I'd have to say it probably was the best time of our marriage. After the year passed, your grandmother decided to return to Cincinnati permanently. When your father learned of the news, he plunged into a panic mode, which I thought was a little odd. Late the following evening, as we prepared for bed, I asked your father why he was panicking so much about his mother returning to Cincinnati? Your father just started saying things like, 'She'll never leave me alone!! She'll never leave me alone!!!'

So, I said to your father, 'Who won't leave you alone, honey, and what in the world are you talking about?' Your father would just respond by saying, 'My mom!!! I know she'll never leave me alone when she comes back to Cincinnati. She'll never let me go!!! Mom said, 'What do you mean she'll never let you go?' Your father would just say, 'When my mom comes home from Columbus, she'll never let me go.' With your father really not giving me any specifics that evening, we soon fell asleep for the next day. So, I asked, "Mom, have you ever found out what Dad was talking about?" Mom said, "Only in part at that point, Son, because I wouldn't find out the rest until your father and I were well into our marriage. But when I did, I certainly knew it wasn't something that I could fix in a jiffy." I said, "So why don't you just tell me what it was?" Mom said, "Son, Mom can tell you this. I learned early on in my and your father's marriage that the problem was somewhat rather strange to begin with. So, I'd rather wait awhile before disclosing everything else because, as I said, I want to see our new relationship do well first."

I said, "OK, fair enough, so can you tell me anything?" Mom said, "Well, since you're not letting things go, I'll give you some back ground." I said, "Good." Mom said, "Your father and I were married the better part of two or three years when some of my siblings noticed your grandmother, Victoria, taking trips to Maine to visit her stepfather, Ben Perkins. At first, we didn't think anything of it because, you know, it was her dad!! And, of course, everyone naturally thought they were just visiting. Well, after a while, her visits with her stepfather started attracting too much attention in all the wrong ways." I said, "What do you mean by that?" Mom said, "Well, your grandmother would come home from those visits trying to, inconspicuously insinuate, that maybe there was something more going on between her and her stepfather, Ben." I replied, "You mean sexually?" Mom said, "Absolutely!!! Hey Son, she came into our house one day strutting her stuff all over the place and telling us just how intriguing her visits were with her stepfather. The truth of the matter was everyone was able to see right through her charade. She wasn't fooling any of us." I said, "Are you sure that a sexual relationship between her and her stepfather is what was really going on?"

"Hey Jack, we weren't crazy. We knew damn well what she was alluding to. She wanted all of us to believe that she was in bed with her stepfather. She would flaunt her stuff all over the place like there was no tomorrow, saying things like, 'My daddy did this!! And my daddy did that!! And then I did this, and then I did that.' Why was that old broad eating up with that madness? She always fell short of actually coming right out and telling us of her sexual exploits with her stepfather. Why don't you kid yourself? That old broad was plain evil." I said, "Did she ever say those things around Grandpa?" Mom said, "Hell no!!! Why, if your grandfather would have known those trips consisted of something like that, he would have gone to Maine himself and killed the man. Yes, sir!!, That old broad knew to keep her mouth shut when your granddaddy was around. Hey Son!! Your grandfather had already killed a man over her nonsense before. What in the Sam Hill was going to stop him from doing it again? Boy!! You better believe she kept her mouth shut when your grandfather was around. Deep down inside, your grandmother knew your grandfather never believed her cocking bull story about that man trying to rape her in the laundromat. And she was damn lucky the police bought her story.

Your grandfather felt terrible about having to kill the man for the rest of his life. That's why he went to the altar right before he died to ask God for His forgiveness. After your grandfather concluded in his heart that your grandmother's story was shady at best, he knew killing your grandmother's so-called assailant was unnecessary for sure. So, there was no way on God's green earth that woman was going to lead on like something was going on between her and her stepfather. Yes sir!! You can believe that with all your heart!!! Don't you kid yourself. She made damn sure she kept her mouth shut with all that mess when your grandfather was around. She knew your granddaddy would have gone up there in person to kill that man with no second thought!! Plain and simple, now that's just the way it was!! But she didn't mind flaunting her stuff all over the place with us. As I remember it, she enjoyed bragging to us about her escapades without ever really giving us any solid details of what actually happened. But one thing for sure, according to her account, was that plenty was going on. Like Mom said, that old broad was evil, if ever!!!

You have to understand something, Son; your grandfather still lived during a time in our country when adultery wasn't accepted like it is today. Your grandfather was considered to be a "southern gentleman" back then. Make no mistake, it was far more expected that a "southern gentleman" take care of things like that should they arise. And if one found his or her life coming to an abrupt end because of their reckless acts of adultery, the general populace had a way of turning their heads on such matters. Yes sir!! It's not like it is today, where adultery is running rampant and even glorified. If people today looked at adultery like they had during your grandparent's generation, our nation wouldn't be in the chaotic mess it's in. So, your grandmother knew she had better not say anything about all of that around your grandfather. But she didn't mind bragging to us about her adulteress affairs.

I'm sorry, Son, Mom is talking too much. You get on with your story." I said, "Yes, that's quite a story, Mom, and a disheartening one at that. At any rate, as I was saying, after the incident with Dad, I returned to school the following morning. After a night like that, I became desperate and in need of something that would make me feel like I had some sort of self-worth. What I mean, Mom, the things that took place with Dad had a way of taking it right out of me, if you know what I mean?" Mom said, "Yes, I do know what you mean, Son." I said, "You know, when children are molested, many of them have a pretty low self-esteem afterward." Mom said, "Yes, I know what you mean, Jack." I said, "You do?" Mom said, "Yes, Son, I do." I said, "Well, how do you know that?" Mom said, "We'll, we will get to that in a moment after you finish what you were saying." I said, "Ok, anyway, after the encounter with Dad, I wanted to feel like I had some kind of worth, so I cheated by stealing answers from a girl who sat next to me. I knew she was an "A" student, and I wanted to be like her for a change.

I hadn't known that I had developed a very low self-esteem from being molested in those woods. The incident had me only producing D's and F's on a regular basis. But turning in "A" paperwork would surely attract new attention, not to mention the submission of it stood out like a sore thumb. So, when I stole the girl's work, the teacher asked me if the job was mine? I assured her that it was. She knew I was lying and immediately adopted a look on her face that suggested I would soon be acquainted with my fate. This particular girl, being the teacher's pet, made things even worse. Now, the teacher was somewhat beside herself and made sure I was immediately skyrocketed to the principal's office. Mr. Amaranth, our principal, was a Korean War veteran who only had one arm. But he did have a brain, and he was accustomed to using it." Mom laughed and said, "You're a mess, Son." I said, "I know,

Mom, but I had no idea I was getting ready to walk into another misfortune. I had been in front of our principal before, and I didn't mind stopping by and seeing him once in a while. But stealing this little girl's work was certainly unusual circumstances for the principal and me. I knew it would take more than a low-key approach to convince our principal that the "A" paper was mine. Much to my surprise, my so-called "integrity" in my principal's mind would be significant in winning him over. Or at least I thought so!! You see, I had a habit of not lying to Mr. Amaranth about anything. Allow me to elaborate, Mom. Mr. Amaranth always had a habit of making me feel better about myself. That's why I found it necessary to visit him once in a while. In short, getting in a bit of trouble once in a while was worth hearing his inspiring speeches. His messages always seemed to entail an adequate amount of self-worth. And since I wasn't equipped to disclose how emotionally crippled I was from being molested, it appeared our principal insight helped make up the difference. Even if I had to undergo a little trouble once in a while to receive such a positive outcome. When Mr. Amaranth got through giving one of his grand talks, I always made sure that I was reasonably enthralled. That way, the occasion at least left the door open for future enlightenment. Of course, he was always glad to deliver at a moment's notice. A little kidding there, Mom. Allow me to say what I mean.

You see, Mom, by having brief visits with Mr. Amaranth in those years, one could always enjoy watching their self-worth grow right through the roof." Mom said, "What!!" I said, "Hey! Relax, I had to get it somewhere. Besides, with abuse soaring in those years, it caused a severe depression of self-worth." Mom said, "You are a mess, Son! You are a mess!!" I said, "Now understand something, Mom. Mr. Amaranth was a man I never lied to about anything. Knowing that he was a reasonable man and that he had a controlling interest in my self-worth always compelled me to tell him the truth about everything. Even if it were going to be a little self-incriminating." Mom said, "You are crazy!!" I said, "Hey, I thought the relationship was working great. I mean, let's face it, it worked far better than the great depression of self-worth. I mean, think about it, Mom. Here you have this principal making sure your self-worth is skyrocketing, and he doesn't even know there's a depression of self-worth going on. Making sure I visited him once in a while guaranteed my stock of self-worth would go through the roof. Of course, every stock has its risk, and mine was to balance the visits with my principal to make sure I didn't actually go to jail for anything serious." Mom said, "Boy, Son, you are a mess!! Seems to me you really were pushing the envelope just to feel human in those years" I said, "Hey, it worked well, Mom. I managed to stay out of jail and keep my stock of self-worth valuable.

I was in a lot of pain in those years. Mom and I received some pretty good pep talks from Mr. Amaranth. Hey, someone had to be educated, and it seemed our principal had a better act than my homeroom teacher. So, I thought, why rock the boat?" Mom said, "Boy!! You are a mess, Son." I said, "All kidding aside, Mom, I felt that telling Mr. Amaranth whatever he wanted to know was my way of asking him to please help me. And yet, as a little boy, deep down inside, I was afraid he wouldn't adequately respond to my silent request for help.

Mr. Amaranth simply didn't have the capacity to see what was really happening in my life. And likely so. And so there I was, this eight-year-old boy trying to communicate with his principal about things I didn't know how to explain. He probably really never knew the challenge it was for me to balance our relationship without going to jail." My mother started crying because she knew all too well that my efforts with Mr. Amaranth were to try and live an everyday life. She realized the challenge my circumstances produced. I explained to my mother that I found my relationship with our principal ludicrous just to feel human. And yet, there I stood, in this encased body of flesh and bones, screaming inside to my principal, why can't you see what's happening to me and please fix it? Mom kept crying, "I'm so sorry, Son, I'm so sorry!!" I said, "You see, Mom, stealing the little girl's paperwork in those years was all I had to feel like I had some type of self-worth. Unfortunately, I ended up lying to Mr. Amaranth, desperate to feel like I was human. And I considered him to be my best friend at the time. So, Mr. Amaranth asked me in his office that day, 'Jackie, did you steal Julie's paperwork?' I said, 'No, I didn't, Mr. Amaranth,' Mr. Amaranth said, 'Jackie, are you sure the work is yours?' I said, 'Yes, Mr. Amaranth, the work is mine.' Mr. Amaranth replied, 'Ok, then I'm going to send you back to class, and I want you to give this note to your teacher.' I said, 'Ok, Mr. Amaranth, I will.'" Skipping down the hallway that day, I was convinced that my self-worth stock had just reached its peak. Having learned what Mr. Amaranth had written in his memo, I became curious about what he had written to my teacher.

So, I stopped in our school corridor to sneak a peek at what my principal wrote. As I began reading his message, my consciousness started to suffer a massive heart attack right away. Much to my surprise, Mr. Amaranth's note informed my teacher not to be alarmed about the "A" paperwork I had turned in. He had stated that since Jackie had never lied to me about anything before, I felt assured that the assignment was his. Needless to say, as I read Mr. Amaranth's message in the hallway that day, my self-worth fell right through the floor. I really liked Mr. Amaranth, and I knew I had just delivered him a low blow that he didn't deserve. I felt like a sap, and I needed to because I knew I was wrong. The reading of Mr. Amaranth's note considerably slowed my step down in our hallway that day. Walking ever so slowly back to class that day, I couldn't help but contemplate what our principal had written to our teacher. Continuing to slow my stride, I realized I never wanted Mr. Amaranth to feel like I did at that moment. So, I vowed in my heart not to ever lie to that man again about anything, and I never did. Not fully realizing the somberness of the moment that day, I later in life became acutely aware that our "self-worth stock" only skyrockets when we do what's right in the sight of God. Mom said, "You love God, don't you, Son?" I said, "Yes, I do, Mom. I studied a lot about Him when I was incarcerated." Mom said, "Good for you, Son. Mom would rather see you a godly man than anything else." I said, "Mom." Mom said, "Yes, Son, what is it?" I said, "You once told me that you understood why molested children can have such low self-esteem." Mom said, "That's right, Son, I did." I said, "Well, how do you know that?"

Mom said, "Because I was molested myself when I was a little girl." I said, "You were!?" Mom said, "Yes, I was Jack. My father, your Grandpa Smith, fought in the Second World War in Germany. Before he was deployed, he used to play around with me in my cradle. He thought because I was young, I'd never remember those incidences." I said, "What do you mean, Mom, by him playing around with you?" Mom said, "Well, when I was a little girl, he'd come in my room and reach in my cradle and play with my vagina. Son, let Mom tell you something. Regardless of who does those things to you, I have no doubt that they rarely ever think about their victim growing up one day. It took a fair amount of time for me to forgive my father and get on with our lives. But I did, and my father and I had the best relationship possible under the circumstances. And both he and I were grateful for that. Because I loved him and I wanted to know him better. So, we worked those things out, and we got on with our lives. But I have to admit, our relationship was never what it could have been had those things not occurred. But, I, too, adopted a pretty low self-esteem out of the whole ordeal just as you had," I said, "I'm glad you told me that, Mom. Now I know you really do understand. Wow, Mom!! I would have never guessed such things happened to you when you were a little girl." Mom said, "How could you, Son? After all, most people don't walk around with a sign tacked to their forehead announcing that they've been molested. So, bear in mind, Jack, when we have our visits, I not only understand some of the things you have suffered, but I often see them coming as you speak." I replied, "Yes, I guess you do."

CHAPTER 6

SEARCHING FOR A MISSING LIFE

"As I was saying, I started experiencing more trouble in the school cafeteria. It forced our principal's hand in having me sent home for lunch almost every day. Walking home for lunch every day proved to be difficult at times. The time allotted for lunch was always taken up by walking back and forth to school. There was no real time to sit down and eat when I got home. My stepmother, Jennie, would usually display an asinine attitude as I sat down to eat my lunch. She knew all along I had no time to eat. Many times, I arrived too late to eat lunch and ended up making my own. After making my lunch, I'd have to leave right away. One day, I walked into my home for lunch and noticed my stepmother Jennie and I were the only ones there that day. Her demeanor seemed somewhat perplexing to me that day. As I was busy making my lunch, she looked at me most peculiarly and asked, 'Why are you doing all of this?' I said, 'Doing all of what?' Jennie said, 'Acting out in all the ways you do?' I told her I don't know. For the first time in my childhood, I felt genuinely sorry for Jennie because I could see she was struggling to find some real answers. Being just a nine-year-old boy at the time, I didn't have the answers she so desperately sought and needed. I really felt for Jennie at that point because I could clearly see she was overwhelmed with all the problems that eight kids could provide. For Jennie to have found the answers she was looking for in those years, she probably could have postponed her second divorce between her and my father. I have no doubt that ten people living in the same household would have made most parents squirm.

It wasn't like I could stand up and say, 'Oh yeah! I forgot to tell you! My behavior is classic of a child who's been molested, abandoned, verbally abused, physically abused, and the recipient of divorce all by the age of seven. Boy, isn't it great?' If anything, I found all of our circumstances to bare no answers at all. Jennie or Dad was not equipped to deal with an indifferent atmosphere. At times, it was miserable for all parties concerned, and there was no real relief or answers in sight. My behavior patterns continued to decline, and I started running away more frequently in search of a missing life. I ran as far and fast as I could for a nine-year-old boy. One time, I chose to run away and follow the route my father so often traveled for work. I thought maybe the answer somehow lay in the wake of those paths. I clung tight to my runaway mission, hoping to find Camelot at its conclusion.

As I ran one day, I managed to cover three neighborhoods on foot before darkness set in. Not knowing anyone, I stopped at an upper-class apartment building located in the Jewish sector of town. With the doormen welcoming me in, I acted as if I had lived there all my life. Stepping on the elevator that evening, the lobby doorman asked, 'What floor do you desire, Son?' I said, 'I'll be going to the eighth floor, but don't worry about it; I'll see my way up.' The doorman answered, 'Very well,' and gestured with his body language to have a good evening. I failed to mention to the doorman that I had just met a strange man on the street suggesting that I could stay with his friend who lived on the eighth floor of the building. Getting off the elevator, I knocked on the door number given to me by the strange man I had met an hour earlier.

As I knocked on the door, a sad voice came from the other side telling me to beat it. This wasn't exactly a time for things to go south, Mom. I was hungry and tired and just wanted to sleep. But be that as it may, it was clear I was being blown off by the stranger who was supposed to save my day. I suddenly realized I would need a good story if I were going to gain favor with the doorman I had just blown off in the lobby. Getting on the elevator and heading back to the first floor, I knew I had a reasonable chance of running into the doorman again. I wondered what in the world I would tell him. Stepping off the elevator to the first floor, I was immediately met by the doorman. The look on his face suggested that he had anticipated my arrival. So, the doorman said to me, 'I take it that things didn't go so well up there?' I told him that my parents were late getting home and asked him if I could wait for them in the lobby. The doorman said, 'That will be fine, Son.' He then proceeded to direct me to the most inconspicuous place in the lobby. I sat down on a beautiful golden-colored couch that was very comfortable. I waited on that couch for a while and acted as if my parents would arrive at any moment. My sudden falling asleep was caught by the doorman moments later. Awakened gently, the doorman asked me if my parents would arrive any time soon? I told him I really didn't know. He suggested that I remove my shoes so I could sleep on the couch until they arrived. I said, 'Really!?' He answered with a big smile and said, 'Yes, really!!' He helped me remove my shoes and told me he would alert me when my parents arrived. I was so tired I didn't think to ask how he would have known them. It became obvious the doorman knew what was going on all the time, Mom."

Mom said, "Sure he did, Son." I said, "I just didn't know what to make of it." Mom said, "Of course not; how could you? You were just a nine-year-old boy at the time. Of course, it wasn't the doorman's fault, for that was still during a time when colored people didn't get involved with white people's personable problems." I asked, "Why not, Mom?" Mom said, "For fear of borrowing more trouble than what it was worth." I said, "Well, I can't argue with that, for that was the whole feeling I had during my acquaintance with the doorman. I was just glad the man elected to deal with me kindly." Mom said, "You can thank God for that man, Son." I said, "You're right, I should.

At any rate, I thanked the doorman for allowing me to sleep on the couch, and I quickly fell asleep. Awakening the following day, I slowly walked to the front door, hoping the doorman wouldn't notice me. I thought if he saw me, he would automatically think I was lying to him about my parents arriving the night before. Not able to detect him anywhere in the immediate vicinity, I quickly approached the front door, hoping to get out of the building before being discovered. Much to my surprise, a clear and kind voice spoke to me from an obscure corner. 'Good morning, Son!' Rubbing my eyes, I said, 'Good morning, sir.' The doorman said, 'Did you sleep well?' I said, 'Yes, sir, I did.' The doorman then walked me through the lobby and out the front door. He paused momentarily and said, 'Son, you try to take care of yourself and stay out of trouble.' I said, 'Thank you, sir.' Walking down the street that day, I realized the doorman knew all along I was a troubled youth and that my parents were never going to arrive. Because we were still at the height of the civil rights era, the doorman elected to be careful not to personalize our acquaintances. I thank God the man had the foresight to see what was happening and simply elected to deal with me candidly.

Walking away from the Jewish sector that day had me suddenly realize my own parents didn't have the same foresight as the colored man had when it came to dealing with me. Realizing that morning I didn't have the means to take care of myself, I regrettably headed home. Continuing my search for a missing life, I contemplated running away once again. But as I arrived home that day, and much to my surprise, I was given some good news for a change. With our family being native to Cincinnati, my stepmother Jennie learned of a rather unique camp site for kids in the Northern Kentucky area.

The name of the campsite was Camp Robert Mi-chum. With Jennie and Dad startled by my last runaway, it appeared they both were actually seeking ways to improve my situation. This came as a surprise to me because neither Jennie nor Dad seemed to be concerned most of the time. Or at least it came across that way to me." Mom said, "What do you mean, Son?" I said, "Well, Dad was so busy trying to take care of ten people that it appeared Jennie was trying to get everything she possibly could get from him. Whatever it was, I figured things had gotten serious enough that both Jennie and Dad took note of my situation. My stepmother Jennie told me that Dad was making arrangements for me to attend an exclusive campsite in the Northern Kentucky area.

A day would pass by only to hear both of them discussing the matter. Dad wanted to know what type of expense this so-called exclusive campsite would incur. Jennie told Dad it would cost three thousand dollars for a three-week stay. Dad wanted to know if all of it came with an ice cream cone. It was indeed a lot of money for 1966. But you have to remember, Mom, we lived in a "thriving economy" at the time, and businesses were accustomed to getting what they asked." Mom said, "Boy!! That sure isn't the case nowadays. Hey, you don't have to tell me. I was married to Harvey O'Connor at the time, and we were doing very well together. So, I can definitely identify with what you're telling me, Son."

I said, "At any rate, Dad bought me a big camping trunk so I would have a place to put my things while I was away at camp. And off to Camp Robert Mi-chum I went. I had hoped in my heart that things would finally be okay with a lasting solution to our family problems. Arriving at the campsite that day, I noticed its grandeur and beauty had surpassed anything I had ever seen before. It actually brought to mind something one could expect to see in the movies." Mom said, "Do you mind describing it to me, Son?" I said, "No, not at all, Mom."

I said, "Mom, the place was well kept with beautiful cut lawns rolling as far as the eye could see. There were little cape cod cabins spread out throughout the property for the boys to reside in. Huge oak trees ran around the camp perimeter. As the days passed, I admired those old oaks being shifted back and forth from gentle winds. It gave one a sense of peace and adoration for God's creation." Mom said, "I bet they were beautiful, Son." I said, "Yes, they were, Mom. With the staff being so kind and helpful in every way, I thought for sure I found my Camelot. Even if it were only a moment in time. I certainly welcomed that kind of peace in my life." Mom said, "You really needed peace at the time, didn't you, Son?" I said, "Yes, I did, Mom." Mom said, "I have no doubt it was a beautiful place, Son, and I'm so grateful you got to attend." I said, "Mom, I had so much fun and appreciation for all that was being done for me. One of the most impressive things I saw was the dining room decor they had for the kids. Absolutely unbelievable!! The food was just impressionable, and there was plenty of it. Fit for Kings!!! Our boys would ever so gorge themselves like gluttons.

The dining hall brought to mind of eating at a five-star restaurant. I had never seen such table settings as these before. These tables were giant round oaks that were equipped with ornamentation suited for visiting dignitaries. They easily sat twelve to sixteen people. In the center of each table lay the number of the cabin in which those particular boys resided. If your cabin won their white clove inspection, that cabin could have anything on the menu the following day, no questions asked. Our cabin number was seventeen, and we only won once. Of course, what we didn't know at the time was that all the other cabins only won once.

Three times a day, one could hear a huge brass bell ringing over the entire camp-site. One hundred and forty-eight boys walked through those dining room doors to tuck themselves in at their appointed seats. Gladly gazing at our food, the boys would drool in anticipation, wanting to eat. Waiting for our pastor to say grace, one couldn't help but admire the great oak beams that ran across our dining room ceiling. Day after day, it would bring news about events to endeavor in. Swimming, horseback riding, arts and crafts, and even live theater were so interestingly woven into our program." Mom said, "Wow, Son! That sounds great." I said, "It really was Mom; it was grand in every way, and I didn't expect all of that at one time. I was blessed to get a break from the so-called normal way of life. But unexpectedly, another boy whom I hadn't known attended the same campsite that year. Mom, allow me to elaborate on the background of his situation. Some four years earlier, my sister Dorthy told me about some boy who liked to pick on the girls after school. To my surprise, she never shared with me that she was one of the recipients of this boy's attacks. Or at least not until her last day of school, (which is one year.)

Dorthy was walking home with her girlfriends that day when suddenly it started to rain pretty hard. Out of nowhere, this boy picks up speed on his bike and heads toward Dorthy and her girlfriends. One of the girls noticed the boy's fast encroachment and shouted out, 'Watch out!!!' Dorthy wasn't able to respond to her girlfriend's warning and suffered being run over by the boy's bike. The boy literally managed to run over Dorthy's entire body. As Dorthy and I grew up, she would describe to me how horrible the experience was." Mom said, "Why that sucker? I guess you're going to tell me he was at the same campsite as you?" I said, "Unfortunately, yes, he was, Mom.

But I had no idea he resided in the very same cabin with me. Four years had passed since he had struck my sister with his bike. One night in our cabin, just before everyone fell asleep, the boy began bragging about running over a little girl on the last day of school one year. He told his story with a sense of pride and arrogance. As his story unfolded, I couldn't help but notice the amazing parallels Dorthy's story had some four years earlier. With the boy enjoying the delivery of his story, he explained how pleasing it was to hit one of the girls with his bike. I gathered from his story he enjoyed watching Dorthy's terror as he rapidly encroached on her at a high rate of speed. Especially the part where he collided with Dorthy to watch her face slam against the concrete. He said he thoroughly enjoyed watching his rear tire roll across Dorthy's back as he passed over her body. So, I decided to interrupt his story and ask him if he remembered the little girl's name that he had run over? He answered me ever so enthusiastically and said, 'Dorthy Cummins.' As most other kids fell asleep that evening, my sleep failed me because of the madness that ran through my mind." Mom said, "Son, what did you think of his story?" I said, "Well, Mom, knowing the boy was a few years older and seeing how his story concluded, I had hoped that Batman would soon arrive to take up my cause. But seeing how big the boy was before going to bed made me think that I needed to be at least the equivalent of Superman to rectify the situation." Mom and I laughed. "Planning the boy's fate that evening proved to bring long and challenging thoughts, but regardless of the cost to me, I vowed in my heart to avenge my sister's past tragedy.

With the boy and I staying in the same living quarters, it positioned both of us near the tether-ball court. I observed that the tether-ball court had a dirt base. One had to be careful when playing on this particular court because of the broken glass lying in the northern part of the court. Our staff really didn't want the kids playing in that specific part of the court, but we did anyway. One day, Mr. Jerk finished his tether-ball game, winning against his opponent. Of course, in order for him to continue playing the game, the rules would require a new challenger. And like the mighty warrior I thought I was, I stepped up into the court to challenge the boy to a new game. The game started off really nice until he suspected that I wanted to fight him. Gladly accepting my invitation, the boy began smashing me into the ground right away. Not too good of a start, Mom." Mom said, "Doesn't sound like one, Son." I said, "Knowing that I wouldn't emerge as Superman anytime soon, I needed a plan B in order to stand any kind of chance at all. Experiencing stars and lightning from several of the boy's punches had me immediately looking for some way to get the situation under control. I suddenly saw a stick laying just inside the top of the tether-ball court. Realizing I was playing the game in my bare feet, I knew there would be a reasonable chance of cutting my feet if I were to pursue that stick for a defense. But at the same time, I knew I had to obtain that stick if I were going to stand a chance against my opponent. Plain and simple, the other boy's ability to stomp me far out reached my anticipation. I also realized it would take great determination to secure the stick. Ignoring the cost of having my feet cut from the glass, I fought desperately, inching my way to the top of the tether-ball court. After an intense struggle, I finally gained full possession of the stick. As I took possession, my mind immediately told me that I was at least the equivalency of Superman. So, I commenced beating the boy's legs and ankles until he fell to the ground. There was only one problem with being Superman that day, Mom." Mom said, "And what was that, Son?" I said, "Each step I took to strike my opponent brought new cuts to my feet. With the fight being broken up by our staff, I was asked why there was so much trouble with the other boy?

I explained to our staff that the boy had run over my sister with a bike some four years earlier. To our staff's dismay, a supervisor asked, 'Is there anything else we should know?' As I look back on the situation and know that my feet now bore new scars, it gave great credence as to why God once said, 'Vengeance is mine, Saith the Lord.' Mom said, "Son." I said, "Yeah, Mom, what is it?" Mom said, "There is something fundamentally wrong with your story that doesn't quite add up." I said, "Yeah, and what might that be?" Mom said, "Well Jack, little boys don't hold grudges from age five to nine. They forget about things quickly and move on to something else." I said, "That's usually true, Mom, so what's your point?" Mom said, "When the situation with your sister's attacker rekindled itself, you chose to get involved and avenge your sister." I said, "Yeah, and so what of it?" Mom said, "Son, that's not real revenge, that's a little boy that should've forgotten your sister's tragedy long ago. When your opponent told his story in the cabin that night, you felt a war going on inside of you, didn't you?" I said, "How would you know that, Mom?" Mom said, "It stood out like a sore thumb when you were telling your story, Jackie." I said, "Mom, you're addressing as Jackie like people did in the 1960s. Why are you calling me Jackie when you know everyone calls me Jack?" Mom said, "Because in this story you are the little boy. Would you like to share with Mom how you really felt that night in the cabin?" I said, "Yeah, I guess maybe I could.

After I fought Dorthy's former assailant, I went over and over in my mind as to why I had done that. I even would remind Dorthy once in a while why I avenged her honor by fighting the boy. She was glad at first and acknowledged my efforts. But two or three years would go by, and I would remind her again how I championed her. Of course, by this time, she had heard the story several times and had adopted a perplexed look on her face as if to ask, why do you keep bringing this occasion up?

So, I simply wouldn't bring the story up anymore." Mom said, "I suspect you know why you kept telling your sister the story, don't you, Son?" I said, "Yes, I do, Mom." Mom said, "Well, will you tell me why?" I said, "Yes, I guess I can." Mom said, "Go ahead, Son, and tell me why you kept bringing up how you championed your sister."

I said, "Well, when the boy told his story that night of running over Dorthy, I didn't realize at the time, but something desperate was going on inside me that day. That is to say, when I challenged the boy to a tether ball game, that was my chance to champion Dorthy's misfortune. And yet, deep down inside, I had always wanted someone to champion my life causes. By championing Dorthy's misfortune, the experience of fighting her former attacker brought me as close as I could possibly feel if someone were to be my champion. I just hadn't expected to be hurt in my attempt to champion Dorthy's cause. In retrospect, I had hoped one day, someone would champion me as well. I was abandoned by your mom at the age of four, experienced your and Dad's divorce at age five, and molested at the age of five and seven. I desperately wanted a real champion in my life. And if I couldn't have a champion in my life, I thought maybe I could champion Dorthy's life regardless of what the cost was to me. Fighting the other boy kind of gave me the feeling of what it would be like to be championed by someone else. Still, all was not lost, for when I entered my incarceration period at a much later date, I learned that my champion had always existed. He was now ready to champion me. And He has been my champion in every sense. I learned to love Him far more than I could have ever hoped to love my earthly father. Wonderful Counselor is His name, and being my champion was His aim."

Mom said, "I'm glad you shared that with me, Son, because that's exactly how I felt when I was a little girl. So, what did you do next?" I said, "I packed to go home from our campsite and thought to myself, how could I have ever calculated running into this boy at our campsite. Be that as it may, Dad arrived later that day to take me home. He would have to visit the camp's office to finalize funding for my stay. Of course, I waited in the car with much anticipation, hoping the camp staff wouldn't bring the incident to Dad's attention. With Dad having to pay the remainder of the bill, I knew their staff would have plenty of time to address the issue.

As I waited outside, I fought the suspense for about an hour and a half. It felt like I was in a vice for a lifetime. Not wanting to be in trouble with Dad proved the wait to be arduous and agonizing. Dad had just purchased a new 1966 Bonneville convertible, and I thought I was going to fry in its back seat that day. Finally, Dad and Jennie appeared, opened the car doors, and quietly got in. Thinking the worst, I tried to ask Dad most inconspicuously if everything was okay? Dad answered by saying, 'Jackie, Dad's not mad at you for warming that boy's ass. He ran your sister over with a bike, and the fool had everything coming that you gave him. You were just a couple years too late in giving it to him. The people here will just have to get over it. The kid was a schmuck, and that's all there was to it. So let us just go home and forget the whole matter.' Riding home that sunny day gave me fleeting memories of my lost Camelot. But not being deceived by my temporary euphoric atmosphere made me ponder what would happen next in the world?

Being settled at home from camp for a few months brought in our annual Thanksgiving dinner. Serving these types of dinners certainly was a tremendous strength of our stepmother, Jennie." Mom said, "I'm sure it was, Son." I said, "Well, Mom, I have to give credit where credit is due, and our stepmother really was a great cook." Mom said, "It's okay, Son. Mom's not offended." I said, "Yes, you are, let's face it, Mom. No maternal mother wants to hear how well the stepmother did in her place." Mom said, "Don't get smart with me, sonny boy, because I'll run your butt right out of here like a locomotive!!! Let's face it, as you would say, your asinine comments don't exactly lend themselves to us building the best relationship under the circumstances, do they?" I said, "You're right, Mom, they don't. So, therefore, I apologize, and I'll try to do better by refraining from such comments in the future." Mom said, "Thank you, and now you may proceed with what you were saying."

I said, "You know, Mom, I know you realize the negative atmosphere I have so often associated with Jennie when speaking about her. But her cooking surely was one of her great strengths. I was hoping to find the proper time where I could simply elaborate on some of her good qualities as well." Mom said, "I know that, Son; none of us are all bad." I said, "You're right. In short, only telling Jennie's faults certainly wouldn't be a fair assessment of who the whole person was. One thing for sure, when it came to preparing Thanksgiving dinner, Jennie was second to none."

Mom said, "I'm glad you guys knew her in that capacity, Son." I said, "Mom, it's just I have a hard time telling the good about Jennie when I think of the beatings Jerry suffered at the end of her ironing cord. Sometimes, those types of memories don't sit so well with me. And yet I know she was operating under less than desirable circumstances at the time." Mom said, "I know that, Son, just as much as when you sometimes verbally strike out at me for abandoning you. You sometimes act as if that's all there was to it." I said, "What do you mean by that?" Mom said, "Well, when most parents abandon their children, it is probably fair to say that's pretty much the end of the matter. But that wasn't the case at all with me, Son." I asked, "Really, and how's that?" Mom said, "When I left Dorthy and Jerry and yourself that day, I left for the sake of my own sanity. Mom just couldn't take all that madness anymore. For me to continue to stay in that type of relationship with your father would have been insanity for me. But to say that I didn't reach out shortly after my departure would be a far cry from the truth. Because I did."

I said, "Really!!" Mom said, "Oh yeah!! You see, shortly after Harvey and I were married, we decided the best thing to do was to adopt you, Dorthy, and Jerry and have one big family. I certainly agreed with Harvey, and we moved forward with adopting all three of you. So, when your father and I went to court over the matter, he managed to get a good lawyer and won the judgment to keep you, Dorthy, and Jerry with him. This shocked the hell out of Harvey and me because, in those years, the judge usually ruled in favor of the mother. In fact, it was very common for a judge to rule in favor of the mother most often. How your father managed to pull that one off still baffles me to this day.

But I can tell you this, when the court proceedings were moving forward, your father was behind me saying things like, 'No one else is going to raise my babies!! I'm the great JC!!!' Mom said, "Well, who in the hell did the great JC think I was? I am the mother of his babies. And I do have a right to have my babies at home with me. So, Harvey and I finally had to give up our court proceedings for the three of you. We realized it wasn't a matter of your father loving you three as to why he fought so hard for you." I said, "Well then, what was it?" Mom said, "Harvey and I could clearly see it was far more a matter of your father's pride to win. You see, Harvey and I felt your father wanting to win the custody case for you three wasn't exactly out of love for the three of you. Son, don't take me wrong. I'm not sitting here telling you that your father didn't love you, Dorthy, or Jerry. That's not what I'm saying at all. I'm just saying that your father's false pride far outweighed the proper concern he should have had when it came to winning the custody battle. His pride wouldn't allow him to suffer the embarrassment of knowing that Harvey and I could have just as effectively reared you three. So don't allow anyone ever to tell you that those efforts weren't made to keep all of us together because they were. And it's not like I haven't mentioned these things to your sister before because I have. But she loves to maintain her position of "it just wasn't enough." Well, that's just another one of her versions of passing judgment on me. I forgot she's right up there with God. She, and only she, sees things from their true perspective. Well, regardless of how Dorthy felt, there was no way in hell I was going to throw away a happy marriage with Harvey just so I could go back and live a miserable life with your father. And your sister can believe that with all her heart. As a matter of fact, she can take that one to the bank if she wants to. Your father had his chance with me, and he willfully threw it away. Yes, sir, he kicked me around enough that I finally started to believe him!!! Shame on me for not waking up much sooner. But I'll tell you this, Son, one day, Mom is going to close her eyes for good. And when that happens, your sister's eyes will finally open. But the problem with that is, it will be too little, too late, for both your sister and me. Well, you go on with your Thanksgiving story because that's the way it really was."

I said, "Well, as I was saying, homemade cooking was Jennie's code. Yes, no one in the whole world could make rice like our stepmother, Jennie. After Jennie died, I challenged Dorthy, Louise, and Lucy to make the same rice pudding Jennie made so well while she was alive. All three failed, and they never tried again. Well, at any rate, after Jennie finished preparing Thanksgiving dinner, we all sat around the table, listening to Dad's uncanny ability to tell his jokes." Mom said, "Your father was good at that kind of stuff, Son," I said, "Yes, he was, Mom. I remember once thinking to myself, boy!! If I could only tell jokes like that someday. But knowing wholesome times like those were short-lived, trouble would soon be on the horizon. Case in point. In the summer of 1967, I was hit by an oncoming car while walking home from school one day. As I was crossing the street, I noticed a brand new 1967 bluish-green Pontiac Catalina encroaching on me rapidly. It was too late to evaluate its speed, so the car suddenly struck me. It knocked me airborne across the street, only to hit a steel telephone pole. After landing on the ground, I was somewhat confused as to whether I was even hurt. With a knot on the back of my head about the size of a baseball, a woman standing next to me suggested that maybe I should remain lying on the ground until the ambulance arrived. My hospital stay lasted three weeks. It left me with a brain concussion, bruised ribs, and a twisted right ankle. Much to my surprise, when I returned home, I noticed the neighborhood children had planned a homecoming party for me. Sitting there enjoying their presents, I commenced building a model airplane. I was elated the neighborhood children had gone out of their way to see me happy. With that being the case, suddenly and out of nowhere, Dad starts SCREAMING at me for reasons I can't explain to this day." Mom said, "Had you done something wrong, Son?" I said, "That's just the thing, Mom, I had no idea. I mean, I'm just sitting there enjoying my toys with the neighborhood kids, and Dad is going off like a bomb. I mean, I had no clue as to what the heck merited that type of behavior. It caught me off guard, to say the least. The other kids who were playing with me were just as appalled as I was. You could look around the room and feel the thickness of the atmosphere."

Mom said, "So, did your father ever explain the problem to you? I said, "He told me that I was ungrateful and that I didn't know how good I had it. As he continued screaming at me, he would say things like, 'Who the hell do you think you are!!! Well, answer me!!! Who the hell do you think you are!!!' I said, "Not knowing how to respond to his question, all I could think of was what I heard the minister say in church one day." Mom said, "And what was that, Jack? I said, "He emphasized to everyone one afternoon that we were all God's children. But in remembering what he said and hearing all of Dad's screams at that moment, I didn't think it was the best time to inform Dad that we were all of God's children. But not understanding why Dad was screaming surely took away any joy the neighborhood children had planned for my homecoming. I was sick of the verbal abuse, and I hated it with EVERY FIBER of my being!! Not knowing whether Dad would turn violent, I remember thinking to myself, I have got to get out of here at all costs if it is the last thing I do!!! Here, the neighborhood kids wanted to show their kindness and concern for my hospital stay, and my dad is going off!!! It was as if he couldn't accept other people treating me well. The stress and traumatizing effect it had on me was to leave my home as soon as I could. So, I soon elected to run away again. This time, Jerry would join me. As the evening encroached, Jerry and I decided to run away. Walking down the street, Jerry decided to enter a neighbor's garage to find a blanket so we could cover up for the evening.

When Jerry entered the garage, I felt so ashamed because I was supposed to be the big brother and not fear doing such things. Instead, I watched my little brother do the dirty work of stealing the blanket. Mighty brave of me, wasn't it, Mom?" Mom said, "Oh, Son, it's not like Jerry broke into Fort Knox. He was just securing a blanket for the two of you. You can't think less of yourself just because you chickened out." I said, "See, Mom, even you feel like I was a chump!!" Mom said, "Oh, Son, you're making too much out of it!" I said, "Maybe so, but at any rate, Jerry and I found a treehouse that night and managed to sleep inside of it. With the treehouse well above the ground, we both felt it would be reasonably safe enough to sleep in.

Rising the following day, we continued playing with the neighborhood kids as if nothing ever happened. Both Jerry and I chose to ignore our personal circumstances at home as if they didn't exist at all. We both had a conversation that day about what we could eat without returning home. I suggested to him that we could probably eat apples off the trees for a little while. We really had no intention of ever returning home again." Mom said, "Son, I never imagined my boys having to look elsewhere for their happiness." I said, "Well, Mom, as the day lingered on, we played with other kids in the neighborhood. As Jerry and I played, we suddenly saw a policeman walking up to a neighboring house. We thought he might decide to stop where we were playing. Well, we were right. So, the Policeman asked, 'Are you fellows okay?' Answering the officer, Jerry and I stood up and said, 'Sure!!' The officer said, 'Do you boys know that we have been looking for you the last two days?' We said, 'No!' The officer said, 'Well, come with me, boys.' We said, 'Yes, sir.' A few minutes later, the police pulled up to seat Jerry and me in their cruiser. When my brother and I arrived home, there were at least ten police cars already there. Jerry and I wondered what the big brew ha ha was all about. We actually thought something else was going on other than us being the subject. You see, in those years, if there had been a big conglomeration of police cars, it was usually because something significant was going on. Obviously, Jerry and I hadn't thought of ourselves as

SEARCHING FOR A MISSING LIFE

something important. How can you be beaten within an inch of your life with an ironing cord and still feel that you have some sort of self-worth?

I don't think Jerry ever really knew that Dorthy and I were in proximity when he took those beatings from Jennie. Dorthy and I stood there and watched the blood protrude from some of Jerry's welts where Jennie had beat on him like a drum with that ironing cord. It was awful. Jerry's screams were chilling as he begged for mercy. And there was nothing Dorthy, nor I, could do to help him. Every time Jennie decided to beat Jerry, all we could do was hate the moment and hope that Jennie would stop. Unfortunately, there was no such luck. And neither was Dad there to deter the situation. In those years, if a step-parent wanted to beat you, it was looked upon as something normal and acceptable.

Jerry's beatings would run through my mind like a picture show when he and I would run away. I didn't want him to be around the situation anymore, and neither did Dorthy. With so many police cars there that day, we were shocked that someone else did not even care. Many spectators were there as Jerry and I stepped out of the police car. We were escorted into our home by two police officers. Dad's facial expressions were that of a stone wall. He held a look on his face that suggested he had all the publicity he could ever use." Mom said, "Boy, I bet he did." I said, "Mom, with the interaction the police had with the spectators, you would have thought that maybe Jennie and Dad needed to take a second look at things. But you know how that goes. Human nature never sees itself as the problem. Instead, it always sees the problem in other people. At any rate, when the police left, Dad felt brute force would serve as the answer to correcting the problem. So, he closed the family room off and beat me with a leather belt." Mom said, "When your father and I were married, he thought brute force could handle every situation back then as well." I said, "I know what you mean, Mom. Once, when I was six years old, Dad beat me so hard that he decided to time the beating in five-minute increments. At six years old, I knew what it was like to be beaten for fifteen minutes in five-minute increments. Dad allowed a two-minute break after each five-minute beating. My body became so numb from the beating I couldn't feel the pain anymore. It was as if all the pain was one source of the same pain." Mom said, "Son, where did all that take place?" I said, "In the basement when we lived over on Minion Avenue. I can't remember what the beating was about, but I certainly remember the incident. The beating threw me into a state of shock, and I had to stay home from school for about ten days until the bruises cleared. When our school called our grandmother to ask about my absence, she would tell them I was sick. It is hard to explain that type of beating if one has never experienced it." Mom said, "I don't think I want to hear anymore today. Come on, Son, give Mom a kiss, and we will talk tomorrow." I said, "Okay, Mom, you take care of yourself, and I'll see you tomorrow."

Walking down my mother's corridor that evening brought to mind how many years had already passed between the ages of four and twenty-six. It was as if a lifetime had already passed without any real relationship with my mother. So, I vowed in my heart that the time being was as good as any to make up the difference. After all, twenty-two years had passed without really knowing her. I knew if I didn't at least try, I would probably regret it later on. And yet, I was aware there would have to be more of an effort on my side to fully forgive her for abandoning me at four years old. Returning the next day, I explained to my mother that I had run away once more before being placed with Aunt Penny. Mom said, "What do you mean you were placed with your Aunt Penny? Didn't they know turning you over to her was like a train wreck waiting to happen? In short, as I remember your aunt Penny, she was a nut looking for a bolt in the hope of threading her brains back together." I said, "Well, I can't argue with you there, Mom, but I decided to run away again. I guess you can say I was still looking for a missing life.

This time, running away would only take me as far as our backyard. Slipping out of the house one evening, I had the utmost intention to run as far and fast as I could. But a sudden heavy rain thwarted my effort. The rain started coming down in sheets as I left out the back door of our home. Knowing that I couldn't get far without being drenched, I had to think of something fast. So, I noticed some rubber-back carpets lying across our fence line. These rubber-back carpets would lay in the doorways of Dad's cleaning accounts. He'd bring those 3x5 carpets home, scrub them with his shampooer, and then hang them on the fence to dry. Moving quickly to escape the rain, I grabbed one of them and draped myself in it. I positioned myself in our backyard on a slight natural incline to help repel any water around from where I lay. Having draped myself with this type of carpet gave me a great advantage of securing my comfort and staying dry." Mom said, "How was that, Son?" I said, "Well, Mom, as I remember it, I would lay on the ground so the rubber side of the carpet could repel rainwater away from me. The other part of the carpet was obviously the soft part that kept me dry and comfortable. I was glad it was summertime, so I wouldn't catch a chill or a cold.

During the night, I looked through a small opening of the carpet, pondering my circumstances. The rain continued raging as I watched little drops of water slowly drip from the carpet edge directly in front of my face. With the water not being able to penetrate where I lay, it left me with an odd sense of security that God was there in some way. For a moment of time and space, I felt indubitably safe and wondered what would become of my life. As I awakened from my sleep, I was told, 'You'll be going to live with your Aunt Penny.' I had no idea my stay with her would soon introduce another wreck in my life." Mom said, "Yeah!! You better believe it because as I remember your Aunt Penny, she had a habit of not only engineering her own wrecks, she has done well at orchestrating other people's wrecks." I said, "Times were changing in those years, Mom. And the civil rights era was reaching its climax. By 1967 and 1968, our country had fifty-eight cities burning with looting and rioting. The atmosphere was highly charged between the black and white races of its day.

Before I left to go live with Aunt Penny, Dad got me to help him clean up the Murdock & Murdock building downtown for the last time. Dad, Jennie, and I were in the Murdock building one evening when a full-scale riot took place just outside the door where we had been working. With our work finished, we sought to exit the building to no avail. The riot had already encroached on the front of the building, prohibiting us from leaving the foyer. Hesitating as to how we could manage to make it to our car, the sudden appearance of four police officers arrived to help guide our escape. When clearing the building, we observed two other officers issuing twelve-gauge shotguns to other officers on duty that day. The next moment, two other officers pointed their shotguns toward the riot in the hope of slowing the crowd. Suddenly, the advance of fifteen to twenty pedestrians threatened our immediate vicinity with a firebombing. The police had taken stricter positions with their shotguns in order to deter any further encroachment of rioters.

With Dad, Mom, and myself being briskly escorted to our car, the police were delighted to see that Dad drove a convertible. The police noticed the car top in the down position and ordered all three of us to leap over the car walls for an immediate escape. With the three of us landing in our car, Dad quickly started it with the eagerness to leave the proximity spontaneously. Suddenly, the police noticed further encroachment of rioters and pointed their shotguns toward their advancement. Several closer rioters heeded the police warning, and their compliance afforded us an immediate and successful escape. As we sped away, I maintained an accurate view of the site only to witness the remaining escalating violence and firebombing. It was like pulling out of hell with no time to lose. The following day the media had shown much of the damage on television. That same day, Jennie decided to coast through the affected areas in order to size the enormous destruction left behind by rioters. Dad's cleaning accounts were primarily in areas where most of the rioting accrued. Dad's concern for his life forced him to remain armed while conducting business. In the upcoming months, Dorthy and I would reluctantly have to deal with many racial issues.

Meanwhile, Dad and Jennie moved me to Aunt Penny's house, which was located in Bond Hill. I held hope that the move would somehow solve many of our family's problems. At first, things appeared to be okay. But I soon learned that Aunt Penny was just as much of a screamer as Dad was. And at times, even more so. Aunt Penny's screaming definitely set me on edge, and I knew the move would be just more of the same. My Aunt Penny was probably the rudest person I had ever met in my entire life. Not to mention how she loved to be obnoxious with almost everyone. She kind of prided herself on that type of approach.

I was equally convinced my Aunt Penny thrived on misery as well. She was the type of person who would walk into a public store, and if she didn't get her way, she would "scream" at the manager and call him every name one could possibly think of. It appeared she liked throwing her weight around because my Uncle Less was an attorney. You just didn't make scenes like that in the 1960s, Mom, and if you did, you stuck out like a sore thumb. In today's society, madness is now a regular procedure!!! When my Aunt Penny would have her public rages, I'd be so embarrassed I would just walk away, hoping that no one had seen me with her." I said, "Mom," and Mom said, "Yes, Son.? I said, "Do you remember when Aunt Penny married that Jewish lawyer by the name Less Goldman?" Mom said, "Well, I wasn't there for their wedding, if that's what you mean. However, I do remember your Uncle Less being pretty politically active in the late 1940s and fifty's. As a matter of fact, I thought your Uncle Less far outclassed your Aunt Penny. Plain and simple, I thought your Uncle Less was too good for your Aunt Penny, and she certainly didn't deserve him." I said, "What do you mean?" Mom said, "Son, I couldn't stand your Aunt Penny because she could just be as evil as your grandmother Victoria. And she even had the gall to give her baby away in a bar back in the 1940s. She could have at least adopted the child out as opposed to giving her child away in a bar. I mean, what the hell was she thinking about. Think about that, Son. What kind of mother would give her child away in a bar. Would you please explain that to me?"

I said, "I don't think I can, Mom." Mom said, "You better believe you can't. Why would any woman give her child away in a bar? They have totally flipped their lid. Hell, when I left you, Dorthy, and Jerry, I wouldn't have ever considered leaving you in a bar with some stranger I didn't even know. Jack, I'm not justifying it was right to leave all three of you. I'm just saying if a parent is going to leave their children behind, one would certainly not want to leave them in a bar with a perfect stranger?" I said, "I understand your reasoning, and I'm glad you didn't. But the effect it had on Dorthy, Jerry, and myself certainly had its consequences regardless of where you left us, Mom." Mom said, "With that, I have no doubt, Son." And my mother walked over to hug me and cried in my arms for her decision to leave us twenty-two years earlier.

CHAPTER 7

DIFFERING PERSPECTIVES

Hugging my mother while she cried, I reminded her that it wasn't my intention to make her feel bad about leaving us. I told her that I thought she and I had advanced far enough in our relationship that it was not necessary to harbor any more ill will. I realized at the beginning of our reunion that that's precisely what I used to do. After a good hug, Mom resumed her story by saying, "Any time your Aunt Penny came around, like your grandmother, she'd always enjoy leading me a dog's life in any way she could possibly find. Her husband, Less, was just the opposite of her, for he treated me with kindness and respect. I don't know what your Uncle Less ever saw in that broad, especially since he is an attorney. He must have been drunk when he married her, only to wake up the next morning to discover his first case was a nightmare." I said, "You know, Mom, when I moved in with Aunt Penny, Uncle Less was always nice to me." Mom said, "I'm glad he was, Son." I said, "Uncle Less once told me all the things that would happen to me if I weren't able to put my life back in order. He was right; all those things eventually happened.

Another time, he told me he was imprisoned in Ohio State Penitentiary for embezzling three and a half million dollars from a large corporation in the late 1950s." Mom said, "That's true, Son, I remember when all that madness took place. That bologna was all over the 6:00 o'clock news and was very embarrassing for days on in our whole family. And the authorities didn't have any problem putting your uncle in the booby hatch either." I said, "Uncle Less also told me he and two other attorneys arranged the embezzlement so Uncle Less would be the fall guy in their plot." Mom said, "I don't know about the specifics, Son, but I guess if your uncle told you those things, it's probably true." I answered, "While Uncle Less was imprisoned, he became briefly associated with gangster Yon Licavoli. Licavoli was a powerful gangster who ran bootlegging operations out of Detroit in the 1920s and 30s. He was later arrested for murder and was serving a life sentence in the Ohio State Penitentiary when Less arrived there to serve his sentence for embezzlement.

With Uncle Less being an attorney, Licavoli asked him to read his court transcript in the hope of finding a loophole for an eventual release. After Uncle Less read the man's transcript, he assured Mr. Licavoli that he had been railroaded. It was commonly known that the Purple Gang in Detroit in those days were primarily of Jewish decent." Mom said, "How would you know all that, Son?" I said, "We'll, I'll get to that in a moment, Mom. Anyways, for the sake of successful assassinations and other operations, outside Irish gangsters would conspire with the Purple Gang to take on some of their contracts. An Irish gangster by the name of Al Sinclair joined the Purple Gang in 1920." Mom said, "Now you stop right there, Son!! How do you know these things?" I said, "Would you just wait a minute, Mom?" Mom said, "I'm sorry; go on with what you were saying, Jack." I said, "Al Sinclair, at just twenty years old, quickly became a bagman for the Purple Gang. A bag carrier to your mom would be a person who carries large sums of money from point A to point B. Sinclair was involved in five different shootouts with the FBI during his criminal career and was shot by federal agents only to narrowly escape death. He was also suspected of helping set up the Bugs Siegle hit in Vegas in June of 1947. To my surprise, Al Sinclair and I became friends after his interview with a national magazine in 1972. The magazine article had shown Sinclair to be one of the few old-time American gangsters still alive." Mom said, "Son!!" I said, "What, Mom?" Mom said, "Why would you want to get involved with a man like that?" I said, "Because Jerry and I wanted to be gangsters, and that's precisely what we did. And as you can see, by the time Al Sinclair came on the scene, Jerry and I were not of the opinion that "Leave it to Beaver" was a preferable way of life, so why not give the underworld a shot?" Mom said, "That's not funny, Jack." I said, "It wasn't meant to be funny, Mom."

Mom said, "Yes, I know, but those things got your brother killed, Jack." I said, "Is it your purpose to bust my chops over it?" Mom said, "No! But you and your brother could have gone to college and had a better life, Son!! I said, "That's true,

Mom, but with all due respect, is that the way things turned out for you?" Mom said, "Don't get smart with me, Jack. You just get on with your story before I throw your butt right out of here!!" I said, "Well, Mom, I'll just come back tomorrow when the atmosphere is not so highly charged." Mom said, "Well, that's fine with me too!!!" Walking toward Mom's door, she asked, "Son?" I said, "Yeah, Mom, what is it?" She said, "Are you really going to come back tomorrow?" I said, "Yeah, Mom, I just need a little time off." Mom said, "Okay, I'll see ya tomorrow." That next morning, I asked my mother to hear me out. Mom said, "Okay, go ahead with what you were saying, Son." I said, "I wanted you to know that it wasn't like Jerry and I got down in some kind of huddle one day and decided that we were going to be gangsters." Mom said, "Well, I hope not." I said, "Well, we didn't. Furthermore, as I started to say yesterday, if one wanted to be a gangster, what better person to rub elbows with than a gangster who had been written up in a national magazine?

The article featured Al's history and his affiliation with several known Mafia families during the 20s, 30s, and 40s. Finally, in 1948, Sinclair was arrested and spent the next twelve years in Sam Quentin. After Al's release in 1960, he knew he had a drinking problem during his former life, so he joined Alcoholics Anonymous in the hope of combating the problem once and for all." Mom asked, "Is that where you met Al Sinclair, Son?" I said, "Yes, Mom, I met him in 1967 right before moving in with Aunt Penny and wouldn't see him again until 1972. As you already know, Dad had been attending Alcoholics Anonymous when I first met Sinclair. Al had been going to AA meetings for a couple of years. One day, two unknown men decided to enter the 405 Oak Street Center, where AA meetings were being held. Both of these men were of Italian descent and had been sent to visit Al from one of the New York crime families. Don't ask me what crime family, Mom, because I didn't know back then, and I still don't know to this day. And even if I did, I would never disclose that information to you." Mom said, "Well, trust me, Son, I wouldn't want to know anyway."

I said, "At any rate, Al had discussed the matter of two men entering our center one day." Mom said, "Well, trust me, Son, I really don't want to know that part." I said, "Mom, that's always a good position to be in when that type of information starts to flow. Anyway, with these two men knowing Sinclair was a stand-up guy from the old days, they sought to recruit him for what had become the modern organized crime.

Al quickly turned their offer down, explaining to them that he actually lived by the 12 Steps that hung on the wall. The two gangsters quickly realized Alcoholics Anonymous had become a fundamental way of life for Al. Realizing Al wasn't going to budge from his new way of life, the two men gracefully bowed out, never to return.

The two men leaving quietly gave credence to the new Mafia, not wanting to make any unnecessary noise. Once, Al admitted to me that he had committed many of his crimes in the old days just short of a drink. Involved in two different gang wars in the late 20s and 30s, Sinclair was responsible for 21 murders between 1923 and 1931. Breaking bread with the mob for the last time in 1948, Al Sinclair would go on to spend the next twelve years in Sam Quentin. After his release from Sam Quentin in 1960, he married a former madam he knew from the 30s, and they lived out the rest of their natural lives in a four-unit apartment building located in Covington, Kentucky. I wanted you to understand something here, Mom." Mom said, "And what's that, Son?" I said, "Rarely do these types of gangsters end up living their natural lives out in peace. It just doesn't work that way all the time. How Al Sinclair ended up as a historical figure in a national magazine is definitely a rarity. But as a teenager, I loved the idea of rubbing elbows and being affiliated with one of the most notorious gangsters in American history. For unknown reasons, I really never understood my short eleven-year affiliation with Al Sinclair. But with being released from prison at twenty-six, I finally realized my affiliation with Sinclair was to learn lessons that never should have been necessary to begin with. Essentially, I had become an occasional guest at Al and Marie's home before my imprisonment. I admired Al's original wardrobes, which he wore in his 20s and 30s. There in Al's closet were multiple pinstripe suits with handkerchiefs depicting the bygone era. I was fascinated with all I saw and wanted to be just like him.

Coveting some of Al's original shoulder holsters, I once said to him, 'Someday, I'll be the best man to wear your wardrobe, Al.' Unknowingly to me at the time, Al Sinclair of the 1920s Purple Gang would soon become my mentor in my upcoming crime years. But more on that later. The Irony was this, Mom, "What's the odds of my Uncle Less doing time with Yon Licavoli of the Purple Gang and me getting to know Al Sinclair from the same criminal empire?" Mom said, "I have no idea, Son." I said, "With both of these men working for the same crime family in the 20s and 30s made mine and Uncle Less's acquaintance pretty bazaar. Considering the fact that I never saw Uncle Less again after the age of fifteen, he would have never known that Al Sinclair and I would become friends a short time later.

Of course, and just as well, I would have never known Al Sinclair and Yon Licavoli knew each other from the Purple Gang during the 1920s and 30s. Nor had Al ever disclosed any of the gang's operations to me. I guess you can attribute that to Al knowing that Dad had once muscled for Sammy Eisner of Newport in the 1950s." Mom said, "Boy, Son, you are a mess!!" I said, "Well, Mom, that was then; this is now." Mom said, "You're darn lucky you didn't end up like your brother, Jerry." I said, "I couldn't agree more. And furthermore, if it had not been for God's intervention while I was still in prison, I have no doubt I'd still be involved in organized crime to this day, or in prison, or dead." Mom said, "You better count your lucky stars." I said, "No, Mom, there's no luck to it. Either one is blessed, or he is not blessed. You see, Mom, luck is what you need if you are going to play the lottery. In short, if you are not blessed, you are going to need all the luck you can get. And since there's a tremendous shortage of luck, you'd be better off being blessed. And since I was never good at playing the lottery, I'd much rather be blessed for doing the right thing." Mom said, "Boy, you've got that right."

I said, "At any rate, upon Uncle Less's release from prison, he was greatly ashamed of not being able to practice law anymore. This goes without mentioning him being marked as a public offender. Because of public embarrassment, Uncle Less and Aunt Penny eventually moved to Florida. They are both still there to this day. But for 1967, I still resided with both of them in Bond Hill. Which was still partly known in those years as a Jewish sector of town. Being under the custody of Aunt Penny proved to be challenging at times." Mom said, "I can attest to that." I said, "At the time, I was enrolled in Bond Hill Elementary School. It was still during the height of the Civil Rights era, and it really had me on the edge." Mom said, "What do you mean, Son?" I said, "Well, I didn't understand at ten years old just exactly what the black race wanted, but whatever it was, they felt it merited chasing me home almost every day after school. Being chased home by black youth became a regular procedure. No one cared to explain to me what the heck was going on. All that was being offered was violence and no answers in sight. Many times, I'd have to leave school prematurely to avoid being jumped. Leaving a couple minutes early each day always helped me get a jump on my departure." Mom said, "Son, when the black kids chased you home, had any of them ever caught up with you?" I said, "No, but the experience did wonders for me a few years later when I joined the track team." Mom said, "You are a mess, Son, you're just a mess!!!" I said, "Uncle Less encouraged me to join the Boy Scouts back then, so I did. I had to quit a short time later because of escalating violence in our neighborhood where the scout meetings were being held. One time, a black student sat directly behind me in class when I was attending Eastwood Village Elementary over in Oakley. Of course, you know that school doesn't even exist anymore.

At any rate, this black kid kept smacking me on the back of my head until I was forced to respond. Grabbing him by his neck and chest, I started running across the room with him. We arrived at a sink where we used to clean up after our science projects. I commenced beating the youth's head on the sink until he promised to leave me alone. The fight was broken up before either one of us was seriously hurt. Thinking of the incident some years later, I felt that the civil rights era brought about many unjustifiable violent acts for both black and white races of its day. It was common to witness racial fights almost every day after school. Some students even threw bricks at each other as they walked home from school. Unfortunately, one of those bricks struck a black girl whom almost everyone liked. The incident seriously hurt the girl, and to the end, I have never known. With the violence at an all-time high, it found its way to our home as well." Mom said, "What do you mean, Son?" I said, "Well, being taunted every day by black students proved not to be enough. It appeared that Aunt Penny wanted some of the action as well. I felt like asking her to take a ticket and stand in line. That is to say, if Aunt Penny wanted to pound on me, make no mistake, she would." Mom said, "If that broad were here right now, I'd choke the life right out of her." I said, "Okay, Mom, plain and simple, Aunt Penny was slap happy. That is to say, she would slap you just out of (GP), general principle. I would use my arms to hide my face when she would commence slapping me. As I tried to defend myself, she'd use upper cup slaps to penetrate my defense so as to continue her slapping fiesta." Mom said, "I'll kill her. I'll just kill that broad." I said, "Mom, for one, she lives in Florida, and you don't have the health to do anything. And two, if you don't chill out, I'll have to leave again and discontinue my story." Mom said, "OK! OK!! Go on with what you were saying." I said, "With Aunt Penny's upper cup slaps completely straightening out my posture, it opened the door for her to land her famous left and right hooks. I thought maybe she was trying to make the boxing team before the year closed out. And if she wasn't, I reminded her that the boxing federation could possibly be interested in such performances." Mom said, "That's not funny, Jack." I said, "I know it's not, Mom. It just helps me live with the past abuse I suffered on her behalf.

Hey, make no mistake, Mom, Aunt Penny enjoyed ringing my bell. As in so much, I'd have daydreams about someone coming over and stomping her. Boy!! Before she completed some of her sessions, I was hoping it came with an ice cream cone. One time, the slapping session went on for so long I had to viciously threaten her to get her to stop slapping me." Mom said, "What did you say to her, Son?" I said, "I just told her if she didn't stop hitting me, I'd be forced to strike her back. And if she thought I was kidding, just continue and watch what happens." Mom said, "What did she do, Son?" I said, "She stopped slapping me. Thank God, she believed me. She just stood there looking at me dumbfounded, as if I were out of line for trying to stop her abuse. I then informed her that if Uncle Less tried to do anything, I would call Dad when he was good and drunk and tell him what was going on. I reminded her how Dad loved to fight when he was intoxicated. I really wasn't worried about Uncle Less because he was always nice to me. I just wanted to cover that base in case she thought Uncle Less was someone she could scare me with. And, I knew she really didn't want Dad coming over because you know how Dad likes to break people up like a pretzel when he was drinking." Mom said, "So, did she say anything more?" I replied, "Mom, it was one of the most awkward moments of my childhood. I couldn't believe what I was saying to my aunt just to get her to stop slapping me. In short, I think Aunt Penny and I were somewhat taken back from the entire situation. That is to say, she was definitely appalled that I had a convincing argument that Dad would break her up if she didn't stop slapping me. I was puzzled because I realized at that very moment I was threatening my father's sister, who should have been protecting me. For a bleak moment in time, it was the loneliest feeling a child of ten could ever experience. The one man I really needed to help secure me in those years was no more than a fleeting illusion in my mind. And why? Simply because Dad hadn't yet learned to control his own demons. And yet, I longed for that so much in my heart. I longed for a true champion that could save my life before it was too late. Sadly, I realized and accepted that it wasn't going to be my father at that point. His drinking and character defects were starting to systematically destroy him."

My mother just started to cry. I went over, hugged her, and said, "It's okay, Mom, it was a long time ago." Mom said, "No, it's not okay, Son; it was a train wreck waiting to happen right from its beginning. I had to contend with your Aunt Penny myself when your father and I were still married. And she was no pushover either!!" I said, "What do you mean?" Mom said, "Well, mine and your father's marriage was pretty much coming to an end, and I didn't know how much longer I could take it. Between your father drinking and his mother trying to hold on to her little boy!! I knew something had to give sooner or later. This would be an evening when your grandmother Victoria and your Aunt Penny arrived at our home all drunk-ed up. I was concerned for our evening because I knew it was just a matter of time before your father would join his darling of a mother and his sister Penny in their drunken rage. And it was just as I thought, eventually, that he did. Most of the time, your father would drink with his mother, Victoria.

But this particular evening, your Aunt Penny and your grandmother would arrive at our home with all their venom intact. And trust me, Son, you don't have to tell Mom anything about your Aunt Penny. That broad was a jerk from the word go!! She liked to do her drinking and whoring around just as much as your grandmother did." I said, "What!?" Mom said, "That's right, Son, it was no big secret in those years! Why they even whore around together as a mother-daughter team at one given point?" I said, "Wow! Are you kidding?" Mom said, "You better believe it. Why, when your grandfather brought Victoria back from Maine, she was the biggest whore running around Foster, Kentucky. She ran around that town with some other woman by the name of Alta. Those two loved to go out and paint the town red!! And for what town people were saying back then, it appeared your grandmother and your Aunt Penny were doing it up with as many men as they could. The behavior of those two idiots created a very uneasy atmosphere for the entire Cummins family. At that time in history, your grandfather had already done well at establishing the Cummins family's reputation. You see, Son, that was still during a time when people just didn't do things like that. Back then, a person's reputation was noted by what type of family he or she had been reared in. Not so much today in our time.

Yes, sir, it was vital in those years to have been from a reputable family with good character traits. It wasn't like it is today, where people are running to and fro, and no one even knows who the hell they are or what they are even doing. So, when your grandmother and your Aunt Penny decided to do their whoring around, it attracted a lot of attention for the Cummins family. Why did that old broad embarrass the hell out of your grandfather? Those two stood out like a sore thumb far too often. It got so bad with Alta and your grandmother that the older people of the town called a meeting, wanting to run both of them out of town. One day, the town council got together and requested that your grandfather leave immediately with your grandmother. They wanted your grandmother out of there!!! Foster, Kentucky, was a small, quiet town, and those old people got tired of putting up with your grandmother's madness. Let Mom tell you something, Son. When a whole town hall wants to get rid of you, it's not because you've been voted most likely to make the deaconess.

Well, at any rate, it's like I was telling you, your grandmother Victoria and your Aunt Penny decided to come over one evening to our home. Those two broads hated my guts because I didn't mind reading their pedigree just the way it was. I mean, don't take me wrong, Jack, we all have our sins, but let's face it, I'm over here trying to raise you babies, and these two idiots are all drunk-ed up. Your father is getting ready to join them at any moment. I mean, what the hell is that!!? What made things worse was all three of them would get drunk-ed-up together and try to make me out to be the bad guy. Hey, baloney!! Those two broads needed to get out of my house so I could raise my babies. And your father would just let them sit there and get drunk and raise hell. He was so busy helping them destroy our home that he forgot which side he was on. I mean, forgive me if I'm wrong, but doesn't the Bible say anything about forsaking all others when it comes to a marriage? I mean, the man couldn't see the forest for the trees. Son, Mom's not telling you I was some perfect mother, but I had my hands full with those two idiots. Certainly, with your dad and your grandmother Victoria, but now I have to contend with your Aunt Penny as well. And your father wasn't helping matters anymore by not telling them to go home.

Instead, he'd join them, and it would make me want to pull my hair out!! Now that's the way it was, like it or not!!" I said, "Mom." Mom said, "Yes, Son, what is it? I said, "Get back to what you were saying about how Aunt Penny and Grandma came over that night and got drunk with Dad." Mom said, "Oh yeah! As I was saying, the two of them came over one night and got all drunk-ed up with your father. After your grandmother got drunk, she would start in on me. And when that old broad got drunk, she thought she was Phyllis Diller!!! You remember back when Phyllis Diller had that big long black cigarette holder she smoked from?" I said, "Yes, I remember that." Mom said, "Remember when Phyllis would take a big puff and say something like, 'Darling!!! How are you doing, ha, ha, ha?'"

I said, "Yes, I remember that too, Mom. Of course, that was kind of Phyllis Diller's signature move or trademark, if you will?" Mom said, "Yes, that's right, Son. Well, anyway, your grandmother would go out and buy one of those ridiculous cigarette holders that Phyllis Diller had and start acting like she was Phyllis Diller!!! She'd get all drunk-ed up and puff on that thing and then blow the smoke right in my face. After which, she would say things like, 'Why did you take my son from me?' Why did that old broad make me sick by saying things like that? I just wanted to reach across the table and slap her silly!!! How on God's green earth could I have taken her son from her? Why, I had no idea what the heck she was even talking about. I was legally married to your father!! And for her to make a comment like that made no sense to me at all, Jack. But it wouldn't take too long into my and your father's marriage before I found out exactly what she meant." I said, "You know, Mom, you have made those types of comments before. Now, just what the heck was it that grandma was alluding to in her comments that you have so conveniently evaded from telling me?" Mom said, "Son, you asked me to tell you about the night your Aunt Penny and your grandmother came over, and that's exactly what I'm going to do for right now."

I said, "OK, so you really don't want to tell me?" Mom said, "Hey, you rang my bell. Do you want to hear about your Aunt Penny and your grandmother coming over that night or not?" I said, "Go on with what you were saying, Mom." Mom said, "Well, at any rate, when your grandmother Victoria started popping her mouth off, your Aunt Penny soon jumped in and wanted some of the action. So, your Aunt Penny said, 'That's right!!! Why did you take my brother from our mother?'

Penny no more got those words out of her mouth before your grandmother Victoria reached across the table and slapped me silly. Well, Son, you know if you slap me as sure as God made green apples, I'm going to have to check into your existence. Yes sir, that's all it took for me. So, I pinned your grandmother down on the floor and commenced slapping her face beyond belief!!! Why don't you know, your Aunt Penny couldn't stand for your grandmother being pinned down, so she decided to jump me from my backside when I still had your grandmother on the floor." I said, "Well, where the heck was Dad during all of this?" Mom said, "Well, he was just sitting there at the kitchen table all drunk-ed up, taking it all in. So, when your Aunt Penny jumped me from my backside, I reached behind me and grabbed her by the neck and pulled that broad right on over!!! Why that fool hit the floor right next to her DARLING of a mother. About the time your Aunt Penny hit the floor, I realized her face was perfectly aligned with your grandmother's head. I began to make a punching bag out of both of them whores!!! Why those two clowns tortured me during my whole seven-year marriage with your father. Especially your grandmother, Victoria. Why I was so sick of that broad I made the day of reckoning come true!!! And with both of their heads aligned right beside each other, I tried to slap both of those fools into oblivion. Yes sir!!! I slapped those two whores into next week, and I was loving every minute of it. Well, it was about that time your father had enough. He wasn't accustomed to seeing his sister and his DARLING of a mother get their ass whipped right in front of him. Trust me, Son, the occasion hadn't set so well with your Daddy. As in so much, he got somewhat enraged about it.

So, your father got up out of his chair, came over, and jerked me off of both of them in lightning speed. When he stood me upright, he threw me into the shower stall. He then punched me in my side, cracking two of my ribs. It was all Mom could do to keep my breath and still remain standing in that shower. I couldn't believe your father had turned against me, knowing what all your grandmother and aunt had put me through during those seven years of our marriage. With your father punching me in that way, it obviously hurt me physically. But the hurt in my heart over the whole situation was far greater, and it was doing me in. I knew that moment it wouldn't be long before I would have to leave your father for good. I had had enough, and I didn't want anymore!!! And if that old broad wanted your daddy that much, what the hell, let her have him!! Your father knew I wanted to leave when we got up the next morning because I was in a lot of pain from the night before. I needed to go to the hospital, and your father knew it.

When your father and I woke up the next morning, we sat there for a minute or two before we both noticed you could hear a pin drop in the whole house. So, I said to your father, 'Jake, I'm in a lot of pain. Would you please go down to the store and get me some feminine napkins because I really can't make it there to get them myself?' Well!! Don't you know the great JC just sat there and indicated to me that he may or may not go down to the store and get what I needed? Well, he no more than got those words out of his mouth, and I screamed at him, saying, 'If you don't move your ass off of this couch and go down and get me what I need, I swear as sure as God made green apples, I'll walk out of here today. I promise you; you'll never see me again!!!' Now your father knew I meant business, and he got up out of there with a sense of urgency to get those feminine napkins. He knew I wasn't having anymore!! Of course, his sense of urgency in wanting to do the right thing would only last until his next drunk." I said, "What do you mean by that, Mom?" Mom said, "Well, he'd get all drunk-ed up again and get up in my face and say things like, 'Well, who would want you anyways? Where would you go? Ain't nobody wants you, woman!!! Why do you think someone is standing in line just so they can have you? Ha, ha, ha, who are you kidding? Ain't nobody wants you, woman!!'

Son, Mom can't tell you how those words cut right through my heart. Well, he found out who wanted me when Harvey O'Connor came on the scene about a year later. When your father and I finally got divorced, Harvey and I got married. It turned your father's head around full speed!!! He wasn't sitting there singing that tune anymore about who would want me. Your father found out in a hurry who would want me and appreciate me!! It shocked your father's socks right off. Why, that sucker wasn't singing that tune anymore. It looked to me like the situation had Jake's full attention. Yes sir!! In the first few years Harvey and I were married, your father would call our house and want to see me. Harvey would tell him he could come over and visit for a while if he'd like to." I said, "Harvey said that, Mom?" Mom said, "Yes, he did, Son. Harvey and I had a good marriage, and Harvey knew your father was still hurting inside from losing me. So, he'd let your father come over once in a while to visit me while Harvey went to work." I said, "Mom, wasn't

Harvey concerned about leaving you two alone while he was at work?" Mom said, "No, he wasn't, Son. Harvey was a mature man, Son. He was a man of peace, and he knew I wouldn't do anything to hurt our marriage. You see, Son, those few visits Harvey allowed your father and I to see one another was for your father's benefit, not mine. Harvey was a smart man, Jack. Those visits were designed to let your father down easily because Harvey knew your father was really hurting inside. The man's strategy and wisdom worked very well because it wasn't long after our first visit that your father concluded I wasn't coming back.

Yeah, you can't tell Mom anything about your Aunt Penny, Son. Like Mom said, that broad was a jerk from the word go, and so was her drunken mother. Son, Mom's not sitting here telling you that your grandmother or aunt didn't have any good qualities. I'm just saying those two broads didn't mind treating me like a fool at all. Now, that's just the way it was, plain and simple. Neither one of them had any respect for me at all. Not only that, they had no qualms in exerting their will on me at all costs and even at a moment's notice. So, you don't have to tell me anything about your Aunt Penny because I got a full dose of that idiot that would last me a lifetime."

I said, "Mom, I hope you really understand. I didn't want to strike Aunt Penny the day she was pounding on me." Mom said, "Oh, I know that, Son. You just didn't want to be hit anymore." I said, "You're right, I didn't." Mom said, "I had my share of your Aunt Penny, Jack, so I know what you went through." I said, "Mom, I know it's getting late, but I'd like to tell you a funny story about Aunt Penny." Mom said, "Okay, Son. Then Mom wants to wrap it up because I'm getting tired, and I want to turn it in." I said, "Okay, no problem. Well, one day, Aunt Penny came over to visit. She had just finished using the upstairs bathroom when she decided to come downstairs using the front stairwell extending to our front foyer. When she stood at the top of the stairs, ready to come down, Dorthy and I just happened to be playing on each side of the foyer that day. Both Dorthy and I knew that the carpet was slick at the top edge of the first step. In our observance of seeing Aunt Penny about to take that first step, we realized we had forgotten to tell her that the area was slippery. You see, everyone else who resided in the house knew about the slickness of that first step. But with most of us having to deal with that step before, we would simply step over the first step and proceed downstairs. Of course, this habit of everyone else stepping over the problem area didn't exactly lend itself to warning Aunt Penny of any danger. With no one warning her about the carpet, she slipped to the top edge and began the ride of her life!!!" Mom said, "Oh my, you don't say!!" I said, "Oh yes, I do say!!! As she slipped on that first step, her feet fell out from beneath her, and she rode the rest of those steps down like Bronco Billy!!! Man, it was a sight to see, to say the least. I guess I don't have to tell you how heavy Penny was, but Dorthy and I watched all her blubber, shake, rattle, and roll with each step she passed all the way down!!!" My mother and I started laughing so hard. I said, "Why, Mom!! You would have thought Aunt Penny had just joined the rodeo and was designated to make first prize!!!" My mother and I just laughed all over the place.

I said, "Well, needless to say, Aunt Penny was pretty embarrassed when she discovered Dorthy, and I had witnessed her arduous ride down the steps that day. Dorthy and I were laughing so hard that we ran around the corner in the hope of muffling our laugh from Aunt Penny. There was no such luck. We were busted to the max. When Aunt Penny discovered we were laughing at her, she yelled out, 'I can hear ya out there. You better shut your mouth before I shut it for you.' Mom said, "Well, Son, that was a good one, but Mom's going to bed right now." I said, "Okay, Mom, I'll see you tomorrow." Mom said, "Alright, Son, I'll see you tomorrow. Lock the front door for me on the way out." I said, "You bet. Good night, Mom." "Good night, Son." The next day, I told my mother that the Child Welfare Department requested a meeting with Dad, our stepmother Jennie, and me. All three of us found ourselves soon sitting in their office. As soon as the three of us took a seat, the case worker opened up right away with her sixty-four-thousand-dollar questions. She asked, 'What's going on?' No one seemed to have the answers to her questions that day. She addressed Dad by asking, "Mr. Cummins, what do you think is wrong with your son, Jack?" Dad shrugged his shoulders, lifted his hands, and said, "I don't know. I was hoping you could tell me. After all, you are the case worker." With the case worker not really responding to Dad's comment, a few moments elapsed when she asked my stepmother, Jennie, "Mrs. Cummins, what do you think is going on with your son, Jack?" My stepmother quickly answered and said, "Well, like Jack's father has already said, I really don't know. We were hoping you could shed a little light on the subject so we could better understand the situation." The social worker did not give any answers to what she thought the problem might be, so she decided to ask me, "Jack, why do you run away from home so much?" I said, "I don't know." Well, as you can see, nobody seemed to have any answers that day. So, the agency took me out of our home and placed me in a temporary shelter for juveniles. The establishment was called Allen House, and I was placed there in October of 1967. I had just turned ten that past August.

The Allen House was located on the west side of Cincinnati, just off Gurley Road. The main objective of the shelter was to provide temporary quarters for battered and emotionally disturbed children. These same children would eventually be placed in a more permanent setting at a later date. However, none of us really knew how long we would reside at Allen House before being placed anywhere. My first trip to Allen House would last 14 months before being transferred to the Children's home over on the east side of town. Allen House had its challenges, but I liked it far better than being at home with my stepmother and father. Don't take me wrong, every child wants to have a happy home with their own siblings. But in my case, I'm sure you can see by now that being placed outside my home was probably better for me at that point. I admit, though Allen House wasn't always the best of circumstances in every detail, it indeed gave me a chance to just be a kid. Most of the children at Allen House were disturbed with a history of multiple abuse issues. I watched many who were released early, only to return crying from their visit. Some children cried because they really wanted to go home again. Others cried because they still had love and abuse issues all mixed up in their head. I thought most of us had done really well under the circumstances, considering our background. Even though most of us came from a challenged environment, residing at Allen House provided the children with time to start responding as normal

To my readers, the gentleman seen on this page is a personal friend of mine. His presence depicts the following story of Mr. Charles Roddy, who was once an educator and principal for the Cincinnati Board of Education. Welcome to a follow educator, Mr. Tony Collier.

children. Plain and simple, we were no longer operating in an abusive atmosphere. It doesn't mean that the same type of abusive behavior never occurred in Allen House because it had.

However, I usually found such behavior perpetuated by its residents as opposed to staff members. It's not that our staff were totally exempt from such behavior because that view wouldn't really warrant an accurate picture. And unfortunately, some Allen House staff members were involved in sexually abusing our children. Most of these incidences were recorded in the mid to late 1970s and well into the 1980s. But no such incidences of staff molesting children took place while I was there in the 1960s. Or at least not to my knowledge. Plain and simple, there were far more moral standards being adhered to at Allen House in the 60s than in the late 1970s and 80s. I had heard about these types of things long after my time.

Therefore, we didn't have to contend with these things as other children did in the late 1970s and 80s. I thank God for that because it allowed Allen House to accomplish its objectives for its children. And that was to enable children to be children. There were other strange incidences that the children perpetrated. For example, I was once sitting in our dining room when, one afternoon, I noticed a black girl standing behind me, hitting me on the back of my head with a large serving spoon. When I acknowledged her presence, for some unknown reason, she decided to discontinue hitting me. But I had no idea as to why she was striking me to begin with. Another time, five black girls attacked me in our recreation room. They commenced beating the hell out of me with pool balls and cue sticks. After seeing stars and lightning from their many blows, I became somewhat confused as to why they wanted to take my clothes off. At first, I thought maybe they were trying to rape me. But that wasn't the case at all. It became apparent that they just wanted to humiliate me by exposing my genitals to other children who happened to be in the recreation room that day.

After they jerked my pants off and exposed my nakedness, they threw my body on the floor and stomped me a little more. Crawling away from their kicks, I managed to pull my body under a large pool table in the hope of concealing my nakedness from the rest of our children. The girls who attacked me that day suddenly feared being caught, so they ran out of our recreation room. As they fled down our corridor, I heard their fading laughs and remarks about exposing my nakedness. Feeling battered by their beating, I didn't have enough strength to pull my pants up and conceal my nakedness. So, I lay there under the pool table in a feeble position, trying to forget what had just happened. Though I wasn't sexually assaulted, I still felt totally raped of all my dignity in every way. Not able to help myself from the lack of strength, I suddenly noticed a little girl crawling under the pool table to join me.

Not knowing what she wanted, she decided to lay next to me for a while. She began rubbing my arm until she gained my complete confidence. She then offered to help me pull my pants up to conceal my nakedness from the rest of the room. She gently coached me to my feet to help me pull my pants up. As I adjusted my pants, I suddenly realized her kindness far outweighed any embarrassment I would have held for being naked in front of her. Walking away slowly, I noticed how some of the other children were mesmerized by how the little girl handled my situation. Most others resumed playing while our staff members never had any clue of the entire incident.

Later in life, I was asked why the attack from five female black youths? I answered the inquiry by commenting, "I presume the girl's actions were fueled by the civil rights era for one reason or another. But whatever their reason, I was grateful for the other little girl who helped me during such a dark and bleak moment in my life." As you can see, some of us had our challenges. However, the nine-year-old girl who helped me that day shone like a beacon in my mind for most of the rest of my life. I thought about her from time to time, hoping that she had lived a good life. Many of the children at Allen House metaphorically adopted one another as brothers and sisters. For instance, when we knew someone would be leaving Allan House to obtain a better outcome, it was common for other children to hold a going away party for the departing child. We would wish that particular individual good tidings in their journey, knowing all along it was like losing a brother or sister. Not to mention the calculation that ran through our minds of whether or not he or she would even make it. All we had was one another, and we'd try to hang on to that for all it was worth until the departing person left. Some would awaken early the following day to walk down the corridor to see such a person for the last time. Many others would run to the closest window to watch our friend be seated in a car with their prospective driver. Knowing that we would probably never see them again, the fading automobile stood as a reminder of when we were all still together. God was there with us all along; we just never knew it.

We really felt connected and wanted the best for one another. Seeing another child go home or placed elsewhere brought much sorrow in not knowing what would become of their lives. And that's not to mention if we would ever see them again. It tore us apart as metaphoric siblings. To begin with, we were not lost on why we were there. We shared our pain together with a sort of silent love for each other. So, if one were being transferred, we would commonly meet the night before in what was referred to as the Teen Room. This would be the last time to share company with the departing child before leaving the following day.

Many hugs and kisses were exchanged, engulfed with many tears for the departing party. We all offered our hearts in hand, hoping the person leaving would be successful in their new life. Going home would be a test for many of us, and we knew it. For that matter, even a temporary visit could be challenging. For instance, one year, I went home for the Christmas holidays. As I ate Christmas dinner that evening, my father decided to verbally go off on me for reasons unknown to me to this day. With Dad knowing I had been placed in Allen House for a while, it appeared he wanted to assure everyone that he was still the boss. "You know how that can be at times, Mom." Mom said, "Yes, I do, Son." I said, "At that point in Dad's life, he simply didn't have the maturity to demonstrate that his home could be led in love." Mom said, "I know, Son." I said, "At any rate, being an Allen House resident gave me the power of choice. Not wanting to put up with Dad's verbal abuse, I simply rejected his explosive behavior by asking him to return me to Allen House immediately after dinner.

I remember my request coming across as a total shock to Dad at our dinner table that evening. Nevertheless, my request was honored, and I returned to Allen House after dinner. It was as if someone had reached across the table during dinner and put a stop trap on his verbal abuse. Never before in the history of our home had Dad's verbal abuse been shut down at a moment's notice. And the antidote responsible for that is the power of choice. I was the one person in our home that evening who wasn't willing to accept the verbal abuse anymore. It appeared that some people from our father's generation felt that they had a carte blanche pass to treat almost anyone else the way they wanted, regardless of how it may affect the other person.

My request to return to Allen House after Christmas dinner set Dad back on his heels. Too bad my example didn't motivate other siblings to realize that they, too, didn't have to accept abusive behavior being fostered off as love. Of course, my siblings weren't in the same position I was to just get up and walk out. And, of course, I knew they wouldn't because they were used to operating out in fear with no real refuge in sight. The sad part is, I don't think my sister Dorthy had ever come to see abusive behavior for what it really is, dysfunction, dysfunction, dysfunction!!! She simply tolerated it, considering that a bit of abuse was okay. Or that it will somehow just go away someday. Baloney, wake up; it's a total waste of people's lives. Seeing my father taken back from my boldness not to accept his verbal abuse had him suddenly realize that Allen House would support my decision to return. In short, my father now knew I wasn't going to put up with his outrages under any circumstances. This came to him as a shock. It does to most abusive people. They somehow feel they reserve the right to treat you any way they want. Sadly, most people who are being abused, regardless of the type, often give power to their perpetrators, feeling that they have done something wrong. Baloney!!! That's just not true. People can stop the abuse. We must learn, as God's people, to stop operating out of fear. We can do this by asking God in prayer to create circumstances to break the abusive cycle that many of us feel so desperately trapped in. God will deliver you through earnest prayer. We have to remember the abuse cycle is never broken by remaining in the abuse for any reason. When kids are growing up, they simply don't have a choice, but as adults, we not only have a choice, we need to stop operating out of fear." My mother said, "Son, it sounds like you have really learned from some of these things." I said, "Like you, Mom, learning just a few of these things and then acting on them to see change wasn't easy."

At any rate, I was still in the Allen House in the late 1960s as racial riots continued to rage all around us. We would hear a lot about the riots from outside sources. We weren't locked up, so it was pretty easy to obtain any information we wanted. At times, people would sneak through the back woods of Allen House to meet with us at our fence line. This was one way outsiders used to keep us abreast of what was happening in our surrounding neighborhoods. Our staff did well in keeping the general attitude of our children optimistic when it came to racial problems. They knew we had trouble brewing all around us in small groups. Of course, we had some children who were hell-bent on disrupting our populous at all costs. At one given point, a few children managed to provoke a small riot in the backyard of Allen House in 1968. About thirty of our children were involved. Much to my surprise, one of our black staff members by the name of Mrs. White, broke up the riot at a moment's notice. All of our children respected Mrs. White and dared not fool with that woman about anything.

Thanks to her efforts, order was soon restored, and everyone returned to their daily business. I had no doubt in my mind Mrs. White had preferences in her life that she would have liked to see change for the sake of the black race. But she wasn't willing to advocate violence or the use of it in order to bring about those changes. I admired her for her approach. For she certainly understood Dr. Martin Luther King's message of non-violence. To have kept such a great attitude right smack dead in the middle of the civil rights era, when hope for so many weighed in the balance, was indeed a testimony to her willingness to be the example as opposed to being the problem. Clearly, she stood as a shining beacon for her day. Her example still stands out in my mind to this day." Mom said, "I bet it does, Son." I said, "Yes, it does, Mom. We also had a small schoolhouse in the backyard of Allen House.

And I really mean that's exactly what it was, Mom, a small two-room school house. A light-skinned black gentleman was its principal. His name was Mr. Charles Roddy. He would occasionally remind all the Allen House staff that he didn't work for Allen House. He reminded them that he worked for the Cincinnati Board of Education. That way, should he need to correct Allen House students, he would be able to do so without any interference from Allen House staff. Or any other matter at that. None of the Allen House staff ever challenged Mr. Roddy's authority, and of course, we didn't either. His very walk was exuberant of order and a sense of equity and quiet compassion for everyone. That's the man I remember Charles to be. With Mr. Roddy being our school principal, I eventually learned he was originally born and reared in Birmingham, Alabama. Our schoolhouse only had two big rooms in use at the time. One teacher would teach 2nd, 3rd, and 4th graders in one room, while Mr. Roddy taught 5th, 6th, and 7th graders in the other. Now you have to understand something about Mr. Roddy, Mom. He certainly wasn't dealing with a normal class setting one would find in a public school system today. These classes were different from the standpoint that most of their students came from a challenged background to begin with. So, you may be a little surprised with Mr. Roddy's approach in regard to guiding his class as opposed to public classrooms of today." Mom said, "Hey, no problem, Son, move forward with what you were saying." I said, "Many times, our children would starve for approval and acceptance from having been reared in an abusive environment. It was common for some to go out of their way to get the attention they craved. This often showed up in the form of a fight, a verbal argument, or some disagreement. They just wanted attention, and so Mr. Roddy would make sure they got it.

We lived in a highly charged country at the time, and most things were handled differently to begin with. That is to say, much of what was considered normal in those years would be regarded as entirely politically incorrect today. Not to mention, our countrymen are so willing to cram our courts full of frivolous lawsuits. Everything wasn't perfect back then, but I'm equally convinced we wouldn't have as many problems today if we'd just use some common sense. Some of our classmates would want to fight over childless nonsense. Mr. Roddy would just let them fight it out. But he'd make sure they wouldn't kill one another as they do today.

For that matter, no one ever thought about killing each other as they do nowadays. Mr. Roddy felt letting most kids get things off their chest in those years generally brought the problem to a conclusion. Mr. Roddy had a large thirty-two-gallon metal garbage can that usually sat right next to his desk. One day, a fight broke out between two of our boys. By the time the fight concluded, one of the boys had been stuffed in Mr. Roddy's garbage can. Mr. Roddy and the rest of the class laughed so hard that they all realized how ridiculous the situation was to begin with. Even the two boys who were engaged in the fight saw how stupid their predicament was, and they, too, decided to join the rest of the class in laughing at themselves. At times, Mr. Roddy could tell I wasn't doing so well. So, he'd take me to his office where we could just talk. He was the man who always encouraged me to do better. Sometimes, I just wanted to go to his office and talk with him because I enjoyed his company. That's not to mention wanting to hear all of his life stories, which I loved so much. He'd never turned me down for a visit, and yes, I became his pet. So, he always had the time and patience for me. I was so grateful for him in those years. And if I needed the whole class period to hang out in his office, he'd let me.

Of course, hanging out in his office for the whole period was a rare occasion, but nonetheless, he'd let me stay in his office and talk to him if I needed to. As I said, Mom, it wasn't often, but it was as if Charles knew when I needed the extra time in order to make it through the day. With Mr. Roddy being reared in the deep south, one of their traditions down there was to cut a locket of one's hair for keepsake. Another tradition was to stop time on a clock at the passing of one's life. Mr. Roddy had a habit of cutting a locket of hair from each one of his favorite students over the years he was principal. I sensed I was on the list, and he cut a locket of my hair one day when I was just eleven years old. My hair was red at the time.

Years later, when I turned nineteen, I stopped at the Allen House to see Mr. Roddy for the last time. He was getting ready to retire and go back to Alabama. During our conversation, I observed him removing a clear plastic bag from his office wall locker. I asked him what was in the bag. He said, 'A locket of hair I cut from your head some eight years ago.' I noticed the color of my hair had changed considerably in eight years. I'm glad I had a chance to see him one last time before he left for Alabama. As I commenced to go that day, he handed me that locket of hair that was soon accompanied by a handshake and a smile that lasted a lifetime. I was never to see Mr. Roddy again. As I walked away that day, I was somehow compelled to remember a short story Mr. Roddy had told me." Mom said, "And what was that, Son?" I said, "As Mr. Roddy and I stood in the schoolyard one day, he asked me, 'Jack, how old are you, Son?' I said, "Ten." Mr. Roddy said, "Well, Son, how long do you think the world has been here?" I said, "Well, according to our textbooks, about four and a half billion years." Mr. Roddy said, 'Okay, then if the world has been here for four and a half billion years, and you have only been here ten years, how much in the world do you think you'll change?' I said, "I don't know." Mr. Roddy said, 'Well, Son, rest assured, not much.

You see, Son, the moral of the story is this, the world ain't the way it could be, should be, or even ought to be. You see, Son, the world is simply the way it is.' The validation of his story couldn't have come at a better time, in the sense that I was starting to pay my bills on a regular basis. With me knowing Mr. Roddy, I could only imagine him telling me this story because maybe he held such high hopes for a better equality of life during the civil rights era. Some sixteen years would go by before sharing his story with a ten-year-old boy playing a basketball game one afternoon. The boy wandered over to talk with me at a time. I shared Mr. Roddy's story with him just the way Charles had told me when I was ten. A whole year went by before I saw the boy again. I asked him if he had remembered Mr. Roddy's story from the previous year. Much to my surprise, he quoted Mr. Roddy's story word for word. I was pleased to know that, so long as that boy lived, Mr. Roddy's story would never die. With the boy having the capacity to live well into the twenty-first century, I had the oddest feeling that someday, another little boy was about to learn Mr. Roddy's story.

At any rate, the holidays would roll around in the Allen House. One hundred and twenty-nine children gathered in the dining room for our holiday meal. One of our matrons liked appointing me to give the meal prayer. I can still hear her voice in the background of our dining hall, trying to persuade another matron to allow me to provide the meal with a prayer. She would say, 'Let Jack say the prayer! Get Jack to say the prayer!! He really knows how to pray.' I'd end up thanking God for our food and that type of thing. In retrospect, I really don't think I gave such good prayers as this particular matron led on. As I remember, in saying the prayer, it became apparent to me that the matrons enjoyed the protestant terminology and jargon that was being used during the prayer. I simply didn't know how to address God correctly and genuinely while praying. For that matter, I hadn't realized what a real prayer was. But that's the only way I knew how to pray back then, Mom." Mom said, "That's okay, Son, if that's all you knew at the time, that's all you knew!!" I said, "But it was kind of nice to have the matrons ask me to give the prayer anyway. You know how it is with kids who have been formerly abused. They don't think that much of themselves, to begin with. With that being the case in my life, I appreciated when matrons would ask me to give the prayer, for it provided a real shot in the arm for me. Of course, normal children have the same need for the same shot. It just doesn't take as much gunpowder to convince them of their self-worth." Mom said, "You're probably right, Son." I said, "For instance, even as an adult, I still felt crippled inside from the abuse as a child. I learned to hide it well from others. You sort of fake it until you make it, if you know what I mean. Some of that "making it" would require an ample amount of counseling and personal growth over some time. It's a process, not an event.

And that's not to mention you'll need a lot of God's help as well. I found in my life in order to make a comeback from a shattered background, one would have to seek God out on a regular basis. To think that I could achieve personal growth and overcome spiritual defects of character without God's help was like entertaining the idea that an automobile had the capacity to pull a freight train." Mom said, "Now, Son, Mom has undergone a lot of counseling in my case to get things worked out." I said, "Mom, I know that worked for you, and I'm glad it did. But when I went to work in my own life, professional counseling wasn't an immediate option. However, I take my hat off for the work you've already done. Most people don't want to talk to a therapist. And quite frankly, they are usually in fear of what they may find." Mom said, "Well, Son, I managed to accomplish with psychiatry what you have accomplished with religion." I said, "Yeah, but that's not the whole picture, Mom." Mom said, "No, I guess it's not. But for me, I had to counsel on and off for fifteen years in order to process all that crap I had been through in my life." I said, "Yes, I see what you mean. You know, Mom, as I grew older, I'd catch myself watching a movie where some star was achieving fantastic success at overwhelming odds against himself. When the star's success in the movie continued to grow, I would cry silently inside. Because I desperately wanted to achieve something worthwhile in this life just as the star had!! But when I would go to do whatever it was that I thought was worthwhile, I sometimes would literally shut down inside and wasn't able to overcome the emotionally crippling effect that the abuse had left behind, thus prohibiting the very success I desired. And that same feeling is still there to some degree today. It never went away in its entirety. And yet, I realize that I have achieved more on a regular basis over a period of time. It just took a lot of patience to see that come about over time. Though I knew these feelings of disappointment were still there, I became willing to accept that a piece of my pie was missing. That is to say, emotionally, mentally, psychologically, and especially spiritually. So, I looked to God to make up the difference in my life and He has.

And sometimes, that was a bitter pill to swallow because I wanted to be like everyone else on this planet. These feelings of despair and doom didn't mean that I could never be successful. They suggested that, in some areas of my life, it would take the extra effort to overcome and achieve success. I had to accept that there were holes punched in the foundation of my life to begin with and that it would take time to get well and overcome life's difficulties. I also found that some defects of character could only be overcome to a certain degree. And when other problems would rear their head, I would go to God and ask Him to make up the difference in combating them. I had to learn that what God granted in my life was enough. I found that I could move forward and be successful by seeking God out on a regular basis. He really is the only hope I've got, Mom." Mom said, "Mom believes what you are saying is true for you, Son." I said, "I'm not saying religion is the only way, Mom. I'm just saying for me to get the help I needed- in a significant way- couldn't be done without God's help.

Mom, not to change the subject, but I feel many people with an abusive background can fully understand overwhelming feelings of defeat to their very core." Mom said, "Hey, you don't have to tell me; you're preaching to the choir. I felt overwhelmed trying to achieve anything as a younger woman. When my father had done those things to me as a little girl, they damaged my personality and character to the point of stunting my personal growth. And then I felt devastated for some years to come. The irony is, in many ways, I couldn't see the effect of being molested. Yet, in other ways, the effect literally blindsided me." I said, "I know that's true, Mom. Sadly, too many people who have been molested go to their graves, never developing any of their given abilities. They seem to live a life of internal shatter with no hope of recovering. In my case, I desperately needed to stay close to God if I were going to make it at all. And I knew that wholeheartedly during my initial stages of incarceration. Make no mistake about it; staying close to God had to be real to me. I knew if I were going to keep my life in order, I would have to focus on God's Will as opposed to my will (rather than if that appealed to me). I read about people with the same background as mine, and they ended up drinking themselves to death. Some of them used drugs all their lives. Others ended up homeless, destitute, and even committed suicide. It's not just me saying these things, Mom; there's a whole host of research that supports what I'm saying. So, I knew I was definitely going to need spiritual help if I was going to be successful in any capacity." Mom said, "Considering your brother Jerry had committed suicide, do you think your father ever messed around with him like he had with you?" I said, "I really don't know, Mom. From what I can remember, Jerry didn't have any of the classic signs of being sexually abused. Furthermore, even if Dad had, how could one ever know that. We don't want to jump to any conclusions and accuse Dad of something we know nothing about."

Mom said, "Oh, I know that, Son, nor is accusing your father my point. I was just curious as to if something like that could have happened to Jerry long before his death." I said, "I guess anything is possible. Mom, however, as I said before, in Jerry's case, I really hadn't noticed the character traits of someone who had been sexually molested. But I definitely saw character traits of Jerry suffering verbal, emotional, physical, and psychological abuse. Hands down, I could attest to all of that!! I have no doubt some of those conditions could have been a major factor in Jerry's life when he subsequently decided to take his own life. I, for one, can verify Jerry didn't have such a healthy self-esteem and sought out other things in his life to make up the difference. Such as the taking of illicit drugs and being involved in criminal behavior. Of course, I was just as guilty for the same things. I have no doubt both Jerry and I felt that living a criminal lifestyle, somehow, was going to fulfill our lives in some way. It so happened to be, for Jerry and I, we would end up dealing with people who had no qualms about burying you in the middle of a cornfield should something go wrong with our acquaintance. It wasn't much of a life to live. So, for God to have saved me out of all of that when I was so willing to remain in it, I consider that a miracle." Mom said. "Son, did you and Jerry really want that way of life?" I said, "By all means, Mom, both Jerry and I loved it. Again, that way of life had Jerry and I believing we had conjured up some type of self-worth. In other words, when Jerry would board twenty-million-dollar yachts in Miami solely to deal cocaine in the hundreds of kilos, I think those experiences had Jerry feeling pretty important." Mom said, "But that's insane, Jack." I said, "I know that now, and so do you, but when one hasn't been reared in a wholesome atmosphere, it can often lead to grand illusions. Even if the risk there threatens your very life. As a matter of fact, the bigger the risk, the grander the illusion. That's how Satan's mind works when sucking people into evil pursuits.

That's why I have so often conveyed to younger parents, 'If you are not willing to rear your children in a wholesome atmosphere, then you can look forward to your children developing into tomorrow's criminals.' You see, what happens to most people on different levels is this, Mom. One inconspicuously starts to believe that he or she can embrace an illicit way of life without any real consequences or ramifications. We all have our brand of such thoughts, whether we acknowledge them or not. Some choose to take that concept further, as Jerry and I had. Dealing with dangerous gangsters was Jerry and my brand of that illusion. We thought it would somehow fulfill our life in some interesting way." Mom said, "Why, that's crazy, Son." I said, "You're exactly right, Mom, it is. And I'm sure Jerry couldn't agree more if he were here today. Especially when he sat there on those yachts and watched other people lose their lives from being torn apart by sharks. I have no doubt the experience had Jerry totally reevaluating his relationship with the Cuban Mob. I'm sure it made a lasting impression on him, to say the least. How do you think watching those kinds of things affected Jerry's mind, Mom? Do you think he felt an overwhelming feeling of wholesomeness as he watched those men die? Not on your life, he didn't!! I have no doubt Jerry's false concept of self-worth went right out the window when witnessing such hideous crimes in international waters. I knew exactly how Jerry felt and how I ignored those very same feelings and warnings." Mom said, "You had those same things happen to you, Son?" I said, "Sure, Mom." Mom said, "You mean you also witnessed those sharks killing people like Jerry?" I said, "No, Mom, I dealt with an entirely different criminal organization than Jerry had. These gangsters were of Italian descent. I had no illusions that they, too, could be just as ruthless as the Cuban Mob that Jerry had dealt with. In fact, one of the Italian Mobs' specialties in dealing with someone was to make sure you would totally disappear should something go wrong. And they had some pretty convincing methods of making sure you understood that. It's not like today, where you get some thug doing a drive-by shooting, and he thinks he's doing something. Why, those idiots are just making a lot of noise that would soon lead to their arrest. In my time, the Mob prided themselves on having you disappear without anyone ever knowing how that came about.

That's one of the reasons that made them suckers so dangerous. They had mastered your departure so well that oftentimes, the police would discover your remains decades later. One of them was to grind you into a million pieces, making sure no one ever found you. They really liked using this particular method because it was definitely foolproof. Nothing like authorities trying to find fine dust scattered in the middle of a field. With the efforts of any law enforcement agency ever seeing you in that condition, we were truly in a billion to one if ever. And the Mob knew it. That's the way they took advantage of murdering many people. Grinding someone into fine powder was pretty foolproof for the Mob. And in my particular case, the Mob made special arrangements for me to see if I could figure out when and how they were going to whack me." Mom said, "They wanted to kill you, Son!!?" I said, "Yes, they did, Mom, and only by the grace of God would I escape their grasp. Trust me, when these people go whack somebody, they are not accustomed to missing. But escaping their grip not to whack me wouldn't happen overnight. I had to live with an enormous amount of fear for some time. And it taught me a lifetime lesson not to ever ring the Mob's doorbell again." Mom said, "My God, Son, what happened!!?"

I said, "Well, Mom, the year was 1977, and the Mob was still at the height of their power. The Vietnam War had just concluded a few years earlier, and it just so happened that I knew a drug lord when I was still in the Marine Corps. As I got to know this guy, I became privy that he was supplying four different Marine Corps bases with assorted drugs. With both of us soon to be discharged from our service, I wanted to keep in touch with him for future drug deals. Being fresh out of the Marine Corps and looking for action, I was suddenly recruited by an Irish gangster. My job was to make sure large shipments of PCP coming in out of L.A. would go undisturbed from being ripped off by other drug dealers. As a new enforcer of an independent crew, we started receiving large quantities of pure PCP that could have been easily cut ten times over and then some. You could smell the stuff a half block away if one were familiar with what PCP smelled like."

Mom said, "Son." I said, "Yeah, Mom." Mom said, "What's PCP?" I said, "It's a strong hallucinogenic that also carried the slang name of Angle Dust back in the day. A lot of people died from the sale of it back then. But at any rate, my job was to protect shipments as well as the drug deals themselves. I largely utilized prior military knowledge to achieve the task. The boss of our crew soon realized my approach was effective and asked if I needed anything else to maintain persistence? I responded, 'Yes, I do.' I asked him if I could enlist one more former Marine I knew who served in force recon during the Vietnam War. They usually hadn't done things this way, but with them witnessing a few of my performances, they decided to grant my request. As I introduced the other former Marine to our crew boss, it essentially gave birth to our involvement with organized crime and its makings. My new partner and I were happy as hell because we were both trigger happy and looking for action any way we could get it." Mom said, "You two must have been out of your minds!!" I said, "Yes, we were, Mom, and enjoying every minute of it." Mom said, "Why, you're crazy, Son!!" I said, "Yes, I guess you could say that. I chose this particular partner because of his experiences in Vietnam. That is to say, he trained with the Navy Seals to overthrow ships at a moment's notice. He was the type of guy who could board a ship, slam you on the flight deck of it, and tie your hands behind your back with a rope that was being fed from his pocket, all in a matter of seconds. And I needed him. And though we both were trained in gaining ground, I admired his discipline in knowing when not to fire his weapon. Being trigger-happy is one thing, but being stark stupid is another. I know this to be true because the very thing we were recruited for became the very thing we ended up doing to other gangsters of our day.

Mom said, "What do you mean, Son?" I said, "Well, at a much later date, my partner and I decided to commit armed robberies against other known drug dealers, taking their money and drugs. Such robberies went off very well and without a shot ever being fired. Working with my new partner was unlike any other armed robbery I had ever participated in." Mom said, "What do you mean by that, Son?" I said, "Well, earlier in my life, four of us went in to rob this place one day only to discover that one of us was armed during the robbery. By the time my new partner and I had finished our second robbery, I realized it just wasn't my cup of tea." Mom said, "Well, I guess we can all breathe a sigh of relief." I said, "Mom!! Going into an armed robbery with someone who's trigger-happy when they don't need to be is stupid. In fact, I went to my partner one day and requested that he and I no longer do them, because I'd much rather sell someone something than stick them up. We both laughed and we never performed another armed robbery again. Mom said, "Well, wasn't that nice of you two? Had the two of you also considered attending Sunday School as well?" I said, "Mom!! Do you want to bust my chops, or do you want to hear my story?" Mom said,

"I'm sorry, Son, I just wanted to jerk your chain a little. Boy, Son, you say those things as if you were out just having lunch." I said, "Not exactly, Mom. We were moving so fast in those years that dinner would have been required as well." Mom said, "Son, you are a mess, and I mean, you are a mess!!! We never heard of such things when I grew up. But enough about when I grew up, I wanted to know why those Italian gangsters wanted to kill you." I said, "Well, as I was saying, I knew a drug lord when I was in the Marine Corps that supplied drugs to a nearby base. When we were discharged, we decided to stay in touch. With me being new to organized crime, I wanted to make a name for myself other than protecting drug investments and collections. I wanted to be seen as someone significant to our crew boss. In short, my vanity was starting to get the best of me, and I wanted to make a name for myself.

I have to admit here, Mom, vanity is one of Satan's favorite things to ensnare people. But displaying one's vanity while dealing with ruthless gangsters can get you killed every time. Not to mention how they love to be in line first to cut your throat." Mom said, "Wait a minute, Son, you said something about collections?" I said, "Yeah, so what!" Mom said, "What was that all about?" I said, "It wasn't really a big deal, Mom. When people wouldn't pay their fronts off, they'd send Bardo and me to visit them." Mom said, "What's a front, Son?" I said, "That's when an upline dealer fronts a sum of drugs to sell, and their payoffs weren't being made." Mom said, "What if the person wasn't able to pay off?" I said, "There was no such thing, Mom. These deals weren't layaway deals at Walmart. If you were moving Mob dope back then, there usually wasn't a problem with people making their payoffs because most people desired long-term health benefits. Some smaller dealers had problems collecting, but they were pretty much on their own. If you had Mob dope fronted to you, and you weren't making your payoffs, you could pretty much expect a visit right away.

I thought we didn't need to talk about this part, considering you already know that's how Jerry died." Mom said, "Yes, I know that, Son, but I was just curious as to how Jerry's death could have occurred." I said, "Oh, I see." Mom said, "So what if you and this guy, Bardo, had to go visit someone that wasn't paying off?" I said, "Actually, we never had too much of a problem collecting because no one wanted our second visit." Mom said, "What do you mean by your second visit?" I said, "Well, on the first visit, we'd just tell them that if they didn't have a certain amount of money by a certain time, things could get very uncomfortable for them. We would then remind them that our second visit was never profitable for all parties concerned. Of course, our second visit was usually executed without them ever knowing our arrival time." Mom said, "So, did you ever have to make a second visit?"

I said, "I recalled having to make three first-time visits, (with a fourth visit,) seemingly ready to explode into second visit criteria. Bardo enjoyed hurting people, so he usually led by example. He loved his work so well that he always had me watch his progress in action. But on one particular occasion, Bardo was curious as to what I would do if I were handed the rings to make a collection. Jerry happened to be there that day, and he indicated to both Bardo and me that he suspected this particular individual would rip him off. And since Bardo handed me the rings that day, we both arrived at Jerry's choice of location. When Jerry's associate walked into the room that day, the seats were arranged in such a manner that Jerry's associate would be forced to sit to the left of me. As Jerry's associate sat down, he noticed a bowl of Acapulco gold sitting on the coffee table. Its leaves were as bright as yellow pencil shavings. I invited him to roll a joint to set the mood for our business. With his hands occupied rolling the joint, he quickly started to say a lot of nothing, and I knew this was my cue to get the drop on him first. Pulling out a .380 automatic from my back, I jammed the gun to the right side of his head and suddenly asked him, "Do you enjoy breathing?" His demeanor changed spontaneously, coupled with the offer to pay us in full right away. Not paying attention to what he had to say, I, in an instant, slammed his face into the bowl of Acapulco gold that sat on the coffee table. I held the gun to the back of his head and informed him that it would have been much better for him to come to that conclusion earlier. He suddenly started shaking and begging me for his life. Seeing that the bowl of Acapulco gold was restricting his breathing capacity, I shoved his body to the floor, enlightening him that he couldn't get any closer to his grave even if he wanted to. He assured Bardo and me that our payoffs would always be on time and that no other visit would be required. I congratulated him for being such a good student and encouraged him to always make the grade. As Bardo and I left that day, he was no longer concerned about whether or not I could make a collection. He told me that I not only passed with flying colors but literally scared the hell out of him as well. Without Bardo ever really knowing, I was just performing what came naturally to me as a former Marine. I loved it because I was good at it.

Heck, Mom, I was just glad it was over because if the guy had resisted in any way, I would have had to pop him in order to make my point." Mom said, "Son." I asked, "Yeah, Mom?" Mom said, "Would you have really popped the guy as you have said?" I said, "It largely depended on how much money someone owed and what the higher-up orders were for that particular person. Smaller amounts brought convincing injuries. But for a large amount, say in the hundreds of thousands, I have no doubt Bardo would have wanted me to empty his life out. It really didn't matter anyway because the Chicago Police found his body in a dumpster three months later for trying to rip someone else off. After hearing about his death, I knew for sure I had given him the benefit of the doubt during his stay in Cincinnati." Mom said, "Son." I said, "Yeah, Mom?" Mom said, "Will you be honest with Mom about something?" I said, "Sure, Mom, what is it?" Mom asked, "Have you ever killed anyone?" I said, "I think you already know the answer to that, Mom." Mom said, "No, I really don't know, or I wouldn't be asking." I said, "Well, that's easy to say; the answer is no. I was never asked to whack anybody back then, and so I never did. Although I have to admit, I found myself in several situations where having to whack someone could have been the end result had not the circumstances changed for the better. For if they hadn't changed spontaneously, it would have made whacking a particular individual very necessary." Mom said, "Never mind!! I think I already know the answer!!" I said, "Why are you busting my chops on this, Mom? I've been honest with you!! Grant you, I did things back then I didn't necessarily want to write home about, but whacking someone wasn't one of them, so let it go!!" Mom said, "I don't believe you!!" I said, "Boy!! You're really blowing me out of the saddle with this thing. What's up!!?" Mom said, "Well, I want to know if my baby boy ever killed anyone or not, and I have a right to know that!!! I grabbed my mother by both sides of her head. I pulled her face close to mine until our eyes met. I said, "Okay, Mom!! Does it look like anyone in here took somebody out?" Mom stared into my eyes for a few seconds and said, "No!! My baby boy never killed anybody!!"

I said, "Ya see, I told you, you are just getting yourself all worked up over nothing!!" Mom said, "Well, it's not like you're sitting over there telling me about Goldie Locks and the Three Little Bears, Jack!!" I said, "I can't argue with you there, Mom, so let's take a break for today and visit another time, okay?" Mom said, "Okay, I'll see you tomorrow." I said, "Okay, I'll see ya then." Walking away from my mother's home that day, she yelled out, "Are you sure you never killed anyone!!?" I said, "Yeah, mom, I'm sure." Mom said, "How do you know you haven't!!?" I said, "Because the police always have a way of never letting you live those things down!!" Mom said, "What if the police never knew?" I said, "There's no such thing, Mom, they always know!!" Mom said, "Oh, okay, I'll see you tomorrow!!" I said, "Okay, Mom, I'll see you tomorrow."

Arriving the next day, Mom still wanted to know why a particular Italian gangster wanted me dead. So, I said to her, "Mom, as I was telling you yesterday, I wanted to be perceived by our crew boss as someone significant as opposed to the rest of our crew. I decided to call a drug lord I knew when I was still in the Marine Corps. I knew this particular guy dealt large quantities of drugs, and I figured if I could tie down a big deal with him, it could possibly impress our crew boss. I knew from time to time, our crew used Mob money to finance larger deals we couldn't handle. I figured, why not use their money for the deal I had in mind. I was approached one afternoon by two guys in our crew, suggesting that maybe I was moving too fast by asking the Mob for their assistance. They asked me to reconsider all my options before ringing the Mob's doorbell. I knew they were right, but my vanity and ego dictated to me that I knew what I was doing. So, I became more determined to do the deal with the Mob. After all, doing business with the Mob was starting to really stroke my ego in all the right ways." Mom said, "Do you mean to tell me that your ego was about to get you killed!!?" I said, "Yep, I think you are starting to get the picture, Mom. I knew a guy I had grown up with on the west side. He had worked with the Mob on several occasions, and I decided to go through him to see if my deal would be successful.

When my friend approached the Mob for me, they wanted to know all about me and my offer. They also spoke to another one out of our crew, who wanted to know who I was and how long I had been in business. After they were satisfied with what they heard, they made arrangements for me to meet them right away." Mom said, "I thought you said it was your deal, Son." I said, "Essentially, it was Mom, but my connection to the Mob had an invested interest at that point." Mom said, "How so, Son?" I said, "My connection, The Bear, was now middling the deal for the Mob while I stood to middle the deal for my L.A. Connection. Who was none other than a drug lord I had met while still in the Marine Corps. At any rate, my partner who would middle the deal for the Mob was none other than The Bear of Cincinnati. He had just as much to fear if something were to go wrong. In short, it was The Bear that essentially introduced me to the Mob. He was the one I was telling you about who got pistol-whipped across the hood of a police car during our arrest. But he is dead and gone now, Mom." Mom said, "You should be grateful you're not dead and gone."

I said, "I can't argue with you there, Mom." Mom said, "So go on with what you're saying." I said, "Well, at any rate, two weeks later, a Mob driver picked me up in a black Fleetwood Cadillac and transported me to the Greater Cincinnati Airport. I had never met the driver before, and from the looks of his face, I could see that he wasn't exactly interested in having a cozy conversation with me. Needless to say, the drive to the airport that day was just as quiet as taking a ride in a noiseless hearse. This is not to mention the sudden thoughts I had in realizing that I could be the next corpse if something were to go wrong. When I arrived at the airport, the Bear introduced me to three Italian gangsters who were waiting in the Delta Airlines' lobby. I later learned that all three of these men were actually made men from a known crime family. It just so happened that their leader and I would make final arrangements on the deal before boarding our flight bound for L.A. The other two mobsters accompanying him stood close behind him, wearing stone faces that could have been easily chiseled into anyone's gravestone upon request.

With these two watching my every move, I suddenly asked their boss, "I take it you've got the money?" Reaching inside his suit jacket, he pulled out an envelope that easily held twenty grand in new crisp hundred-dollar bills. He encouraged me to examine the rest of the envelope. I noticed there wasn't hardly enough money for the entire deal. After reviewing his envelope, I commented, "And what about the rest of it?" He responded by rolling his eyes to the left of him, where a man held a briefcase in his left hand. Understanding his drift, his eyes suddenly rolled to the right of him, where they landed on a man who gingerly stepped forward. The body language of these two men screamed with assurance that nothing would be taken prematurely from the briefcase. I was assured these two were armed, and from the looks on their faces, I was convinced their attendance that day wasn't for the purpose of watching a parade.

For a brief moment in time, I couldn't believe I was standing in the presence of a Mob lieutenant at just twenty years old asking him if he had his dog and pony show together." Mom said, "Yeah! I can't believe it either, so either you were stark crazy, or you couldn't wait to prove it to them." I said, "Mom!!" Mom said, "Go on with your story, Son." I said, "Before boarding the aircraft, all five of us elected to utilize Delta's curb service to ensure our arms would be transported with us. In those days, you could still smuggle arms aboard the belly of a plane. A feeling of doom immediately fell over me as the five of us boarded that jet bound for L.A. For the first time in my life, I felt the weight and gravity of what it was like to be in the company of men who would literally waste you and not think anything of it. I had no doubt in my mind that if something were to go wrong in L.A., I would never see the light of day again. It had to be the longest five-hour flight of my entire life. During the flight that day, The Bear and I decided to go over every detail of our deal. It was as if The Bear and I were trying to convince each other that everything was going to be okay. No doubt about it, we were!! With our plane soon to land, I noticed the same stone faces on our new accomplices hadn't changed one twitch. They looked just as convincing in L.A. as when we had first boarded our flight in Cincinnati.

The fear I naturally adopted during our flight gave intense birth to a clinging reminisce of my entire life. This is when I suddenly realized I wasn't watching a movie on television. I was a literary actor who participated in real life. And I knew, to the core of my being, if things didn't go well, I would definitely end up like they do in the movies. Arriving in L.A. we all rented three different cars and headed down San Bernardino Highway armed to the teeth and headed for our destination. Observing other passengers commuting to work that day bore looks that were not so inviting to any of us. It was as if I, too, now wore the same stone face that seemed to be so prevalent on Marceli and his men. Arriving at our destination, we slowly pulled into a driveway, only to be stopped by a barred gate and a greeting guard. The guard engaged himself in a short call, which allowed us to pass.

As we approached my L.A. Partners' estate, the sizing of its premises became automatic to avoid any ambush. Getting out of the car, The Bear, myself, and one of Marceli's men were welcomed in by an approaching maid. Walking through the front foyer, I was immediately met by Tom, my L.A. Connection, and two other gentlemen I hadn't known at all. Realizing I hadn't seen Tom since being discharged from the Marine Corps, I shook his hand and then introduced The Bear from Cincinnati. Tom then introduced himself to Marceli's associate, and he introduced two of his men to The Bear and myself. As Tom asked the maid to make everyone a drink, I suddenly interrupted Tom with a question. I said, 'Tom, do you have a moment?' Tom said, 'Of course, Jack, what can I do for you?' I said, 'In light of our former association and for the sake of Marceli and others wanting to join us, I would like to request that one of Marceli's men check the rest of the premises accompanied by my associate, The Bear?' Tom said, 'By all means, Jack, I would have been disappointed if you hadn't asked.' So, Tom motioned a man to accompany The Bear and one of Marceli's men to do a friendly search to secure the area.

Tom's maid elected to continue serving drinks while the search was being conducted. Tom said, 'Well, Jack, it looks as if you are just as careful as when we did business in the Marine Corps. Of course, I wouldn't have expected anything less from you.' I said, 'Well, Tom, what can I say? You taught me well, and with a million dollars in Marceli's suitcase, I have no doubt you would have wanted me to do the same for you had the deal been ours back in the Marine Corps.' Tom said, 'Of that, I have no doubt, Jack.' Tom then walked ahead of everyone, inviting us to join him in his den. A few moments later, Marceli's man returned with The Bear, indicating that the rest of the estate was secure. So, I motioned for The Bear to have Marceli and the rest of his men come inside. Marceli and two other associates got out of their car carrying a suitcase full of money. They headed for the entrance of Tom's estate. As we awaited Marceli's arrival, I took the liberty of asking Tom if he had all of Marceli's dope that he come for? He assured me that he did and that everything was going to be just fine. Breathing a sigh of relief, we all waited for Marceli to enter Tom's foyer. Once he had, I commenced introducing everyone, which was soon followed by the maid making more fabulous drinks that no one had ever drunk.

The first deal of the day was set for one hundred thousand pharmaceutical Royal 714 Quaalude's. The narcotic was super popular in the 1970s, and my partner Tom in L.A. claimed to have had an angle with the pharmaceutical company that made them. You can see why it attracted the attention of the Mob mom, as there were millions to be made. The second order of the day was that one million pharmaceutical Quaalude's would be sold every two weeks to Marceli for the sum of ten cents per Quaalude. The street retail value of a pharmaceutical Quaalude at that time varied between two and three bucks a piece if that tells you anything, Mom." Mom said, "Yeah, it does. It tells me the Mob was getting ready to clean up." I said, "And like how, as you so often say, Mom. Suddenly, out of nowhere, Tom announces that the pharmaceutical Quaalude can't be part of the deal. With the pharmaceutical Quaaludes being the main attraction as to why Marceli and his men came, it suddenly looked as if I needed to make arrangements for where I wanted to be buried. No doubt Tom's new announcement came as a surprise to everyone.

With no time to lose, I immediately spoke up to Tom and said, 'You know, Tom, I spent the better part of three weeks in a phone booth to make sure you and I were on the same page. And now you're telling us that, somehow, the deal you and I spoke about on the phone is now obsolete?' With no immediate response to my question, I reminded Tom that the pharmaceutical Quaalude's were the main reason why Marceli and his men had come to L.A. I said, 'And since that was clear to you from the beginning of our conversation, it's only my guess you'll be taking care of what Mr. Marceli came for, right?' Awaiting Tom's answer, I couldn't believe how fast things were going south. With Tom being somewhat apprehensive in his response, the entire room suddenly thickened with enormous tension. Three of Marceli's men wouldn't take their eyes off of Tom's men. The tension became so thick one could cut it with a knife. Knowing that Marceli was paying close attention to all that was being said, I noticed a grayish stone look that fell across his face. Realizing what that look could mean for me and everyone else, I pulled a gun out and stuck it to Tom's head. I then barbarously asked Tom, 'Do we have a misunderstanding here!!!?' Two of Tom's men started to get up from their chairs when suddenly their heads were met with guns from Marceli's men. It was only then I realized putting a gun to Tom's head actually sparked the whole room to panic. Under the circumstances, I felt it was necessary to demonstrate to Marceli that I meant business and that there was never any intended deception on my part as to why we were there. I figured by putting a gun to Tom's head, Marceli would certainly see whose team I was on. Instead, the incident backfired on me, and Marceli calmly brought order to our meeting. Marceli looked at Tom and said, 'Regardless of our highly charged atmosphere and due to the fact that my men have complete control of yours, I would like to explore all of our options before any unnecessary action is taken.' Tom agreed and asked his men to relax. Marceli's men were also asked to holster their guns, and I felt like an idiot for citing the whole room to ensure disaster. With Marceli spontaneously handling our crisis, it left me with no doubt that he was accustomed to handling such circumstances in the past. I was undoubtedly glad he was taking control of the situation, but I wasn't convinced that all was well.

As a matter of fact, with Marceli now controlling the conversation, I wasn't exactly convinced that Camelot would be its outcome." With my mother laughing, I said, "Hey, Mom, Tom had plenty of dope. It just wasn't the kind promised to Marceli when The Bear and I rang his bell in Cincinnati." Mom said, "And so, with the deal not being what you said it was going to be, is why Marceli wanted you dead?" I said, "I believe you are starting to get the picture, Mom. It's like I've told you in past times, when it comes to dealing with men like Marceli, it better be everything you said it was going to be, or else. No, ifs, and, or buts about it. If it's not what you said it was going to be, it's over. Well, at any rate, when Marceli concluded his discussion with Tom, it became apparent to me that Tom had no more than a bait-and-switch proposition for Marceli. Which, of course, wasn't going to help me at all.

Simply put, Marceli went to L.A. strictly for the pharmaceutical Quaalude's. So, everyone was back to square one because Marceli wasn't in the market for Tom's new offer. Which meant Marceli was going to whack me just out of (GP) General Principal. Make no mistake about it; that's precisely how things work out in the Mobs world. Tom's whole approach was to lure a large buyer, like Marceli, into buying kegs of reds and whites that were popular on the West Coast at the time. Mom said, "Son." I said, "Yes, Mom, what is it?" Mom said, "What is a keg of reds or whites?" I said, "A keg of reds is a hundred and forty-four thousand hits of bootleg barbiturates, and a keg of whites was the same amount, only bootleg amphetamine. They were being sold in New Mexico, Texas, and California territories at the time and were doing very well. And yes, you guessed it, Tom controlled the distribution of those kegs. It became very much Tom's intention to sell Marceli 500 to 1,000 kegs of reds and whites. However, the problem with Tom's plan was that Marceli went to L.A. to purchase Pharmaceutical Quaalude's. Which at that time were very popular on the east coast. You don't deceive men like Marceli and expect things to turn out like New Year's Eve. It doesn't work that way." Mom said, "Yes, I can see your concern now."

I said, "No, you don't, Mom. I had a front-row seat with Marceli in those years, and my ship was about to sink big time. And blaming my L.A. connection for deceiving Marceli wasn't going to cut the ice. And I understood that the concept is bigger than life itself. It's like I told you before, whatever you tell men like Marceli, it better be everything you said it was going to be. Those are the rules. Marceli continued to hear Tom out until he didn't want anymore. I could clearly see Marceli suspected Tom of setting me up to draw a larger buyer like himself. But even with Marceli knowing that was what Tom was trying to do, it wasn't enough to persuade him not to whack me. Marceli immediately got up from his chair and asked The Bear to join him in his car. "This was not a good sign, Mom." Mom asked, "Why not?" I said, "Marceli not asking me to join them in his car would be a clear indication that Marceli had a different plan. And, of course, I obviously knew I wasn't going to be a part of that plan. I felt the impact of Marceli only inviting The Bear to his vehicle. A thousand words couldn't explain how uncomfortable that feeling was that day." Mom said, "I bet it was, Son." I said, "When The Bear joined Marceli in his car, Marceli pulled out a .45 automatic that had been lying on his lap. He then pulled back the charging handle of the weapon and told The Bear to go inside and blow me away. With Marceli passing up a deal for fifty-five tons of marijuana in Miami, you can see why he was so angry with me being involved with a bait-and-switch proposition that essentially bore nothing. That's why he wanted me dead, Mom. Marceli had passed up a lot of profit on another deal for what he considered to be a bunch of nonsense with me in L.A. And as you have so often quoted to me, he wasn't having any!!! Heads were going to roll that day, starting with mine being first on the chopping block." Mom said. "Son." I said, "Yes, Mom, what is it?"

"With your head being on the chopping block that day, were you still of the opinion that you needed to be seen as more than something significant?" I said, "That's not funny, Mom." My mother started laughing, but I didn't think it was so funny after all. At any rate, when Marceli and The Bear were sitting in his car, The Bear told Marceli he wasn't able to whack me because he had grown up with me. Marceli told The Bear not to worry about it and that he would take care of it himself.

Meanwhile, The Bear got out of Marceli's car, reentering Tom's estate. Standing in Tom's foyer, The Bear and I opened up with what I considered to be our last conversation. During the course of our talk, it became more than apparent that The Bear would be leaving with Marceli and asked me if I would like to join them? I replied, 'Bear!! You know damn well if I get on that plane with you and Marceli, he'll have me whacked no sooner than I get off in Cincinnati.' The Bear wasn't arguing the point because he knew Marceli was trying to use him to bait me to get on the plane. I was disappointed that The Bear even suggested that I should get on the plane after growing up with him. But realizing The Bear was in the same business as I was, it shouldn't have come as a surprise that he would be so willing to help Marceli walk me to my grave. I really couldn't blame The Bear because I knew he was between a rock and a hard spot for his own life as well. So, I tried not to take it personally when he suggested that I get on that plane with him and Marceli that day. After all, The Bear was just doing what gangsters do. And if that meant aiding Marceli to whack me, to save his own life, why should I be so shocked?" Mom said, "Well, Son, Mom has to admit, it looked like you were in a real pickle." I said, "To say the least, Mom, to say the least. However, I was equally convinced that if The Bear had gotten out of Marceli's car and whacked me there, I have no doubt Marceli would have made sure the L.A. police would have had their trigger man right away. You see, Mom, Marceli knew The Bear and I were far enough down the ladder to be expendable without attracting any new attention to himself. I wasn't lost on Marceli's antics because I had been formerly associated with men like Al Sinclair of the Detroit Purple Gang. It wasn't hard to read what was coming next or more than likely to happen next.

Before The Bear left with Marceli that day, I asked him, standing in Tom's foyer, what he would do if he were in my place? He told me he would at least try to salvage some kind of deal that would suffice Marceli. Though his comment made sense to me, I felt he was trying to let me down easily and say his last goodbye at the same time. But as The Bear left that day, he did mention to me that he would at least try to persuade Marceli not to whack me until I had a chance to at least salvage our deal. Knowing Marceli could easily whack me right away, I decided to at least try to bring about The Bear's counsel to me. But I also knew if I were to run and not at least try to salvage Marceli's deal, I could be easily perceived as being part of Tom's bait-and-switch proposition right from the beginning. Which, of course, would have given Marceli all the more reason to empty my life out as soon as possible. With Marceli and The Bear on their way back to Cincinnati, it occurred to me to ask Tom if he even had the pharmaceutical Quaalude's to begin with. But with him inviting me to stay at his estate, I figured I'd wait until the morning to ask.

After all, how do you put pressure on someone that you just held a gun to their head a few hours earlier?" Mom said, "Son." I said, "Yeah, Mom." What did Tom say to you about putting that gun to his head that day?" I said, "Mom, Tom, and I had an extensive background in the Marine Corps long before Marceli's time. Tom was actually a Marine Corps officer who held the rank of Full Bird Colonel. When I first met Tom, I was surprised to learn he was a drug dealer. I felt officers of his stature didn't need to draw that kind of attention to themselves, much less putting their careers at risk. And with a Full Bird Colonel's pay, Tom certainly didn't need the money.

When Tom and I were still in the Marine Corps, he mentioned to me that he didn't care if he retired from the Marine Corps or not. He then assured me that he had been reared in an independently wealthy family and that his service pension just wasn't a priority to him. He also added that the Marine Corps became a waste of his time because he was trying to prove something to his parents that should have never been necessary." Mom said, "And what was that, Son?" I said, "Tom told me because he had been reared in an affluent family, his parents were of the opinion that he virtually didn't have any real intestinal fortitude that would ever amount to anything. So, Tom set out to prove both of his parents wrong by becoming a Marine Corps officer. After becoming a Marine Officer and proving his parents wrong, he sort of bugged out by pushing the envelope of dealing drugs. Tom pretty much started dealing drugs at the close of the Vietnam War." Mom said, "You let me tell you something, Son, both you and your brother were in the Marine Corps, and I never had that kind of image of either one of you." I said, "Maybe you should have gotten a second opinion, Mom. When I met Tom, I was young and impressionable. I thought Tom was pretty cool being able to deal large quantities of drugs and still being an officer in the Marine Corps." Mom said, "There's nothing cool about it, Son. That joker came close to getting your head blown off." I said, "I can't argue with you there, Mom. His actions were aimless then, and he continued that same nonchalant attitude after he was discharged." Mom said, "Boy, you better count your lucky stars that you're even here today!!" I said, "Make no mistake, Mom, I counted all those stars at one time or another, and I give all the credit to God that I'm even alive today. At any rate, when Tom was serving his last tour in Vietnam, he and two other naval officers started transporting heroin into the US. I know it's not right, Mom, and I'm not condoning their actions. Still, Tom, by far, wasn't the only military officer dealing drugs overseas. Trust me, that wasn't the case at all.

The market was wide open in those years, and many military officers took advantage of it. It was so widespread it could have made Veto Genovese of the Genovese family look like a choir boy of his day. And bear in mind, Mom, Veto was once quoted to be the father of the narcotics trade. However, Tom and two other naval officers managed to get their heroin into the United States undetected. The two naval officers Tom associated with knew there would be dogs brought aboard their ship to check for drugs once they docked. Tom made sure a few men in his unit placed the heroin high in the metal rafters, making it impossible for the dogs to smell. Once the dogs supposedly did their job, they were escorted off the ship, and the heroin was quickly removed. When I first met Tom, he was channeling his drugs just outside several Marine Corps bases. Tom had me dealing with one of his chief petty officers back then, known by the nickname of The Candy Man. With me being a mule for The Candy Man, I eventually learned how Tom was getting his heroin into our country.

I thought it was relatively simple but ingenious at the same time." Mom said, "Son, there was nothing ingenious about it. Plain and simple, that jerk was being paid by our Federal Government to protect our country. And now you're telling me that he and two other naval officers were destroying it by transporting heroin into our ports. Horse crap, there's nothing ingenious about all that stuff at all!! If anything, Tom and his two other naval officers were a disgrace to our nation's uniform." I said, "Mom, I am not condoning what they did back then. I'm just sharing with you what happened." Mom said, "Well, thank God!! Because if those suckers had done those things during the second world war, they would have probably found themselves in front of a firing squad." I said, "I can't argue with you there." Mom said, "Well, you better not because I'd have you shot with them!!!" I said, "Settle down, Mom, settle down. It's not worth all your excitement, especially with all these things happening in the past." Mom said, "Well!! Just so that you know how I feel about all that malarkey." I said, "I know you do, Mom, I know you do.

But to answer your question as to how Tom felt when I held a gun to his head that day. Well, he simply stated at breakfast the next morning that I looked cute. However, as a former Marine who held my service in high regard, I found his comment to be quite intimidating. And true to Tom's nature, his nonchalant attitude continued to tick me off, considering the Mob still wanted me dead. Later that day, and much to my surprise, Tom sympathized with how he understood why I'd be under so much pressure. I was glad to see him come to his senses. I was taken by surprise when he recognized the gravity of the situation. I mentioned to him that I didn't appreciate his bait-and-switch tactic he used on Marceli. He finally agreed that I didn't deserve to be in the middle of his bait-and-switch proposition." Mom said, "Well, how nice of him to recognize it." I said, "Yeah, I thought so too. But I had refrained from being flip with Tom, considering I only had about one hundred and ninety dollars in my pocket with a long way back to Cincinnati. It certainly wasn't enough money to catch the next plane out, much less running the risk of encountering one of Marceli's men. While I was still in L.A., I at least wanted to try and find a lucrative deal that would suffice Marceli. And maybe even possibly persuade The Bear to influence Marceli not to whack me. But unannounced to both Tom and me, Marceli had a different plan altogether.

One that has burned in my memory to this day. With my and Tom's differences dissipating, I asked him if he ever had the Quaaludes to begin with. He told me that he hadn't and that he basically used me to lure Marceli into a bigger deal. I began to steam inside when I heard his answer. So., I said to him, 'Are you trying to get me killed!!!? Because if you are, you are off to a great start!!!' Mom said, "What did he say, Son?" I said, "He told me that he had no idea that I was even acquainted with people of Marceli's caliber. I said to Tom, 'I know you don't!!!' Tom answered, 'But I'm not in the Mob, Jack.' I said, 'Yes, but you are not far from it either, are you?

Oh yes, Tom, I agree you were once a Marine Corps officer. Still, I equally recognize that as a civilian, you are just as much of a dressed-up gangster as Marceli is. Maybe not in the Italian Mob, but definitely just as much of a gangster as them.' Mom said, "What did he say, Son?" I said, "Well, let us just say his face wasn't exactly indicative of pleasure. He just stood there with that smirk on his face. Mom, Tom enjoyed having a businessman's front with his former status as a Full Bird Colonel in the Marine Corps. They both fit him well with his luxury estate and having been reared in old money.

Few Mobsters I've known have had the best of both worlds. Can you see how he would be so sold on his own parade?" Mom said, "Sure I can, Son." I said, "But unannounced to both Tom and I, his parade was about to be interrupted. Grant you, Tom felt he was a successful independent gangster, and he was, but for him to have to contend with Italian gangsters such as Marceli would be a whole different ball game altogether. Tom finally realized the gravity of the entire situation and started thinking of ways he could help me and himself. At first, he didn't think helping me actually involved him to be one of the same problems. I really thought he was in denial at that point because, as far as I was concerned, he certainly was in just as much danger as I was. Especially with Marceli knowing I was residing at his residence." Mom said, "Couldn't Tom just throw you out?" I said, "Of course he could, Mom." But for reasons unknown to me to this day, he elected not to. And yes, I was glad because his estate was like a fortress that was even equipped with Doberman Pinscher guard dogs. But I knew we couldn't stay inside forever, and so did our opposition. AS I kept telling mom the story Mom quickly responded, "He had guard dogs?" I responded, "Of course he did, Mom!! Why wouldn't he?" He was independently wealthy, and considering his lifestyle, he was going to need all the help he could possibly muster. (So, I was surprised to notice that he had guard dogs as part of his arsenal, which shouldn't have surprise me at all.) Two of those dogs were at the front gate accompanying his full-time guard, while the other two stayed inside Tom's front foyer. I didn't like Tom's foyer dogs because they landed right next to the pillars of Tom's front door.

And every time I needed to walk by Tom's foyer, those dogs would eye every move I made." My mother started laughing. I said, "That's not funny, Mom. Those things can really tear someone apart." Mom said, "Ah!! A big tough Marine like you! I'm surprised you were even concerned." I said, "I'm not bulletproof, Mom, nor am I Doberman Pinscher proof. Obviously, at that point, neither Tom nor I knew when Marceli would try to make a move. Having those dogs sure helped us know if anyone was in close proximity. With things calm for a while, Tom turned me on to a few of his L.A. connections, hoping they could supply me with large quantities of Pharmaceutical Quaalude's. There was no such luck in this attempt. So, Tom and I relaxed a little, partying around the Los Angeles area in the hope of finding a deal that would suffice for Marceli. Not the thing to do when you're in trouble with the Mob. We found out the hard way that Marceli's schedule wasn't exactly our schedule.

Late one afternoon, Tom and I were approaching the front door of his estate. I enjoyed entering Tom's estate from his front walkway because of the multi-color granite stones that paved the way to his door. The stone glitter brought to mind the same beautiful granite I once observed in the hills of Rome, Italy. Making my last turn to step into Tom's doorway, I noticed through my peripheral vision two men dubiously sitting across the street in an unknown car. I definitely thought something was wrong, so I informed Tom of what I had seen. He told me I certainly had every reason to be on edge but not to chase ghosts around in my mind. I immediately responded by saying, 'Tom! Didn't you just recently claim that I had every reason to be on edge?' Tom said, 'Yes, I did, so what of it?' I said, 'Well, then, I don't know if you've been keeping up with current events, but I fail to believe that Marceli has forgotten your bait-and-switch performance from just a week ago. If anything, my guess would be that Marceli probably doesn't care if he whacks you right alongside me. After all, I don't think he'll just dismiss your royal, elegant performance that stole his time and dime. If anything, he's probably thinking of ways he can effectively empty your life out.' Mom said, "Wow, Son, how did Tom respond to all of that?" I said, "Well, Mom, needless to say, Tom suddenly came away with a different perspective altogether.

With Tom reconsidering our circumstances, he made a call to invite back some of his muscles that had accompanied us during our initial meeting with Marceli. So, when I learned he had made a call like that, I blurted out, 'Don't tell me you're going to invite those goons back!! Don't you realize Marceli's men had the drop on those idiots before they even knew what was happening?' Tom said, 'That's true, so if anything, they have learned from their mistakes, haven't they?' I said, 'Tom!! You're not a commander in the Marine Corps anymore.' Tom said, 'That's true. And since we can't keep our eyes open twenty-four hours a day, those so-called goons you referred to are going to help us cover our butts in the meantime.' I said, 'Oh yeah!!! I can see it all now; the Calvary is on its way!!! And we are all going to be saved by the bell.' Tom said, 'Jack, why don't you have the maid make us lunch before you become a new sense to me.' Not wanting to push the envelope, I said, 'Okay, Tom, I'll ask her to make us lunch.' Tom said, 'Thank you, that will be all for right now.' I said, 'Do you plan to tell the maid what's going on?' Tom said, 'You know, it's better that she doesn't know anything. I'm just going to give her a few weeks off.' I said, 'Well, who is going to make our lunch when she goes?' Tom said, 'Don't you know, the Calvary!' I said, 'Oh my, does this mean I have to give up my room as well?' Tom replied, 'You have the Mob wanting to kill you, and you are worried about giving up your room!!?' I said, 'Just asking, just asking.' Tom said, 'But if you must know, no, you don't have to give up your room, for there's plenty of room on the first floor for all three of your so-called goons.' I said, 'Three?! I only saw two of your men during our deal with Marceli.' Tom said, 'That's true.' I said, 'Well then, who's the third man?' Tom said, 'The third man is like a son to me.' I said, 'Well, let's hope he's far more responsive than the other two.' Tom said, 'He will be because he's a bit more like me.' I said, 'Now that's reassuring, considering the Mob may want to whack you as well.' Tom said, 'But for right now, can you just have the maid make us a sandwich, Jack?' I said, 'Yeah, I believe I can do that, Tom.' Tom said, 'Great, and Jack.' I said, 'Yes?' Tom said, 'Try not to distract the maid so much at her task because I'd like to eat today.' I said, 'Don't worry, I won't distract too much because I'm hungry myself.' Tom said, 'Can you imagine that?'

When Tom's goons returned that day, I observed their behavior for a while and decided maybe it would be better if I guarded Tom's place myself. Mom said, "I take it you weren't so impressed with these gentlemen on their first performance against Marceli's men?" I said, "No, Mom, I really wasn't. But I have to admit, there was one individual of the three that stood out, and I wasn't able to put my finger on it right away." Mom said, "What was his name, Son?" I said, "His name was Derrick. He was the quitting type, if you know what I mean?" Mom said, "Yep, they are usually the ones that are most dangerous." I said, "Yeah, I know what you mean, Mom. Because I have known a few silent-type folks who have gone off like a bomb when things got riled up. And I really felt that, at that point, we needed someone dangerous, considering our circumstances. I didn't want to feel alone in this particular incident. I would have liked a little more help from someone other than the two other guys Tom had. Well, at any rate, a whole week went by without Marceli's men making a move.

Coming downstairs one afternoon, I asked Tom if I could go out and get some air." Tom said, "That's fine, but make sure you take Derrick with you.' I said, 'Ah, you mean that guy that's supposed to be a little more like you?' Tom said, 'You know, actually, he'll be more like himself when it comes to keeping you alive.' I said, 'And how is that?' Tom said, 'Enjoy your day, Jack, and don't do anything I wouldn't do.' I said, 'I'll keep that in mind.' Tom said, 'Derrick, would you please accompany Jack on his outing today?' Derrick nodded yes, and we both walked out together. Driving down the San Bernardino highway, I asked Derrick how long he had known Tom? Derrick said, 'When I was a kid, one of my best friends died in a boating accident, and Tom showed up for the funeral that day with my dad. I didn't know it at the time, but Tom and my father were best friends in the Marine Corp. Later, my father was killed in Vietnam, and my mother ran off with some other guy. When Tom learned of my circumstances, he gained custody of me while he was still married to his first wife. After staying with Tom for a while, I knew one thing for sure.' I said, 'And what's that?' Derrick said, 'After my father was killed in Vietnam, Tom never looked at the Vietnam war in quite the same way. In fact, he became less and less interested in staying in the Marine Corps.' I said, 'Really!?'

Derrick said, 'Jack, just for the record, I'm not personally involved in any of Tom's business affairs. I decided years ago I didn't fit in so well with that part of his life.' I said, 'Yeah, I know what you mean. That definitely explains why we didn't see you that first day when Tom and I met with Marceli and his men.' Derrick said, 'You've got that right.' I said, 'Don't take me wrong, Derrick, but how do you fit in all this?' Derrick said, 'That's just the thing, Jack, I'm not part of Tom's dope machine or any other shenanigan that he may be trying to pull off. I'm just an adopted stepson to him. So, as I was saying, after my real father was killed in Vietnam, Tom sort of went off the deep end. He knew our government was expecting our men to fight that war with one hand tied behind their backs. Of course, that approach got my father killed. Tom is opposed to the new tactics being implemented on the battlefield, and he kind of clocked out. He started to lose respect for the Marine Corps and our government. He demonstrated that by pushing the envelope when it came to taking unnecessary risks. At first, he made some silly mistakes in the field, involving other men's lives. After getting one of them killed, he realized he no longer wanted to be a part of government policies that led to disaster. He felt so bad about one of his men losing his life he suddenly switched gears and started dealing drugs. Of which I have never understood to this day. And so, after my real father was killed, I grew up as Tom's adopted child. But before my real father's death, and long before Tom lost respect for the Marine Corps, I admired Tom and my dad's devotion as Marine Officers. As a kid, I wanted to be just like them. So, when I became an adult, I joined the Navy Seals and became a Naval Officer. After my so-called tour of duty, I elected not to reenlist.' I said, 'Excuse me, Derrick. I didn't want to break up your story, but what prompted you not to want to reenlist?' Derrick said, 'Jack, we were making some of the same mistakes during the Gulf War as we had in Vietnam. It's just that we were making more of them. And I didn't want to end up like my dad.' I said, 'Fair enough.' Derrick said, 'So when I came home from the Navy, I took an administration position with a large corporation. After about two years of that, I became bored and started taking advanced karate lessons in my spare time.

I enjoyed the art so much that Tom financed an orient trip for me to study the origins of karate. When I came back four years later, Tom helped me set up my first karate school. It wasn't long before one of my students won his first state championship. In answering your question about how I fit in Tom's empire, well, that's pretty simple. As I mentioned to you before, I have absolutely nothing to do with Tom's illegal pursuits. And I really do wish he would bring them to an end because he really doesn't need the money. I'm of the opinion that he likes the charge it gives him. However, I do respect Tom's accomplishments as a former Marine Officer and the many sacrifices he made for our country. After I heard about your particular involvement with Tom, I knew you could probably use some help. My being here with you today is basically a favor to Tom and a courtesy to you. Learning that you were a former Marine made me want to help you even more. It kind of reminded me of the days when the Marines used to train with us for their deep-sea training at Quantico, Virginia. At any rate, knowing my dad is basically a well-dressed-up hidden gangster in our society, I'm still his son, and I still love him. And I try to act accordingly, though it has been challenging at times.' I said, 'Thanks for giving me some insight, Derrick. It helps me know what I'm dealing with.' So, I elected to keep quiet for a while as we proceeded down the San Bernardino highway. As we drove on, I couldn't help but think about all the things Derrick shared with me. His perception gave me second thoughts on why I was so involved with the Mob in those years. It was apparent Derrick was pretty loyal to Tom, but not even for his own good. A few minutes had elapsed when I suddenly realized Derrick getting ready to exit the freeway. I abruptly interrupted him and asked him to continue his course down San Bernardino Highway. With Derrick displaying an odd look on his face, he asked, 'Haven't you had an adequate amount of travel today, Jack?' I said, 'Actually, I have. It's just that I was wondering if we could take a ride up to Santa Barbara?' Derrick said, 'Santa Barbara! What's in Santa Barbara?' 'Well, I was wondering if you knew of a restaurant up there named The Cat's Meow?' Derrick said, 'Yes, it's a well-established place that's a little on the high side, if you know what I mean. But if you want something to eat, there are places much closer to Santa Barbra, Jack.'

I said, 'No, that's okay.' Derrick said, 'Well then if you don't want to get something closer, why the big attraction at The Cat's Meow?' I said, 'Well, when I was introduced to one of Tom's connections last week, the occasion seemed to be more of a social gathering.' Derrick said, 'And don't tell me, you met a woman there?' I said, 'How'd ya know!?' Derrick said, 'For someone that has the Mob on their tail, you seem to be somewhat preoccupied.' I said, 'Well, kind of.' Derrick said, 'You mean you don't know if you met this woman?' I said, 'Not exactly, but I learned enough about her to want to check the situation out.' Derrick said, 'And how would you know if she's at The Cat's Meow restaurant?' I said, 'When she and I were at Tom's gathering last week, we weren't able to take our eyes off of one another.' Derrick said, 'Oh! That's a good way to know she's there. You two couldn't take your eyes off one another.' I said, 'No, that's not what I mean. What I mean is I overheard her girlfriend asking her if she still worked at The Cat's Meow.' Derrick said, 'And of course, her girlfriend answered, yes?' I said, 'That part I wasn't so clear about. You see, the level of noise in the room prohibited me from hearing her girlfriend's answer.' Derrick said, 'Well!! Let me see if I get all of this right!! You met some girl with your eyes that might work at The Cat's Meow that may or may not be there today?' I said, 'Yep, I think that raps it up!!' Derrick said, 'Well!! Now that your intuition has totally eclipsed your brain, why don't we both lose our minds at The Cat's Meow?' I said, 'Thanks, Derrick, I knew you would take me up there!!' Derrick said, 'I don't think I would miss this for the world.' And so off to The Cat's Meow Derrick and I went.

On the way to The Cat's Meow, neither Tom nor I had any clue that two of Marceli's men were already following us. Running northeast on Highway 101, Derrick asked me, 'So what does she look like?' I said, 'Ah, man!!! She is the "Cat's Meow" and fine as twine, to say the least!! I have to admit, Derrick, I've always been attracted to brunettes. But this gal is anything but the so-called average blond.' Derrick said, 'Oh, and how do you know that!!?' I said, 'Because it's easy to see that she personally really differed from the rest of the girls at your father's gathering that night.' Derrick said, 'So what exactly does that mean!?' I said, 'Well, she appeared to have more of a wholesome personality as opposed to the rest of the women that accompanied her that evening. It was as if she hadn't been around quite like the others that sat with her that day.' Derrick said, 'Well, maybe she hasn't spent so much time with those women before. Maybe she's little miss muffin that lives on a candle stick farm.' I said, 'Ah, come on, man!!' Derrick said, 'Well, you're sitting over there drooling all over yourself with a smile from ear to ear. Tell me, what does she look like!!!' I said, 'Ok, Ok!! Well, she's about 5'-4" to 5'-6" with gorgeous blonde hair that lands just about halfway down her back. You can tell she's not a bleach bottle blonde either.' Derrick said, 'And how on earth would you ever know that!!?' I said, 'I don't know, Derrick, I just...know!!' Derrick said, 'Come on, Jackie boy, tell me some more!!' I said, 'Well, she has a deep, beautiful tan with dark blue marble eyes that could pierce the soul of a Prince.' Derrick said, 'Yup, you won't have to worry about the Mob killing you. She'll get ya killed first.' I said, 'Come on, man!!' Derrick just smiled and sped the pace of his car for Santa Barbara. Arriving at The Cat's Meow, Derrick and I noticed the place was packed for lunch. When Derrick pulled into the driveway of the restaurant, my heart began pounding faster with the anticipation of seeing Shelly. Derrick asked, 'Hey Jack, you never told me this gal's name.' I said, 'That's easy, remember, she's little miss muffin from the candle stick farm.'

Derrick said, 'Come on!!' I said, 'No, I'm just kidding. Her name is Shelly, and she's beautiful!!!' With Derrick and I walking in The Cat's Meow, it became rather doubtful if we could even be seated right away. There were so many people moving about the place it became questionable if I would ever find Shelly. Derrick excused himself, wanting to use the restroom, and asked me to find us a table. I said, 'Wait a minute, Derrick. How 'bout if I use the restroom, and you find us a table?' At about that same time, I heard Derrick's voice fading as he walked away to find the restroom. He suddenly and scantly looked back to tell me, 'Don't worry, you'll find us a table.' I said, 'Sure!! anything else?' Derrick disappeared into the crowd, leaving me with a waiter who didn't seem to know where he was. So, the waiter bowed in front of me to ask, 'What is your seating preference, sir?' Not seeing Shelly anywhere, I had hoped to direct the waiter to where Shelly would be serving. So, I answered the gentleman and said, 'Wherever Shelly can best serve us.' The waiter commented, 'Ah! But there are two Shelly's, sir; which one are you referring to, sir?' Not expecting that particular answer, I said, 'You know, Shelly, the one with blond hair.' The waiter said, 'I'm sorry, sir, both of our Shelly's have blond hair.' I said, 'Oh yes, I'm sorry, I should have told you, she's the younger one.' The waiter replied, 'Sir, they are both young.' Feeling totally intimated at this point; I asked the waiter to just pick one. The waiter said, 'Very well, sir, follow me.'

A busboy was clearing a beautiful window seat as the waiter and I approached the table where Derrick and I would be sitting. As I sat down, I couldn't help but fantasize about Shelly and I already being placed there to enjoy a candlelight dinner. When the waiter seated me, I realized I had a clear view of the bar area as well. A few minutes had elapsed when Derrick suddenly reappeared from using the bathroom. I shared with him all that had transpired while he was gone. I didn't think he would ever stop laughing." Mom said, "Well, Son, you have to admit those were some pretty unusual circumstances you were explaining to Derrick. It's not every day one would run into two young ladies with the same name and same description, working at the same restaurant." I said, "Well, I can't argue with you there, Mom.

But when Derrick started laughing, Mom, he laughed so hard he fell out of the booth that we were seated in." Caught off guard, my mother started laughing as well. She said, "You have to admit, Jack, that was a ridiculous conversation you had with the waiter." I said, "Would you like me to tell you the rest of the story, Mom?" Mom said, "Oh, now don't be sore, Son; it could have happened to anyone, so just get on with what you were saying." I said, "Well, suddenly, our waitress appeared, and I realized she wasn't the Shelly I was hoping to see. When the wrong Shelly went to get our drinks, Derrick kept laughing hysterically. I asked him if he could stop laughing long enough to afford me a break. He said yes, and then he announced, 'I'm sorry, Jack, I just couldn't help but think about how the Mob wants you dead, and now you have this champion of a waiter leading you around to find some woman that neither one of you seem to know. You have to admit, that's quite a scenario considering the circumstances.' I said, 'Well, Derrick, I'm glad one of us is having a good time.' With Derrick continuing to laugh under his breath, it dawned on me that our waiter would have to get our drinks at the bar in order to serve us. Observing how excellent the wood carvings were around the restaurant, I wondered if the same carvings existed at the bar counter. Glancing at the bar counter suddenly brought me in view of the Shelly I was actually looking for that day. She was serving a peach schnapps to one of her patrons. My heart started pounding ferociously, the same way it had when Derrick and I first entered the Cat's Meow parking lot. I suddenly and immediately brought Derrick's attention to the fact that I had spotted the Shelly I was looking for serving drinks at the bar. Derrick said, 'You found her!!!' I said, 'I believe I have.' Derrick said, 'Well then, where is she?' I said, 'She's the one that's working on the left side of the bar counter closer toward the back.' Derrick's eyes suddenly scanned the bar counter in the hope of finding this beautiful woman I had spoken so much about. When his eyes finally landed on the Shelly I wanted, he spontaneously blurted out, 'WOW, Jack!!! Man!! She really is a knockout!!!' I said, 'Does she look like little Miss Muffin from the candle stick farm now?' Derrick said, 'No, she doesn't, Jack, she's drop-dead gorgeous!!!'

I said, 'I told you she was.' Derrick said, 'Well, are you gonna go up to the counter and talk to her?' I said, 'Yeah!! Just waiting for the right time to approach her.' Derrick said, 'Waiting for the right time?! Why, you had better get there at rocket speed before someone else discovers her candlestick farm.' Slowly getting up to approach Shelly's workplace, I asked Derrick to hold the fort down. Derrick said, 'No problem. I have to use the bathroom again, but I'll see you in a few minutes.'

I said, 'OK, ciao.' With Derrick fading out of sight, I approached the bar counter where Shelly was serving. Knowing that she would eventually return from the opposite end of the counter, I decided to seat myself in an inconspicuous spot. Having seated myself at the opposite end of the counter gave me the clearest view as to how Shelly handled her patrons. With Derrick gone to the restroom, I had no idea he was about to encounter two of Marceli's men. Forgetting about Derrick, I had hoped Shelly would soon notice I wanted to order a drink. But for the time being, I sure enjoyed watching the way she handled herself. I quickly saw other male occupants responding to her every whim as if she were a Goddess. The men were falling all over themselves, trying not to make any noticeable mistake that would ruin their chance to ask her out. With many male fans at her command, I couldn't believe that little Miss Muffin had shown interest in me just a week earlier. Without warning and in less than a moment's notice, Shelly turned, making her way toward me. With her still not noticing me right away gave me an adequate amount of time to observe the brilliant pace she so rightly displayed. And believe me, that pace seemed to suggest nothing less than radiant purpose.

As she encroached closer, I noticed the dazzling persona she held that could have easily exceeded any expectations of some of the top modeling agencies. Walking ever so close to me, my mind pondered what it would be like to be in love with such a beautiful woman. Suddenly and without reservation, she looked right at me and said, 'How did you know I was here!!!?' Before I could even answer her question, she leaned over the counter where our faces met for a gentle welcome and a brief kiss. Answering her question as to how I knew she was there, I simply told her, 'I overheard you tell your girlfriend where you worked. But because I know you're busy, we'd better exchange numbers now.' She said, 'I thought you would never ask!!' Moving ever so quickly to exchange numbers, we both were engulfed with many pleasant smiles peppered with short and savvy conversation. Unexpectedly, Shelly had to return to the opposite end of the bar to respond to what appeared to be a jealous patron. Jealous or not, it was clear Shelly's internal beauty matched that of her outer beauty, and it made me feel like the luckiest guy in the world. With Derrick returning from the bathroom, he surpassed our table and moved briskly toward me. With him drawing close to me, it was obvious his demeanor was wanting to scream a message. Arriving where I sat, Derrick leaned over to whisper in my ear, 'We have company.' I said, 'We do?' Derrick said, 'Yes, we do, and you need to forget about little Miss Muffin for right now and walk away quickly and quietly.' I said, 'Gotcha.' Both Derrick and I moved quickly toward the door. Of course, at that point, Shelly could clearly observe that there was something really wrong. Beholding Shelly's puzzled look, I motioned her that I would call later. We couldn't have left the restaurant any sooner, considering Marceli's men weren't far behind. As Derrick and I jumped in his car, I suddenly looked over Derrick's right shoulder, only to find both of Marceli's men being quickly seated in their car. Knowing at that point that the chase would be on, I thought it would be much better to whack both of them right there in the parking lot. But not knowing what Derrick may have thought of my plan, I decided to clear it with him first.

So, I said, 'Derrick, how did you know those two were in the restaurant?' Derrick said, 'I spotted both of them when I came out of the restroom, and I was darn lucky they didn't see me right away.' I said, 'How do you know they're Marceli's men?' Derrick said, 'I didn't, but it wasn't hard to figure out they were the only two men there that were of Italian descent. And it certainly didn't appear they were looking to have lunch. In short, it appeared they were looking to have us for lunch.' I said, 'You know what I say, Derrick, the gangster stuff goes two ways. If they are so willing to make my acquaintance, why don't I just kill both of them right here?' With Derrick already pulling out of the restaurant driveway, he said, 'That's not going to be a good idea, Jack.' I said, 'Oh yeah!!, and why is that?' Derrick said, 'By all means, allow me to elaborate. I'm sure there are at least three reasons not to whack them here.' I said, 'By all means, enlighten me.' Derrick said, 'Okay, number one, as a former Navy Seal Officer and with you being a former Marine, I do appreciate your willingness to take the fight to them here and now. But since we are not fighting a war, killing them in this parking lot would only assure the Mob's relentless pursuit of you. So far, so good?' I said, 'Yes, so what are the other two reasons?' Derrick said, 'Second of all, I think Tom would expect more out of me other than to murder two men in a parking lot in broad daylight.' I said, 'But it sounds great to me, Derrick, I could use the action. Just think about it, Derrick. You don't have to do anything. Remember, I'm a fully trained former Marine, and that's what we are trained to do, we kill people. They don't care anymore about my life than I care about theirs. So don't worry about killing them. I'll take care of that part myself.' Derrick said, "But I'm not a gangster, Jack.' I said, 'Well, you've got a point there. So, what's the third reason?' Derrick said, 'Third reason?' I replied, 'Yes, Derrick, the third reason, what might that be?' Derrick said, 'Oh yes, the third reason.' I said, 'Yes, that one, what is it?' Derrick said, 'Considering I once had to outrun two Arabs in the Middle East during the Gulf War, I think I can do the same here today.' I said, 'Well, since the Mob wants to kill me just as much as those Arabs wanted to kill you, do you think you can outrun those two idiots?' Derrick said, 'I think we're about to find out, Jack.' I said, 'Wouldn't it be much easier to just kill them?'

Derrick said, 'I'm pretty sure I can outrun these guys, Jack, so just take it easy for right now. Besides, as you say, I can use the action for a change.' I said, 'You can use the action for a change!! Come on, Derrick, are you kidding me?' Derrick said, 'Well, considering that you want to kill them in a public parking lot, it's probably much safer to try and outrun them, don't you think?' I said, 'Maybe!' Derrick said, 'I'll take my chances on outrunning them. That way, if the police catch either one of us speeding, it surely would be a lot less time in jail as opposed to killing them in a parking lot.' I said, 'Well, I guess I can't argue with you there."

Speeding back to Tom's estate, Derrick started weaving in and out of traffic until we lost Marceli's men. In the event that Marceli's men would catch up, Derrick stopped and used a pay phone to inform the front guard to leave the front gate open for a quick entry. Derrick and I arrived at Tom's estate just about an hour and forty-five minutes later from all the excitement. Walking in, Tom asked, 'I trust that you two had a nice day?' Derrick said, 'Not at all. I had to contend with two of Marceli's men while Jack was occupied with little Miss Muffin.' Tom said, 'Little Miss Muffin, and whom might that be?' Derrick said, 'Some woman Jack met at one of your social gatherings last week.' Tom said, 'Oh, I see, it must have been quite a day.' Derrick said, 'To say the least.' When Derrick spoke to Tom that night, Tom requested that everyone stay inside the compound until further notice. Tom made arrangements the following day for security to bring in groceries on a regular basis. Tom's maid never had any knowledge as to what was happening at all. This continued for about another week with no further interruptions from Marceli's men." Mom said, "Son." I said, "Yeah, Mom?" Mom said, "How did you feel at that moment?" I said, "I'll be honest with you, Mom; I felt like we were sitting ducks because I had no idea how long Marceli's men were going to pursue the situation or when they may decide to strike again. We just didn't know. What made things worse was I wanted to meet with Shelly that day, but the Mob wanted me dead as soon as possible. I wrestled with that in my mind, knowing all along I could never involve her. It was agonizing to me." Mom said, "I bet it was." I said, "Mom, I knew if I were to see Shelly again, it could definitely endanger her life." Mom said, "So what did you do?"

I said, "After Derrick and I arrived at Tom's estate later that afternoon, I asked Derrick if I could borrow his car." Mom said, "You're crazy, Son; after all you guys went through, you would put that girl's life in danger?" I said, "After sitting around the estate for another week, I became a little antsy, Mom. So, one day, I approached Derrick in the den and asked him if I could have a minute of his time. He was, in the interim, reading a novel and asked me to give him a few minutes. Bowing out gracefully, I told Derrick I'd be in the foyer when he was ready to see me. Derrick replied, 'Very well, I'll see you there.' So, we met in the foyer about an hour later, and I asked him if I could use his car. Just as Derrick handed me his keys, the phone rang.

Derrick excused himself to answer the phone while I waited inside Tom's foyer. Suspecting who it might have been on the phone, I asked Derrick that very question as he returned to the foyer. Derrick said, 'Your first guess will probably be your best one.' I said, 'Shelly?' Derrick said, 'You get the cookie, Jack.' I told him I'd take the call in my room. Derrick said, 'Very well,' and then he asked Shelly to wait a few moments so I could resume the call upstairs. Shelly and I spoke for the better part of eight to ten minutes, only to conclude that we would meet later that evening. I could tell Shelly found our conversation somewhat odd, considering the marvelous encounter we both enjoyed at The Cat's Meow. So, I met Derrick in the foyer again and asked him if I could still use his car. He said to me, 'Jack, I really don't think that's a good idea considering everyone's circumstances. I'm assuming that your call was from Little Miss Muffin?' I said, 'Yes, it was Derrick.' Derrick asked, 'And now you want to see her again?' I said, 'Yes, Derrick, I would like that very much." Derrick said, 'Jack, if you go see Shelly, you could endanger both of your lives at the same time without getting any help from me or anyone else. Do you understand the ramifications of that? I mean, what do you really hope to gain from a visit that wouldn't be advantageous for all parties concerned?' I said, 'Well, Derrick, I understand that Shelly doesn't understand the gravity of what's happening in my life.' Derrick said, 'That, you have said well. Because it certainly isn't the time to start any type of romance, regardless of how wonderful things went at The Cat's Meow. Jack, plain and simple, with Marceli wanting you dead, you need to ask yourself something.'

I said, "And what is that?' Derrick said, 'I think you need to consider what part of Shelly's life has to do with Marceli wanting to kill you.' I said, 'You're right, Derrick, I'll just have to call her back and try to explain the situation the best I can.' Derrick said, 'Definitely the right decision, Jack. Bowing out gracefully now would better serve Shelly's life in every way. Because, after all, she's totally innocent of your circumstances.' I said, 'You could never be so right, Derrick.' So, I went back upstairs and spent the better part of thirty minutes on the phone with Shelly. Mom said, "Son?" I said, "Yeah, Mom." Mom said, "How did you feel when you had to walk back up those stairs and make that call to Shelly again?" I said, "Mom, I couldn't believe the situation I was in and what I was getting ready to tell that girl. My affiliation with the mob, at that point in my life, was basically costing me what could have been one of the best things that could have ever happened to me. I found the circumstances very agonizing. And yet, I knew I had to go right back up those stairs and try to somehow explain all of that to her. It was absolutely unbearable. And it was a tall order, to say the least." Mom said, "I bet it was, Son." I said, "Boy, you have no idea how I felt that day, and yet, I had to tell Shelly exactly what was going on for her own sake. It certainly was something I would have never dreamed of having to do.

After I got off the phone with Shelly, Derrick asked, 'I'm curious; how did she take it?' I said, 'Well, in a nutshell, she said, 'I would have never in a million years anticipated receiving a phone call like you have given me tonight, Jack. Nor could I ever allow myself to have any part in what you have described to me today.' Derrick said, 'I bet. And with that, Jack, Tom asked me to have you join him in his office.' I said, 'Sure, Derrick, let's go.' When entering the door of Tom's office, he motioned for both Derrick and me to have a seat. Tom opened up by saying, 'Jack, in view of your and Derrick's visit today at The Cat's Meow, it clearly appears Marceli has more of an interest in killing you than he does me.' I said, 'You couldn't be more right, Tom.' Tom continued on, saying, 'I'm sure you can attest to what I'm saying, which is, at least, a reasonable assumption.' I said, 'By all means, Tom, I certainly do. And I can only imagine you are probably just as glad?' Tom said, 'In view of what all has transpired, of course, I'm glad.'

So, Tom asked, 'What do you purpose to do at this point, Jack?' I said, 'Well, Tom, just a few moments ago, you were just as much a payer to Marceli as I still am now. And now that your butt is out of the sling with Marceli, I'm I to take it that you want to wash your hands of me? Is that what I'm hearing, Tom?' Tom said, 'That's not what's in question, Jack. I have no intention of throwing you to the wolves, Jack. I was more interested in your thoughts on what the best course of action you should take at this point is.' I said, 'Ok, since that's the case, I wanted to at least take one more week and try to tie down a deal that would suffice, Marceli. And if I can't, I think after being here seven weeks, it's probably time to go.' Tom said, 'So be it, I hope you are successful in your pursuit, and you are welcome to use any of my connections to that end.' That following week proved to be a relentless drag. I could tell Derrick was a little worn out with the whole situation and just wanted some normalcy in his own life for a change. So, he made arrangements for one of his karate students to keep me company during my last week at Tom's estate. Derrick introduced me to his student that Sunday afternoon. His name was Davy, and he had lost his previous international karate tournament against a Japanese gentleman from the Philippine Islands. Unannounced to both Davy and me, we got a visit one late morning that no doubt left an ever-lasting impression on the two of us. Because Tom had a half-moon driveway, the security guard was accustomed to allowing the mail truck to pass through the gate and make his delivery directly at the front door.

One afternoon, when the mail was being delivered, Davy and I suddenly realized it wasn't the mailman who was making his usual delivery. In fact, it was one of Marceli's men dressed up as the mailman." Mom said, "Oh my God, Son, you've got to be kidding me!!!" "No, Mom, I'm not kidding you, for one of Marceli's men had cased the joint and found a way to get as close to me as possible. It scared the hell out of both Davy and me. This went on for another two days, followed by Tom making sure the guard wouldn't allow the mail truck to pass through the gate anymore. Though Tom felt secure with Marceli not wanting to whack him, he was equally convinced that Marceli definitely wanted to hit me. That is to say, at least until we heard what the "so-called" mailman had to say."

Mom said, "Son, how did you know it wasn't the mailman?" I said, "Well, I happened to be standing outside of Tom's foyer one late morning when the "so-called mailman" approached Tom's mailbox. As the man lifted the lever to open the mailbox, he asked if I was having a lovely day? Not thinking anything of his inquiry, I said, 'Sure, how about you?' The "so-called mailman" answered back and said, 'I'm having a great day myself, but I suspect Marceli is not having such a good one.' He no more got those words out of his mouth when I discovered I was struck through with stark terror in my whole being. I realized at that point that the 'so-called mailman' had definitely represented an organization capable of pure murder." Mom said, "Oh my God, Son, what did you think?" I said, "Mom, my heart almost failed me in a split second. Regaining my composure a few seconds later, I brought to mind that this man could have killed me at a moment's notice with no warning at all. I was spellbound and couldn't move a muscle in my body. After our "so-called mailman" made his short and grand appearance, he got back in his mail truck and pulled away. I knew he could have whacked both Davy and me right there and then. Which in itself told me Marceli had something else in mind altogether. I just didn't know what it was. I knew I had to contact The Bear in Cincinnati if I were to learn what was going on. Hoping there wouldn't be any more visits like that, Davy and I told Tom later that evening what had transpired. Tom suggested we watch too many movies. It kind of angered both Davy and me that Tom wouldn't take us seriously. But behold, that same scenario took place the very next day. But this time, Davy would be the recipient. Davy was returning from a workout when our new mailman looked at Davy and asked, 'Do you think Marceli has forgotten all about Jack?' Davy suspected the man had a hidden gun in his mailbag when the gangster asked his question. Fearing the man would shoot him, Davy said, 'I don't know enough about the situation to even comment on it.'

The mailman answered, 'Doesn't matter; Marceli wanted all parties to understand how convenient Jack can be emptied out.' With a comment like that, I thought maybe Marceli didn't want me dead right away but rather to terrorize me. Well, it goes without saying that Marceli instantly produced a fraudulent mailman, which certainly had my and Davy's undivided attention.

But I needed to find out why Marceli was suddenly working a different angle. Both Davy and I knew Tom probably wouldn't be back for a couple hours. So, we spent a little time going over what had transpired that morning with our "new mailman." During the course of our conversation, Davy mentioned how he couldn't believe how calm I remained during our mailman's visit. I told Davy that sometimes fear can be a great motivator. It had me incite a room full of gangsters just a few weeks earlier over a misconception. So, in view of that mistake, remaining calm during our mailman's visit proved to be a better choice.

I then shared with Davy that fear and intimidation were the foundation and way of life I had chosen. Davy deeply felt he was in over his head and asked to be excused for a moment. Returning a few minutes later, Davy announced, 'Jack, I can't be like you. I live in a constant state of fear and wonder if some unknown person is going to blow my head off. Hollywood produces movies like that. But man!! You're living this crap for real!!! Jack, are you crazy, or don't you have anything else to do!!' I said, 'Calm down, I know how you feel, Davy. I wish I could wake up tomorrow and know that all of this has been a bad dream, or at least the movie you were referring to. But if anything, you know now, it's not a movie, and my associates play for keeps, don't they?' Davy said, 'Yes, they do!!! And you're right, Jack, it's not a movie. And since I haven't signed up for any of your leading roles, unfortunately, I'm going to have to end our association right now. Jack, I'm definitely out of here!!! Nothing against you, but all of this is way out of my league!! I got to go!!!' Out of Davy's own fear, he had left Tom's estate that afternoon, never to return again. I couldn't blame him.

The next day, Derrick, Tom, and I made arrangements for my departure back to Cincinnati. Of course, leaving Tom's estate would present challenges in not being seen. Tom finally saw the validity of our mailman's visit and wanted me to depart as safely as possible. In the interim, Tom was convinced that these types of gangsters can be ruthless. He no longer held the opinion that the Cosa Nostra didn't exist. Tom suggested not taking any public transportation in concern of encountering one of Marceli's men. So, I asked Tom, 'How do you think I should handle getting back to Cincinnati?'

Tom said, 'I want you to hitchhike, Jack.' I said, 'Really!!?' Tom said, 'Yes, really.' I said, 'Tom, I only have one hundred and sixty-five dollars left from when I first arrived.' Tom said, 'Of that, I have no doubt. But I do think it's much safer for you to hitchhike back as opposed to catching a train, plane, or bus. Jack, you need to remember that being in plain sight at a train station or an airport can make you a sitting duck for one of Marceli's men. I said, 'Well, I can't argue with that.' Tom said, 'So when you arrive in Cincinnati, do you have anyone you can stay with on the outskirts of town?' I said, 'Funny that you should ask, but yes, I do. I know a dealer that lives right outside of Cincinnati that not even The Bear knows about.' Tom said, 'Good, you'll need to stay with him until you get this mess straightened out with Marceli. It is my guess that Marceli has something else in mind for you. It would do you well to find out. But when you go to find out, and if you need to contact The Bear, I guess I don't need to remind you not to use any phone?' I said, 'No, Tom, I don't think you'll have to remind me of that.' Tom said, 'You have to remember, Jack, since The Bear was so willing to help Marceli walk you to your grave, I'd be extra careful in your association with him. But right now, I have an appointment, and I have to leave, so I'm truly sorry for all the heartache and inconvenience I've caused you. However, I have left some instructions with Derrick to help you get back to Cincinnati.

By all means, keep me abreast of what develops. But remember, Jack, if you need my help while you're in Cincinnati, only contact me by payphone.' I said, 'No doubt, Tom, and thanks for all you have done for me.' Tom said, 'You're welcome, Jack'. Leaning forward to shake Tom's hand, I never saw or heard from the man again. As Tom left that day, Derrick asked me to come inside the den so we could talk. Derrick said, 'Jack, Tom wanted me to give you this envelope for all your troubles.' I asked, 'What is it?' Derrick said, 'I don't know, Jack, I haven't examined it. Tom just wanted me to give it to you. So, I took the envelope and looked inside. Seeing what appeared to be a sufficient amount of money, I started to slowly grin at Derrick. Derrick said, 'What's in the envelope, Jack?' I said, 'Well, it appears Tom has left me some money. Can you imagine that?' Derrick said, 'Yes, I can, considering all that has come to pass.' I said, 'Yeah, I guess you're right.'

After having a glass of water with Derrick, I said, 'Derrick, Tom left me twenty-five hundred dollars in this envelope.' Derrick said, 'Well, Jack, Tom said that's the least he could do for you considering all your troubles.' I said, 'Derrick, I agree with what you're saying. It's just that I never thought Tom would give me twenty-five hundred dollars.' Derrick said, 'Well, Jack, whatever part of it you don't think you can handle, you can always leave with me.' I said, 'Don't kid yourself. I don't feel that bad about it. After all, that money can help me reestablish again.' Derrick said, 'Yes, I believe that's what Tom had in mind. Providing you're willing to change your life so that your activities don't threaten your very existence.' Mom said, "Son?" I said, "Yeah, Mom, what is it?" Mom said, "You were damn lucky Tom left you anything." I said, "In one way, you're right, Mom. But knowing Tom the way Derrick and I had, I wasn't surprised at all. I just had no idea it was going to be twenty-five hundred dollars' worth of help. Furthermore, you have to remember, Mom, twenty-five hundred dollars back in the mid-1970s was like $4,500 to $5,000 today." Mom said, "Yes, you've got a point there, Son." I said, "However, the money did give me a good start when I got back to Cincinnati." Mom said, "Like I said, you're darn lucky Tom gave you anything." I said, "Yes, I agree, Mom, but all of Tom's money wasn't worth dangling my life in front of the Mob." Mom said, "No, Son, you chose to dangle your own life in front of the Mob." I said, "And that you have said well, Mom, and that you have said well.

At any rate, Derrick explained to me that Tom had made final arrangements for my departure." Mom said, "And so what did Tom have in mind, Son?" I said, "Well, he arranged for two cabs to be parked in front of his estate with their lights out one evening. This allowed me to step out of Tom's front foyer unnoticed. Tom knew it would be hard for me to be seen from the street should any one of Marceli's men be parked close. Well, needless to say, it finally came time for Derrick and me to say goodbye. I have to readily admit here Derrick really wasn't quite the dip I thought he was at the beginning of our acquaintance. Even the other two goons that were with Derrick seemed to have their act together by the time everything was over."

Mom said, "Well, I guess they better be if they're going to be in that business." I said, "That's a reasonable assumption.

In short, Derrick and I enjoyed each other's company under less-than-desirable circumstances. Our affiliation made me realize Derrick had played a significant part in helping me stay alive. How do you thank a guy for taking time out from his regular schedule to make sure someone doesn't whack you? Or show such a loyalty to his father that he doesn't even merit? Where does a man find someone like that, if ever?" Mom said, "Well, again, you can count your lucky stars, Jack." I said, "Looking back, Mom, I'm not so convinced it was my so-called lucky stars that protected my life in those years. I think it was God simply looking out for me because He knew He would eventually call me at one given point. Anyway, after experiencing a newfound respect for Derrick, it was difficult to say goodbye to him.

Nevertheless, I shook the man's hand and thanked him for all he had done for me during my stay. Walking away that day, I wondered in the back of my mind what it would have been like to have lived the life Derrick had already lived. Being seated in a cab that dark evening, Derrick requested that I remain on the floor until the cab driver was well on his way. With the cab driver pulling away, I had the oddest feeling I'd never see Derrick again. My intuition was correct. I never did." Mom said, "You really liked Derrick, didn't you, Son?" I said, "Yeah, I did, Mom. It goes without saying that some of the finest people I have ever known in my life were formerly trained in the military. Like me, none of them were ever the same again. And undoubtedly, Derrick was one of them. Derrick had done more living in thirty-eight years than most men do in a lifetime. At any rate, that evening, the cab driver transported me to a truck stop in Ontario, California. Derrick told me earlier that it would be easier to pick up I-40 East from that particular stop. I couldn't believe I was in Ontario, ready to hitchhike across the United States with twenty-five hundred dollars in my pocket. I found it rather hard to play poor just to get a ride at a truck stop. But I knew if I hadn't, it could be fatal for my own life. I should have been more concerned with being robbed as opposed to making it back to Cincinnati." Mom said, "Makes sense to me."

I was so tempted to leave the truck stop and catch a bus. But not wanting to run into any of Marceli's men, I decided not to. I figured I'd try to catch a bus when I reached Nevada. So, I started asking different truck drivers if they were going that way. I didn't get any takers right away and had to hang out for a pretty long time. There's nothing like having a couple of grand in your pocket and not being able to get a ride. Entering the truck stop restaurant to eat, I noticed a couple sitting at a booth getting ready to leave. Assuming the man had a truck, I tried pitching him the idea of taking me along with him. He told me he wasn't going my way but mentioned his wife, who would be traveling through Las Vegas, and that she would gladly give me a ride. I immediately thought his offer was rather odd because I would have never made the same offer with my wife and two of my children accompanying her. Especially not knowing the person I was offering the ride to."

Mom said, "Boy, you got that right." I said, "But then, the trucker told me it would be okay to ride with his wife. He assured me that if anything were to go wrong, his wife knew how to take care of herself. And that if I were going to try anything crazy, she would just blow my head off with her 357 magnum." Mom said, "What!!? Had you thought of this situation, Son?" I said, "Of course, Mom, with me even being the bad guy, I found this whole conversation too weird for me. I suddenly envisioned some crazy woman killing me in the middle of the Nevada desert; who knows what may have been in her head. I sensed the woman didn't know my personal circumstances, and I certainly didn't want her to do a better job on me than what the Mob was so willing to perform. Yes, sir, her comments sounded way too weird to me. So, I passed on her husband's offer and bowed out gracefully." Mom said, "And like, how!? Too bad you hadn't used that same common sense when it came to doing business with Marceli right from the beginning." I said, "I couldn't agree with you more, Mom. At any rate, I took off from Ontario, California, and headed north to pick up I-40 East. By the end of the day, I had made it across the border into Nevada.

Crossing over into Nevada, I was pretty much dropped off in a ghost town. I was convinced I wouldn't be able to make it out of town before morning. I was stuck with having to sleep in what appeared to be an old wooden structure that was clearly once a bus stop. It looked as if the structure hadn't been used for years and had set a reasonable distance from the highway. After noticing part of the overhang protruding from the main body of the structure, I realized its capacity to block the desert winds at night would be limited. The overhang would barely ward off the water should it rain. But the structure itself had about an 8×10 long bench inside formally used to seat people while awaiting their bus. With sundown rapidly approaching, I knew the old structure would be home that evening. I was grateful for the bench inside because it made a good emergency bed. But knowing the cold desert winds would soon arrive, I wedged myself between two walls that the old structure had to offer.

When darkness finally closed in, I was glad my temporary shelter sat far enough away from the highway not to be readily noticed by passing cars. The unanticipated atmosphere of my new dwelling had me entertaining thoughts of strangers encroaching on me while I slept. Those thoughts kept me awake until about two in the morning when I finally abandoned the concern and fell asleep. Awakened the following day by chirping birds, I vowed to be in a hotel the following evening. But when one is on the run from the Mob, living an abnormal life becomes a regular procedure even if one does have $2,500 in their pocket. After nearly freezing in the Nevada desert that evening, I was convinced Marceli's men couldn't be everywhere. And yet, I knew Tom's initial suggestion of remaining unnoticed was imperative if I were to keep my life. After having breakfast that morning, I headed back to the old wooden structure I slept in the night before. I knew it wouldn't be long before I could catch a ride now that it was daytime. Sitting on the very bench I slept the night before; I noticed what appeared to be a worn-out magazine lying in the corner. Reaching down to read its content, my attention was immediately drawn to the life story of the once-famous gangster, Veto Genovese, Godfather of the Genovese Family. The article claimed Veto had made over four hundred million dollars from his imports of heroin during the 1930s and 40s.

At one point, the columnist had mentioned that Veto Genovese died of a heart attack at the United States Medical Center for Federal Prisoners in Springfield, Missouri, on February 14th, 1969. In conclusion, the article stated that Veto Genovese had become the first gangster in American history to be coin-phrased "Father of Narcotics." I said, "Mom." Mom said, "Yes, Son?" I said, "After reading Veto's story that morning, I couldn't help but contemplate how the article appeared to be addressing me." Mom said, "What do you mean, Son?" I said, "Well, as I read the article, it occurred to me that if Veto Genovese, who once headed up the Genovese Family in New York, could end up dead in a Federal Prison, what made me think I would do any better? After all, it was clear to me at that point in my life that I would never be the affluent gangster that Veto had already aspired to. Or, for that matter, was I even trying to. I would have been considered small potatoes in comparison to a Veto Genovese. But those kinds of thoughts had occurred to me after reading the article." Mom said, "Yes, Son, that makes sense to me." I said, "Men like Marceli were on the same par as Genovese, only a different crime family." Mom said, "What do you mean, Son?" I said, "Well, it was widely suspected that Genovese had ordered Rupolo's murder for testifying against him in the 1944 Boccia murder trial. After the trial, Genovese didn't order Rupolo's death immediately but instead forced Rupolo to live the last twenty years of his life in terror. And that's exactly what Marceli was doing with me." Mom said, "I'm not sure if I follow, Son."

I said, "Well, Mom, in short, Genovese was to Rupolo as Marceli was to me. In other words, Marceli used the very same fear tactics with me as Veto Genovese had done with Rupolo. Not that I testified against Marceli, for there was no trial between Marceli and me during our acquaintance. But as Genovese made Rupolo fear for his life, I, too, was made to fear for my life in much the same manner from Marceli. After my and Marceli's deal went south in L.A, he suffered a mirage of legal difficulties that preoccupied his time. As in so much, The Bear and I became small potatoes in the scope of Marceli's concerns with the F.B.I." Mom said, "Really?" I said, "That's right, Mom!!" Mom said, "Don't leave me guessing, Son, what the heck happened to him?"

I said, "Excellent question, Mom. But for The Bear and I, life would take a totally different twist in the coming months. And trust me, we never dreamed what was about to happen."

Mom said, "What are you referring to son?" I said, "Well, as you already know, I've been writing this story as long as we've been meeting and talking about it. And so, I feel that a good foundation has already been put into place for stimulating and marvelous conclusion. That being said, I'd much rather you read part two like the rest of my readers for the full benefit of satisfaction and amazement." Mom said, "Well son, if that's what you rather have me do, by all means, let's do it together."